An Akkadian Handbook

An Akkadian Handbook

Paradigms, Helps, Glossary, Logograms, and Sign List

Douglas B. Miller
and
R. Mark Shipp

Eisenbrauns
Winona Lake, Indiana
1996

Printed in the United States of America

The Akkadian fonts used for printing the sign list in Part Five of this work are available from Linguist's Software Inc., P.O. Box 580, Edmonds, WA 98020-0580 [tel (206) 775 1130].

Library of Congress Cataloging-in-Publication Data

Miller, Douglas B., 1955–
An Akkadian Handbook : paradigms, helps, glossary, logograms, and sign list / Douglas B. Miller and R. Mark Shipp.
p. cm.
Includes bibliographical references.
ISBN 0-931464-86-2 (pbk. : alk. paper)
1. Akkadian language—Grammar. I. Shipp, R. Mark, 1953– . II. Title.
PJ3251.M75 1996
492′.1—dc20 96-16975
CIP

The paper used in this publication meets the minimum requirements of the American National Standard for Information Sciences—Permanence of Paper for Printed Library Materials, ANSI Z39.48-1984. ♾™

CONTENTS

Introduction

This work is designed as a bridge between introductory Akkadian grammars and the sign lists, lexicons, and full grammars necessary for advanced work in Akkadian. It provides a collection of helps in compact form to streamline the progression from signs to transliteration, normalization, and translation. In addition, certain sections contain compilations not available anywhere else. For this reason, although especially valuable for the beginning student, even those better acquainted with Akkadian will be assisted by this presentation of the material.

Part One contains nominal and verbal paradigms. Old Babylonian forms have been provided, by far the most common dialect presented to beginners. Section Two contains various items, ranging from the order of the alphabet to a list of abbreviations. Included here are extensive lists of numbers, conjunctions, and prepositions. Part Three is a glossary of more than 650 proper names. This is especially valuable because proper names are only sporadically provided in the grammars and lexicons.

In the fourth section, a listing of logograms frequently found in introductory study is given. These are divided by individual and composite constructions and followed by three indexes. The final part contains a sign list with graphic representations of Neo-Assyrian signs. Two indexes, one organized by sign number and the other alphabetically by value, present all but the most rare syllabic and logographic sign values used in the various dialects of Akkadian. Helpful notations to the sign lists of Labat and Borger are provided, along with a chart of correspondences. See the introductions to each section for more information.

The authors are grateful to their professors of Akkadian, C. Leong Seow and J. J. M. Roberts, for all the help and encouragement they have provided with this important but complex language. Professor R. E. Whitaker assisted in numerous ways with the present work, and Gerald M. Bilkes helped with the section on proper names.

DOUGLAS B. MILLER
Tabor College, Hillsboro, Kansas

R. MARK SHIPP
Institute for Christian Studies, Austin, Texas

Bibliography

Achtemeier, Paul J., general ed. 1985. *Harper's Bible Dictionary.* San Francisco: Harper and Row.

Bergsträsser, Gotthelf. 1983. *Introduction to the Semitic Languages.* Translation of *Einführung in die Semitischen Sprachen* (Munich, 1928) by Peter T. Daniels, with additions. Winona Lake, Ind.: Eisenbrauns.

Borger, Rykle. 1981. *Assyrisch-babylonische Zeichenliste.* 2d ed. Alter Orient und Altes Testament 33/33A. Neukirchen-Vluyn: Neukirchener Verlag/ Kevelaer: Butzon & Bercker.

______. 1979. *Babylonisch-assyrische Lesestücke.* 2d ed. Analecta Orientalia 54. Rome: Biblical Institute Press.

Buttrick, George A., and Keith Crim, eds. 1962, 1976. *The Interpreter's Dictionary of the Bible.* 4 vols. plus Supplement. Nashville: Abingdon.

Caplice, Richard. 1988. *Introduction to Akkadian.* 3d ed. Studia Pohl, Series Maior 9. Rome: Biblical Institute Press.

Deimel, P. Anton. 1930. *Šumerisches Lexikon.* 2d ed. Rome: Biblical Institute Press.

Foster, Benjamin R. 1995. *From Distant Days.* Bethesda, Md.: CDL Press.

Huehnergard, John. 1987. *An Introduction to Old Babylonian Akkadian.* Unpublished Typescript. Cambridge, Mass.

Labat, René, and Florence Malbran-Labat. 1988. *Manuel d'épigraphie akkadienne.* 6th ed. Paris: Librarie Orientaliste Paul Geuthner.

Leick, Gwendolyn. 1991. *A Dictionary of Ancient Near Eastern Mythology.* London and New York: Routledge.

Marcus, David. 1978. *A Manual of Akkadian.* Lanham, Md.: University Press of America.

Moscati, Sabatino, Anton Spitaler, Edward Ullendorff, and Wolfram von Soden. 1980. *An Introduction to the Comparative Grammar of the Semitic Languages.* Wiesbaden: Otto Harrassowitz.

Oppenheim, A. Leo, et al. 1956–. *The Assyrian Dictionary of the University of Chicago.* Chicago: Oriental Institute.

Riemschneider, K. K. 1975. *An Akkadian Grammar.* Translation of *Lehrbuch des Akkadischen* (Leipzig, 1969) by Thomas A. Caldwell, et al. Milwaukee: Marquette University Press.

Roberts, J. J. M. 1972. *The Earliest Semitic Pantheon.* Baltimore and London: Johns Hopkins University Press.

von Soden, Wolfram. 1959–81. *Akkadisches Handwörterbuch.* 3 vols. Wiesbaden: Otto Harrassowitz.

______. 1969. *Grundriss der akkadischen Grammatik.* Analecta Orientalia 33/ 47. Rome: Biblical Institute Press.

______, and Wolfgang Röllig. 1967. *Das akkadische Syllabar.* 2d ed. Analecta Orientalia 42. Rome: Biblical Institute Press.

Stamm, J. J. 1939. *Die akkadische Namengebung.* Leipzig: J. C. Hinrichs.

Tallqvist, Knut. 1974 [reprint]. *Akkadische Götterepitheta.* Hildesheim: Olms.

Ungnad, Arthur, and Lubor Matouš. 1964. *Grammatik des Akkadischen.* 4th ed. Munich: C. H. Beck.

Part One: Paradigms

Introduction

This section presents a variety of paradigms. Nominals are given first, including nouns, adjectives, and pronouns. A list of afformatives to verbs and substantives is also provided. These are followed by a full display of the strong verb, G-stem, and (more brief) presentations of the other stems and of the weak verbs. Finally, synopses of the strong and weak verbs that allow direct comparison of forms among the verbal stems and vowel classes are provided.

The paradigms are principally Babylonian—Old Babylonian, in particular. Occasionally other forms have been included. For additional information, particularly notes on dilectal variations, see the grammars listed in the bibliography. The verbal system, with its plethora of vowel classes, can be one of the most challenging aspects of Akkadian for the beginner. For this reason, the derived stems and weak patterns are given in detail. Care has been taken not to provide forms that have yet to be observed in texts, except for those that can reasonably be assured. In some cases, forms of the paradigm verb have been construed from analogous lexemes.

The following vowel class options have been distinguished:

G: a/u, a/a, i/i, u/u (theme vowels)
Gt, Gtn: a, i, u (theme vowels)
N, Ntn: a, e, i, u (theme vowels)
I-aleph in G or N stems: a, e (in addition to theme vowels)
I-w in G or N stems: a, i (theme vowels)
II-weak in G or N stems: ā, ē, ī, ū
III-weak in G or N stems: ā, ē, ī, ū
No distinctions: D, Dt, Dtn, Š, Št, Štn, I-y.

1.1 Nominal Paradigms

Noun and Adjective Endings

	masc	fem
nom s	šarr-um	šarr-atum
gen s	šarr-im	šarr-atim
acc s	šarr-am	šarr-atam
nom pl	šarr-ū, -ānū	šarr-ātum
(adj)	dann-ūtum	dann-ātum
obl pl	šarr-ī, -ānī	šarr-ātim
(adj)	dann-ūtim	dann-ātim
nom du	išd-ān	šap-tān
obl du	išd-īn	šap-tīn

Suffixed Pronouns

	gen	dat	acc
3ms	-šu	-šum	-šu
3fs	-ša	-šim	-ši
2ms	-ka	-kum	-ka
2fs	-ki	-kim	-ki
1cs	-ī, ya, a	-am, m, nim	-ni, ī
3mp	-šunu	-šunūšim/um	-šunūti
3fp	-šina	-šināšim	-šināti
2mp	-kunu	-kunūšim	-kunūti
2fp	-kina	-kināšim	-kināti
1cp	-ni	-niāšim	-niāti

1cs genitive pronominal suffix, attached to nouns that are:

	sing	plur
nom	-ī	-a
gen	-ya	-ya
acc	-ī	-ya

Additional Afformatives

Some of the following are attached to nominals, others to verbals.

-āyum/-āya	gentilic
-am	ventive afformative
-an	nominal/adj. afformative; perhaps individualizing force
-āniš	adverbial afformative
-anni	direct suffix (= **-am** [vent.] + **-ni** [accus. 1cs])
-ānum	indicates professions
-ânum	adverbial afformative (gives prep. an adv. force)
-ī	relational afformative, e.g., gentilic
-iš	(adverbial ending) *as, like*; (terminative) = **ana**, *to*; (comparative) *like*
-išam	(adverbial ending) **-iš** + **-am** (acc) used to form adverbs of time
-īšu	multiplicative afformative; e.g., **šinīšu**, *twice*
-ium	(see **-ûm**)
-ma	*and, but* (connective par ticle); *indeed* (emphatic particle); indic ventive
-māku	particle indicating something potential or imaginary
-man	enclitic particle, "ever", e.g., *whoever*
-me/-mi	enclitic particle introducing direct speech
-nim	ventive; subjunctive
-šum	indirect suffix (dat. 3ms)
-u	subjunctive
-ûm/-ium	gentilic
-um	(locative) = **ina**
-ūni	subjunctive
-ūtum	abstract nouns

Indefinite Pronouns

mimma	*anything, something* (indeclinable)
mamman	*anyone, someone* (indeclinable)
ayyûmma	*person or thing* (is declinable: ayyîmma, ayyîtim)

Independent Pronouns

	Anaphoric			Possessive
	Nom	**Gen.-Acc.**	**Dative**	
3ms	šū	šuāti/u, šâti/u	šuāšim, šâši/a/um	šûm
3fs	šī, šat	šiāti, šuāti, šâti	šiāšim, šuāšim, šâši/am	šattum, šuttum
2ms	attā	kâta, kâti	kâši/a/um	kûm
2fs	attī	kâti	kâšim	kattum
1cs	anāku	yâti	yâšim, yâšu, yâša	
1ms				yûm, yāʾum
1fs				yattum, yattun
3mp	šunu	šunūti	šunūšim	šunûm
3fp	šina	šināti	šināšim	(Ass.) šunūtum
2mp	attunu	kunūti	kunūšim	kunûm
2fp	attina	kināti	kināšim	(Ass.) kunūtum
1cp	nīnu	niāti, nâti	niāšim	
1mp				nûm
1fp				nuttum, niāʾtum

Demonstratives

A. Near Demonstratives (*this, these*) **B. Far Demonstratives** (*that, those*)

	masc s.	**fem s.**	**masc pl.**	**fem pl.**	**masc s.**	**fem s.**	**masc pl.**	**fem pl.**
nom	annûm	annītum	annûtum	annâtum	ullûm	ullītum	ullūtum	ullātum
gen	annîm	annītim	annûtim	annâtim	ullîm	ullītim	ullūtim	ullātim
acc	anniam	annītam			ulliām	ullītam		

NB: For the neuter "*this*" the f.s. form is used.

C. Independent Pronouns (as demonstratives) (*that, those, the aforementioned*) **Determinative-relative Pronouns** (*he of, she of*, etc; also used for possession)

	nom	**gen/acc**	**dat**	**nom**	**gen**	**acc**
ms	šū	šuʾāti(šâti)	šuāšim	šu	ši	ša
fs	šī	šuʾāti, šâti, šiʾāti	šiāšim	šat		
mp	šunu	šunūti	šunūšim	šūt		
fp	šina	šināti	šināšim	šāt		

Interrogatives

	A. Personal Pronouns *"who?"*	**B. Impersonal Pronouns** *"what?"*		**C. Interrogative Adjectives** *"which?"*			
				ms	**fs**	**mp**	**fp**
nom.	mannum	mīnum	minûm	ayyûm	ayyītum	ayyûtum	ayyâtum
gen.	mannim	mīnim	minîm	ayyîm	ayyītim	ayyûtim	ayyâtim
acc.	mannam	mīnam	minâm	ayyâm	ayyītam		

Note:
1. ana mīnim *for what? = why?*
2. ana mīnim > ammīnim

1.2 Verbal Paradigms

The Strong Verb: G-stem

Durative

	a/u	**a/a**	**u/u**	**i/i**
3cs	iparras	iṣabbat	irappud	ipaqqid
(3fs	taparras	taṣabbat	tarappud	tapaqqid)
2ms	taparras	taṣabbat	tarappud	tapaqqid
2fs	taparrasī	taṣabbatī	tarappudī	tapaqqidī
1cs	aparras	aṣabbat	arappud	apaqqid
3mp	iparrasū	iṣabbatū	irappudū	ipaqqidū
3fp	iparrasā	iṣabbatā	irappudā	ipaqqidā
2cp	taparrasā	taṣabbatā	tarappudā	tapaqqidā
1cp	niparras	niṣabbat	nirappud	nipaqqid

Perfect

3cs	iptaras	iṣṣabat	irtapud	iptaqid
(3fs	taptaras	taṣṣabat	tartapud	taptaqid)
2ms	taptaras	taṣṣabat	tartapud	taptaqid
2fs	taptarsī	taṣṣabtī	tartapdī	taptaqdī
1cs	aptaras	aṣṣabat	artapud	aptaqid
3mp	iptarsū	iṣṣabtū	irtapdū	iptaqdū
3fp	iptarsā	iṣṣabtā	irtapdā	iptaqdā
2cp	taptarsā	taṣṣabtā	tartapdā	taptaqdā
1cp	niptaras	niṣṣabat	nirtapud	niptaqid

Preterite

3cs	iprus	iṣbat	irpud	ipqid
(3fs	taprus	taṣbat	tarpud	tapqid)
2ms	taprus	taṣbat	tarpud	tapqid
2fs	taprusī	taṣbatī	tarpudī	tapqidī
1cs	aprus	aṣbat	arpud	apqid
3mp	iprusū	iṣbatū	irpudū	ipqidū
3fp	iprusā	iṣbatā	irpudā	ipqidā
2cp	taprusā	taṣbatā	tarpudā	tapqidā
1cp	niprus	niṣbat	nirpud	nipqid

Injunctive

	a/u	a/a	u/u	i/i
ac pr 3cs	liprus	liṣbat	lirpud	lipqid
ac pr 3fs	lū taprus	lū taṣbat	lū tarpud	lū tapqid
impv 2ms	purus	ṣabat	rupud	piqid
impv 2fs	pursī	ṣabtī	rupdī	piqdī
ac pr 1cs	luprus	luṣbat	lurpud	lupqid
ac pr 3mp	liprusū	liṣbatū	lurpudū	lipqidū
ac pr 3fp	liprusā	liṣbatā	lirpudā	lipqidā
impv 2cp	pursā	ṣabtā	rupdā	piqdā
coh 1cp	i niprus	i niṣbat	i nirpud	i nipqid

Infinitive

(Note: vowels are the same for all classes)

nom	parāsum	ṣabātum	rapādum	paqādum
gen	parāsim	ṣabātim	rapādim	paqādim
acc	parāsam	ṣabātam	rapādam	paqādam

	Participle		Verbal Adjective	
		construct		**construct**
ms	pārisum	pāris	parsum	paris
fs	pāristum	pārisat	paristum	paristi
mp	pārisūtum	pārisūt	parsūtum	parsūt
fp	pārisātum	pārisāt	parsātum	parsāt
(as noun)	pārisū, pārisī			

	Ventive		Vetitive		Stative		
	indicative	**imperative**					
3cs	iprusam		ay iprus	**3ms**	paris	šar	bēl
(3fs	taprusam		ē taprus)	**3fs**	parsat	šarrat	bēlet
2ms	taprusam	pursam	ē taprus	**2ms**	parsāta	šarrāta	bēlēta
2fs	taprusīm	pursīm	ē taprusī	**2fs**	parsāti	šarrāti	bēlēti
1cs	aprusam		ay aprus	**1cs**	parsāku	šarrāku	bēlēku
3mp	iprusūnim		ay iprusū	**3mp**	parsū	šarrū	bēlū
3fp	iprusānim		ay iprusā	**3fp**	parsā	šarrā	bēlā
2cp	taprusānim	pursānim	ē taprusā	**2mp**	parsātunu	šarrātunu	bēlētunu
				2fp	parsātina	šarrātina	bēlātina
1cp	niprusam		ē niprus	**1cp**	parsānu	šarrānu	bēlēnu

The Strong Verb: Gt stem (a)

	Durative	**Perfect**	**Preterite**	**Injunctive**
3cs	ip**t**arras	ip**ta**tras	ip**t**aras	lip**t**aras
(3fs	tap**t**arras	tap**ta**tras	tap**t**aras	lū tap**t**aras)
2ms	tap**t**arras	tap**ta**tras	tap**t**aras	pi**t**ras
2fs	tap**t**arrasī	tap**ta**trasī	tap**t**arasī	pi**t**rasī
1cs	ap**t**arras	ap**ta**tras	ap**t**aras	lup**t**aras
3mp	ip**t**arrasū	ip**ta**trasū	ip**t**arsū	lip**t**arsū
3fp	ip**t**arrasā	ip**ta**trasā	ip**t**arsā	lip**t**arsā
2cp	tap**t**arrasā	tap**ta**trasā	tap**t**arsā	pi**t**rasā
1cp	nip**t**arras	nip**ta**trasā	nip**t**aras	i nip**t**aras
Infinitive	pi**t**rusum			
Participle	mup**t**arsum	mup**t**arsūtum		
	mup**t**aristum	mup**t**arsātum		

Verbal Adjective		pi**t**rusum	**Vetitive**	ay ip**t**aras

Stative	**3ms**	pi**t**rus	**3mp**	pi**t**rusū
	3fs	pi**t**rusat	**3fp**	pi**t**rusā
	2ms	pi**t**rusāta	**2mp**	pi**t**rusātunu
	2fs	pi**t**rusāti	**2fp**	pi**t**rusātina
	1cs	pi**t**rusāku	**1cp**	pi**t**rusānu

The Strong Verb: Gtn stem (a)

	Durative	**Perfect**	**Preterite**	**Injunctive**
3cs	ip**tan**arras	ipta**tar**ras	ip**tar**ras	lip**tar**ras
(3fs	tap**tan**arras	tapta**tar**ras	tap**tar**ras	lū tap**tar**ras)
2ms	tap**tan**arras	tapta**tar**ras	tap**tar**ras	pi**tar**ras
2fs	tap**tan**arrasī	tapta**tar**rasī	tap**tar**rasī	pi**tar**rasī
1cs	ap**tan**arras	apta**tar**ras	ap**tar**ras	lup**tar**ras
3mp	ip**tan**arrasū	ipta**tar**rasū	ip**tar**rasū	lip**tar**sū
3fp	ip**tan**arrasā	ipta**tar**rasā	ip**tar**rasā	lip**tar**sā
2cp	tap**tan**arrasā	tapta**tar**rasā	tap**tar**rasā	pi**tar**rasā
1cp	nip**tan**arras	nipta**tar**ras	nip**tar**ras	i nip**tar**as
Infinitive	pi**tar**rusum			
Participle	mup**tar**risum	mup**tar**risūtum		
	mup**tar**ristum	mup**tar**risātum		

Verbal Adjective		pi**tar**rusum	**Vetitive**	ay ip**tar**ras

Stative	**3ms**	pi**tar**rus	**3mp**	pi**tar**rusū
	3fs	pi**tar**rusat	**3fp**	pi**tar**rusā
	2ms	pi**tar**rusāta	**2mp**	pi**tar**rusātunu
	2fs	pi**tar**rusāti	**2fp**	pi**tar**rusātina
	1cs	pi**tar**rusāku	**1cp**	pi**tar**rusānu

The Strong Verb: D stem (all)

	Durative	**Perfect**	**Preterite**	**Injunctive**
3cs	uparras	uptarris	uparris	liparris
(3fs	tuparras	tuptarris	tuparris	lū tuparris)
2ms	tuparras	tuptarris	tuparris	purris
2fs	tuparrasī	tuptarrisī	tuparrisī	purrisī
1cs	uparras	uptarris	uparris	luparris
3mp	uparrasū	uptarrisū	uparrisū	liparrisū
3fp	uparrasā	uptarrisā	uparrisā	liparrisā
2cp	tuparrasā	tuptarrisā	tuparrisā	purrisā
1cp	nuparras	nuptarris	nuparris	i nuparris
Infinitive	purrusum			
Participle	muparrisum	muparrisūtum		
	muparristum	muparrisātum		

Verbal Adjective purrusum **Vetitive** ay uparris

Stative				
	3ms	purrus	**3mp**	purrusū
	3fs	purrusat	**3fp**	purrusā
	2ms	purrusāta	**2mp**	purrusātunu
	2fs	purrusāti	**2fp**	purrusātina
	1cs	purrusāku	**1cp**	purrusānu

The Strong Verb: Dt stem (all)

	Durative	**Perfect**	**Preterite**	**Injunctive**
3cs	uptarras	uptatarris	uptarris	liptarris
(3fs	tuptarras	tuptatarris	tuptarris	lū tuptarris)
2ms	tuptarras	tuptatarris	tuptarris	putarris
2fs	tuptarrasī	tuptatarrisī	tuptarrisī	putarrisī
1cs	uptarras	uptatarris	uptarris	luptarris
3mp	uptarrasū	uptatarrisū	uptarrisū	liptarrisū
3fp	uptarrasā	uptatarrisā	uptarrisā	liptarrisā
2cp	tuptarrasā	tuptatarrisā	tuptarrisā	putarrisā
1cp	nuptarras	nuptatarris	nuptarris	i nuptarris
Infinitive	putarrusum			
Participle	muptarrisum	muptarrisūtum		
	muptarristum	muptarrisātum		

Verbal Adjective putarrusum **Vetitive** ay uptarris

Stative				
	3ms	putarrus	**3mp**	putarrusū
	3fs	putarrusat	**3fp**	putarrusā
	2ms	putarrusāta	**2mp**	putarrusātunu
	2fs	putarrusāti	**2fp**	putarrusātina
	1cs	putarrusāku	**1cp**	putarrusānu

The Strong Verb: Dtn stem (all)

	Durative	Perfect	Preterite	Injunctive
3cs	up**tan**arras	up**ta**tarris	up**t**arris	lip**t**arris
(3fs	tup**tan**arras	tup**ta**tarris	tup**t**arris	lū tup**t**arris)
2ms	tup**tan**arras	tup**ta**tarris	tup**t**arris	pu**t**arris
2fs	tup**tan**arrasī	tup**ta**tarrisī	tup**t**arrisī	pu**t**arrisī
1cs	up**tan**arras	up**ta**tarris	up**t**arris	lup**t**arris
3mp	up**tan**arrasū	up**ta**tarrisū	up**t**arrisū	lip**t**arrisū
3fp	up**tan**arrasā	up**ta**tarrisā	up**t**arrisā	lip**t**arrisā
2cp	tup**tan**arrasā	tup**ta**tarrisā	tup**t**arrisā	pu**t**arrisā
1cp	nup**tan**arras	nup**ta**tarris	nup**t**arris	i nup**t**arris
Infinitive	pu**ta**rrusum			
Participle	mup**t**arrisum	mup**t**arrisūtum		
	mup**t**arristum	mup**t**arrisātum		

Verbal Adjective pu**ta**rrusum **Vetitive** ay up**t**arris

Stative	**3ms**	pu**ta**rrus	**3mp**	pu**ta**rrusū
	3fs	pu**ta**rrusat	**3fp**	pu**ta**rrusā
	2ms	pu**ta**rrusāta	**2mp**	pu**ta**rrusātunu
	2fs	pu**ta**rrusāti	**2fp**	pu**ta**rrusātina
	1cs	pu**ta**rrusāku	**1cp**	pu**ta**rrusānu

The Strong Verb: Š stem (all)

	Durative	Perfect	Preterite	Injunctive
3cs	ušapras	uštapris	ušapris	lišapris
(3fs	tušapras	tuštapris	tušapris	lū tušapris)
2ms	tušapras	tuštapris	tušapris	šupris
2fs	tušaprasī	tuštaprisī	tušaprisī	šuprisī
1cs	ušapras	uštapris	ušapris	lušapris
3mp	ušaprasū	uštaprisū	ušaprisū	lišaprisū
3fp	ušaprasā	uštaprisā	ušaprisā	lišaprisā
2cp	tušaprasā	tuštaprisā	tušaprisā	šuprisā
1cp	nušapras	nuštapris	nušapris	i nušapris
Infinitive	šuprusum			
Participle	mušaprisum	mušaprisūtum		
	mušapristum	mušaprisātum		

Verbal Adjective šuprusum **Vetitive** ay ušapris

Stative	**3ms**	šuprus	**3mp**	šuprusū
	3fs	šuprusat	**3fp**	šuprusā
	2ms	šuprusāta	**2mp**	šuprusātunu
	2fs	šuprusāti	**2fp**	šuprusātina
	1cs	šuprusāku	**1cp**	šuprusānu

The Strong Verb: Št stem (all)

	Durative (pass.)	Durative (lexical)	Perfect	Preterite	Injunctive
3cs	uštapras	uštaparras	uštatapris	uštapris	lištapris
(3fs	tuštapras	tuštaparras	tuštatapris	tuštapris	lū tuštapris)
2ms	tuštapras	tuštaparras	tuštatapris	tuštapris	šutapris
2fs	tuštaprasī	tuštaparrasī	tuštataprisī	tuštaprisī	šutaprisī
1cs	uštapras	uštaparras	uštatapris	uštapris	luštapris
3mp	uštaprasū	uštaparrasū	uštataprisū	uštaprisū	lištaprisū
3fp	uštaprasā	uštaparrasā	uštataprisā	uštaprisā	lištaprisā
2cp	tuštaprasā	tuštaparrasā	tuštataprisā	tuštaprisā	šutaprisā
1cp	nuštapras	nuštaparras	nuštatapris	nuštapris	i nuštapris

Infinitive šutaprusum

Participle muštaprisum muštaprisūtum
muštapristum muštaprisātum

Verbal Adjective šutaprusum **Vetitive** ay uštapris

Stative				
	3ms	šutaprus	3mp	šutaprusū
	3fs	šutaprusat	3fp	šutaprusā
	2ms	šutaprusāta	2mp	šutaprusātunu
	2fs	šutaprusāti	2fp	šutaprusātina
	1cs	šutaprusāku	1cp	šutaprusānu

The Strong Verb: Štn stem (all)

	Durative	Perfect	Preterite	Injunctive
3cs	uštanapras	uštatapris	uštapris	lištapris
(3fs	tuštanapras	tuštatapris	tuštapris	lū tuštapris)
2ms	tuštanapras	tuštatapris	tuštapris	šutapris
2fs	tuštanaprasī	tuštataprisī	tuštaprisī	šutaprisī
1cs	uštanapras	uštatapris	uštapris	luštapris
3mp	uštanaprasū	uštataprisū	uštaprisū	lištaprisū
3fp	uštanaprasā	uštataprisā	uštaprisā	lištaprisā
2cp	tuštanaprasā	tuštataprisā	tuštaprisā	šutaprisā
1cp	nuštanapras	nuštatapris	nuštapris	i nuštapris

Infinitive šutaprusum

Participle muštaprisum muštaprisūtum
muštapristum muštaprisātum

Verbal Adjective šutaprusum **Vetitive** ay uštapris

Stative				
	3ms	šutaprus	3mp	šutaprusū
	3fs	šutaprusat	3fp	šutaprusā
	2ms	šutaprusāta	2mp	šutaprusātunu
	2fs	šutaprusāti	2fp	šutaprusātina
	1cs	šutaprusāku	1cp	šutaprusānu

The Strong Verb: ŠD stem (all)

	Durative	Perfect	Preterite	Injunctive
3cs	ušparras	—	ušparris	lišparris
(3fs	tušparras	—	tušparris	lū tušparris)
2ms	tušparras	—	tušparris	šuparris
2fs	tušparrasī	—	tušparrisī	šuparrisī
1cs	ušparras	—	ušparris	lušparris
3mp	ušparrasū	—	ušparrisū	lišparrisū
3fp	ušparrasā	—	ušparrisā	lišparrisā
2cp	tušparrasā	—	tušparrisā	šuparrisā
1cp	nušparras	—	nušparris	i nušparris
Infinitive	šuparrusum			
Participle	mušparrisum	mušparrisūtum		
	mušparristum	mušparrisātum		

Verbal Adjective — **Vetitive** ay ušparris

Stative —

The Strong Verb: N stem (a)

	Durative	Perfect	Preterite	Injunctive
3cs	ipparras	ittapras	ipparis	lipparis
(3fs	tapparras	tattapras	tapparis	lū tapparis)
2ms	tapparras	tattapras	tapparis	napris
2fs	tapparrasī	tattaprasī	tapparsī	naprisī
1cs	apparras	attapras	apparis	lupparis
3mp	ipparrasū	ittaprasū	ipparsū	lipparsū
3fp	ipparrasā	ittaprasā	ipparsā	lipparsā
2cp	tapparrasā	tattaprasā	tapparsā	naprisā
1cp	nipparras	nittapras	nipparis	i nipparis
Infinitive	naprusum			
Participle	mupparsum	mupparsūtum		
	mupparstum	mupparsātum		

Verbal Adjective naprusum **Vetitive** ay ipparis

Stative				
	3ms	naprus	**3mp**	naprusū
	3fs	naprusat	**3fp**	naprusā
	2ms	naprusāta	**2mp**	naprusātunu
	2fs	naprusāti	**2fp**	naprusātina
	1cs	naprusāku	**1cp**	naprusānu

The Strong Verb: Ntn stem (a)

	Durative	**Perfect**	**Preterite**	**Injunctive**
3cs	it**tan**apras	it**ta**tapras	it**ta**pras	lit**ta**pras
(**3fs**	tat**tan**apras	tat**ta**tapras	tat**ta**pras	lū tat**ta**pras)
2ms	tat**tan**apras	tat**ta**tapras	tat**ta**pras	**ita**pras
2fs	tat**tan**aprasī	tat**ta**taprasī	tat**ta**prasī	**ita**prasī
1cs	at**tan**apras	at**ta**tapras	at**ta**pras	lut**ta**pras
3mp	it**tan**aprasū	it**ta**taprasū	it**ta**prasū	lit**ta**prasū
3fp	it**tan**aprasā	it**ta**taprasā	it**ta**prasā	lit**ta**prasā
2cp	tat**tan**aprasā	tat**ta**taprasā	tat**ta**prasā	**ita**prasā
1cp	nit**tan**apras	nit**ta**tapras	nit**ta**pras	i nit**ta**pras
Infinitive	**ita**prusum			
Participle	mut**ta**prisum	mut**ta**prisūtum		
	mut**ta**pristum	mut**ta**prisātum		

Verbal Adjective **ita**prusum

Vetitive ay it**ta**pras

Stative				
	3ms	**ita**prus	**3mp**	**ita**prusū
	3fs	**ita**prusat	**3fp**	**ita**prusā
	2ms	**ita**prusāta	**2mp**	**ita**prusātunu
	2fs	**ita**prusāti	**2fp**	**ita**prusātina
	1cs	**ita**prusāku	**1cp**	**ita**prusānu

I-aleph Verb (a class): G stem (a/u)

	Durative	Perfect	Preterite	Injunctive
3cs	iḫḫaz	ītaḫaz	īḫuz	līḫuz
(3fs	taḫḫaz	tātaḫaz	tāḫuz	lū tāḫuz)
2ms	taḫḫaz	tātaḫaz	tāḫuz	āḫuz
2fs	taḫḫazī	tātaḫzī	tāḫuzī	āḫzi
1cs	aḫḫaz	ātaḫaz	āḫuz	lūḫuz
3mp	iḫḫazū	ītaḫzū	īḫuzū	līḫuzū
3fp	iḫḫazā	ītaḫzā	īḫuzā	līḫuzā
2cp	taḫḫazā	tātaḫzā	tāḫuzā	āḫzā
1cp	niḫḫaz	nītaḫaz	nīḫuz	i nīḫuz

Infinitive aḫāzum

Participle āḫizum

Verbal Adjective aḫzum **Vetitive** ay īḫuz

Stative				
3ms	aḫiz		**3mp**	aḫzū
3fs	aḫzat		**3fp**	aḫzā
2ms	aḫzāta		**2mp**	aḫzātunu
2fs	aḫzāti		**2fp**	aḫzātina
1cs	aḫzāku		**1cp**	aḫzānu

I-aleph Verb (e class): G stem (u/u)

	Durative	Perfect	Preterite	Injunctive
3cs	irrub	īterub	īrub	līrub
(3fs	terrub	tēterub	tērub	lū tērub)
2ms	terrub	tēterub	tērub	erub
2fs	terrubī	tēterbī	tērubī	erbī
1cs	errub	ēterub	ērub	lūrub
3mp	irrubū	īterbū	īrubū	līrubū
3fp	irrubā	īterbā	īrubā	līrubā
2cp	terrubā	tēterbā	tērubā	erbā
1cp	nirrub	nīterub	nīrub	i nīrub

Infinitive erēbum

Participle ēribum

Verbal Adjective erbum **Vetitive** ay īrub

Stative				
3ms	erib		**3mp**	erbū
3fs	erbat		**3fp**	erbā
2ms	erbāta		**2mp**	erbātunu
2fs	erbāti		**2fp**	erbātina
1cs	erbāku		**1cp**	erbānu

Alākum *to go* **(irregular)**

	Durative	**Perfect**	**Preterite**	**Injunctive**
G 3cs	illak	ittalak	illik	lillik
(3fs	tallak	tattalak	tallik	lū tallik)
2ms	tallak	tattalak	tallik	alik
2fs	tallakī	tattalkī	tallikī	alkī
1cs	allak	attalak	allik	lullik
3mp	illakū	ittalkū	illikū	lillikū
3fp	illakā	ittalkā	illikā	lillikā
2cp	tallakā	tattalkā	tallikā	alkā
1cp	nillak	nittalak	nillik	i nillik
Gt 3cs	ittallak	ittatlak	ittalak	littalak
2ms	tattallak	tattatlak	tattalak	atlak
Gtn 3cs	ittanallak	ittatallak	ittallak	littallak
2ms	tattanallak	tattatallak	tattallak	atallak

	Infinitive	**Participle**	**Verb Adj**	**Stative**
G	alākum	ālikum	alkum	alik
Gt	atlukum	mutalkum	atlukum	atluk
Gtn	atallukum	muttallikum	atallukum	atalluk

I-w Verb: G stem (a)

	Durative	**Perfect**	**Preterite**	**Injunctive**
3cs	uššab	ittašab	ūšib	līšib
(3fs	tuššab	tattašab	tūšib	lū tūšib)
2ms	tuššab	tattašab	tūšib	šib, tišab
2fs	tuššabī	tattašbī	tūšbī	šibī
1cs	uššab	attašab	ūšib	lūšib
3mp	uššabū	ittašbū	ūšibū, ušbū	lišbū
3fp	uššabā	ittašbā	ūšibā, ušbā	lišbā
2cp	tuššabā	tattašbā	tūšibā, tušbā	šibā, tišbā
1cp	nuššab	nittašab	nūšib	i nūšib

Infinitive (w)ašābum

Participle (w)āšibum

Verbal Adjective (w)ašbum **Vetitive** ay ūšib

Stative	**3ms**	(w)ašib	**3mp**	(w)ašbū
	3fs	(w)ašbat	**3fp**	(w)ašbā
	2ms	(w)ašbāta	**2mp**	(w)ašbātunu
	2fs	(w)ašbāti	**2fp**	(w)ašbātina
	1cs	(w)ašbāku	**1cp**	(w)ašbānu

I-y Verb: G stem (all)

	Durative	Perfect	Preterite	Injunctive
3cs	inniq	īteniq	īniq	līniq
(3fs	tenniq	tēteniq	tēniq	lū tēniq)
2ms	tenniq	tēteniq	tēniq	eniq
2fs	tenniqī	tētenqī	tēniqī	enqī
1cs	enniq	ēteniq	ēniq	lûniq
3mp	inniqū	ītenqū	īniqū	līniqū
3fp	inniqā	ītenqā	īniqā	līniqā
2cp	tenniqā	tētenqā	tēniqā	enqā
1cp	ninniq	nīteniq	nīniq	i nīniq

Infinitive enēqum

Participle ēnequm

Verbal Adjective enqum

Vetitive ay īniq

Stative	**3ms**	eniq	**3mp**	enqū
	3fs	enqet	**3fp**	enqā
	2ms	enqēta	**2mp**	enqētunu
	2fs	enqēti	**2fp**	enqētina
	1cs	enqēku	**1cp**	enqēnu

I-n Verb: G stem (a/u)

	Durative	Perfect	Preterite	Injunctive
3cs	inaqqar	ittaqar	iqqur	liqqur
(3fs	tanaqqar	tattaqar	taqqur	lū taqqur)
2ms	tanaqqar	tattaqar	taqqur	uqur
2fs	tanaqqarī	tattaqrī	taqqurī	uqrī
1cs	anaqqar	attaqar	aqqur	luqqur
3mp	inaqqarū	ittaqrū	iqqurū	liqqurū
3fp	inaqqarā	ittaqrā	iqqurā	liqqurā
2cp	tanaqqarā	tattaqrā	taqqurā	uqrā
1cp	ninaqqar	nittaqar	niqqur	i niqqur

Infinitive naqāru

Participle nāqiru

Verbal Adjective naqru

Vetitive ay iqqur

Stative	**3ms**	naqer	**3mp**	naqrū
	3fs	naqrat	**3fp**	naqrā
	2ms	naqrāta	**2mp**	naqrātunu
	2fs	naqrāti	**2fp**	naqrātina
	1cs	naqrāku	**1cp**	naqrānu

Nadānum *to give* (i/i)

	Durative Babylonian	Durative Assyrian	Perfect	Preterite	Injunctive
G 3cs	inaddin	iddan	ittadin	iddin	liddin
(3fs	tanaddin	taddan	tattadin	taddin	lū taddin)
2ms	tanaddin	taddan	tattadin	taddin	idin
2fs	tanaddinī	taddinī	tattadnī	taddinī	idnī
1cs	anaddin	addan	attadin	addin	luddin
3mp	inaddinū	iddunū	ittadnū	iddinū	liddinū
3fp	inaddinā	iddanā	ittadnā	iddinā	liddinā
2cp	tanaddinā	taddanā	tattadnā	taddinā	idnā
1cp	ninaddin	niddan	nittadin	niddin	i niddin
Gt 3cs	ittaddin	—	ittaddin	ittadin	—
Gtn 3cs	ittanaddin	—	ittataddin	ittaddin	itaddin

	Infinitive	Participle	Verb Adj	Stative
G	nadānum	nādinum	nadnum	nadin
Gt	—	muttadnum	—	—
Gtn	—	muttaddinum	—	—

II-weak Verb (ā class): G stem

	Durative	Perfect	Preterite	Injunctive
3cs	ibâš	ibtāš	ibāš	libāš
(3fs	tabâš	tabtāš	tabāš	lū tabāš)
2ms	tabâš	tabtāš	tabāš	bāš
2fs	tabaššī	tabtāšī	tabāšī	bāšī
1cs	abâš	abtāš	abāš	lubāš
3mp	ibaššū	ibtāšū	ibāšū	libāšū
3fp	ibaššā	ibtāšā	ibāšā	libāšā
2cp	tabaššā	tabtāšā	tabāšā	bāšā
1cp	nibâš	nibtāš	nibāš	i nibāš

Infinitive bâšum

Participle bāʾišum

Verbal Adjective bāšum **Vetitive** ay ibāš

Stative	**3ms**	bāš	**3mp**	bāšū
	3fs	bāšat	**3fp**	bāšā
	2ms	bāšāta	**2mp**	bāšātunu
	2fs	bāšāti	**2fp**	bāšātina
	1cs	bāšāku	**1cp**	bāšānu

II-weak Verb (ī class): G stem

	Durative	Perfect	Preterite	Injunctive
3cs	iqīa/âš	iqtīš	iqīš	liqīš
(3fs	taqīa/âš	taqtīš	taqīš	lū taqīš)
2ms	taqīa/âš	taqtīš	taqīš	qīš
2fs	taqiššī	taqtīšī	taqīšī	qīšī
1cs	aqīa/âš	aqtīš	aqīš	luqīš
3mp	iqiššū	iqtīšū	iqīšū	liqīšū
3fp	iqiššā	iqtīšā	iqīšā	liqīšā
2cp	taqiššā	taqtīšā	taqīšā	qīšā
1cp	niqīa/âš	niqtīš	niqīš	i niqīš

Infinitive qiā/âšum

Participle qāʾišum

Verbal Adjective qīšum **Vetitive** ay iqīš

Stative	**3ms**	qīš	**3mp**	qīšū
	3fs	qīšat	**3fp**	qīšā
	2ms	qīšāta	**2mp**	qīšātunu
	2fs	qīšāti	**2fp**	qīšātina
	1cs	qīšāku	**1cp**	qīšānu

II-weak Verb (ū class): G stem

	Durative	Perfect	Preterite	Injunctive
3cs	ikân	iktūn	ikūn	likūn
(3fs	takân	taktūn	takūn	lū takūn)
2ms	takân	taktūn	takūn	kūn
2fs	takunnī	taktūnī	takūnī	kūnī
1cs	akân	aktūn	akūn	lukūn
3mp	ikunnū	iktūnū	ikūnū	likūnū
3fp	ikunnā	iktūnā	ikūnā	likūnā
2cp	takunnā	taktūnā	takūnā	kūnā
1cp	nikân	niktūn	nikūn	i nikūn

Infinitive kânum

Participle dāʾikum

Verbal Adjective kīnum **Vetitive** ay ikūn

Stative	**3ms**	kīn	**3mp**	kīnū
	3fs	kīnat	**3fp**	kīnā
	2ms	kīnāta	**2mp**	kīnātunu
	2fs	kīnāti	**2fp**	kīnātina
	1cs	kīnāku	**1cp**	kīnānu

II-weak Verb (ū class): D stem

	Durative	Perfect	Preterite	Injunctive
3cs	ukān	uktīn	ukīn	likīn
(3fs	tukān	tuktīn	tukīn	lū tukīn)
2ms	tukān	tuktīn	tukīn	kīn
2fs	tukannī	tuktinnī	tukinnī	kinnī
1cs	ukān	uktīn	ukīn	lukīn
3mp	ukannū	uktinnū	ukinnū	likinnū
3fp	ukannā	uktinnā	ukinnā	likinnā
2cp	tukannā	tuktinnā	tukinnā	kinnā
1cp	nukān	nuktīn	nukīn	i nukīn

Infinitive kunnum

Participle mukinnum

Verbal Adjective kunnum **Vetitive** ay ukīn

Stative				
	3ms	kūn	**3mp**	kunnū
	3fs	kunnat	**3fp**	kunnā
	2ms	kunnāta	**2mp**	kunnātunu
	2fs	kunnāti	**2fp**	kunnātina
	1cs	kunnāku	**1cp**	kunnānu

Some Forms of the Geminate

G-Stem

	Durative	Perfect	Preterite	Imperative
3 cs	—	iddanin	—	dubub
3 mp	—	iddannū	—	**fem.** dubbī
	Infinitive	**Participle**	**Verb Adj**	**Stative**
	danānum	—	dannu	**3ms** dān
			fem. dannatu	**3fs** dannat

N-Stem

	Durative	Perfect	Preterite	Imperative
3 cs	iššallal	ittašlal	iššalil	—
3 mp	iišša(l)lallū	ittašlallū	iššalillū	—
	Infinitive	**Participle**	**Verb Adj**	**Stative**
	našallulum	muššalillum	—	našallul

Ntn-Stem

	Durative	Perfect	Preterite	Imperative
3 cs	ittanašlal	ittatašlal	—	—
3 mp	ittanašlallū	—	—	—
	Infinitive	**Participle**	**Verb Adj**	**Stative**
	itašlullum	muttašlillum	—	—

III-weak Verb (ā class): G stem

	Durative	Perfect	Preterite	Injunctive
3cs	ikalla	iktala	ikla	likla
(3fs	takalla	taktala	takla	lū takla)
2ms	takalla	taktala	takla	kila
2fs	takallî	taktalî	taklî	kilî
1cs	akalla	aktala	akla	lukla
3mp	ikallû	iktalû	iklû	liklû
3fp	ikallâ	iktalî	iklâ	liklâ
2cp	takallâ	taktalâ	taklâ	kilâ
1cp	nikalla	niktala	nikla	i nikla

Infinitive kalûm

Participle kālûm

Verbal Adjective kalûm **Vetitive** ay ikle

Stative	**3ms**	kali	**3mp**	kalû
	3fs	kalia/ât	**3fp**	kaliā/â
	2ms	kaliā/âta	**2mp**	kaliā/âtunu
	2fs	kaliā/âti	**2fp**	kaliā/âtina
	1cs	kaliā/âku	**1cp**	kaliā/ânu

III-weak Verb (ē class): G stem

	Durative	Perfect	Preterite	Injunctive
3cs	išemme	išteme	išme	lišme
(3fs	tešemme	tešteme	tešme	lū tešme)
2ms	tešemme	tešteme	tešme	šime, šeme
2fs	tešemmê/î	teštemê/î	tešmê/î	šimî/ê, šemî
1cs	ešemme	ešteme	ešme	lušme
3mp	išemmû	ištemû	išmû	lišmû
3fp	išemmeā/â	ištemeā/â	išmeā/â	lišmeā/â
2cp	tešemmeā/â	teštemeā/â	tešmeā/â	šimiā, šemeā
1cp	nišemme	ništeme	nišme	i nišme

Infinitive šemûm

Participle šēmûm

Verbal Adjective šemûm **Vetitive** ay išme

Stative	**3ms**	šemi	**3mp**	šemû
	3fs	šemia/ât	**3fp**	šemiā/â
	2ms	šemiā/âta	**2mp**	šemiā/âtunu
	2fs	šemiā/âti	**2fp**	šemiā/âtina
	1cs	šemiā/âku	**1cp**	šemiā/ânu

III-weak Verb (ī class): G stem

	Durative	Perfect	Preterite	Pret+Subj	Injunctive
3cs	ibanni	ibtani	ibni	ibnû	libni
(3fs	tabanni	tabtani	tabni	tabnû	lū tabni)
2ms	tabanni	tabtani	tabni	tabnû	bini
2fs	tabannî	tabtanî	tabnî	tabnî	binî
1cs	abanni	abtani	abni	abnû	lubni
3mp	ibanniū/û	ibtaniū/û	ibniū/û	abnû	libniū/û
3fp	ibanniā/â	ibtaniā/â	ibniā/â	ibniā/â	libniā/â
2cp	tabanniā/â	tabtaniā/â	tabniā/â	tabniā/â	biniā/â
1cp	nibanni	nibtani	nibni	nibnû	i nibni

Infinitive banûm

Participle bānûm

Verbal Adjective banûm **Vetitive** ay ibnû

Stative	**3ms**	bani	**3mp**	baniū/û
	3fs	bania/ât	**3fp**	baniā/â
	2ms	baniā/âta	**2mp**	baniā/âtunu
	2fs	baniā/âti	**2fp**	baniā/âtina
	1cs	baniā/âku	**1cp**	baniā/ânu

III-weak Verb (ū class): G stem

	Durative	Perfect	Preterite	Injunctive
3cs	imannu	imtanu	imnu	limnu
(3fs	tamannu	tamtanu	tamnu	lū tamnu)
2ms	tamannu	tamtanu	tamnu	munu
2fs	tamannî	tamtanî	tamnî	munî
1cs	amannu	amtanu	amnu	lumnu
3mp	imannû	imtanû	imnû	limnû
3fp	imannâ	imtanâ	imnâ	limnâ
2cp	tamannâ	tamtanâ	tamnâ	munâ
1cp	nimannu	nimtanu	nimnu	i nimnu

Infinitive manûm

Participle mānûm

Verbal Adjective manûm **Vetitive** ay imne

Stative	**3ms**	manu	**3mp**	manû
	3fs	manât	**3fp**	manâ
	2ms	manâta	**2mp**	manâtunu
	2fs	manâti	**2fp**	manâtina
	1cs	manâku	**1cp**	manânu

Quadriliteral Verbs

1. The Š Group

The first radical is *š*, and *l*, *r*, *m*, or *n* is in *4th* or *3rd and 4th* positions; conjugated similar to D.

	Durative	Perfect	Preterite	Impv
G Strong	i/ušqammam	uštaqammim	ušqammim	šuqammim
G III e	ušpêl	uštepēl	ušpē/īl	—
(plural)	ušpellū	uštepēlū	ušpēlū	—
Gt	uštaqmam	uštataqmim	ušaqmim	—
Gt III e	uštepêl	—	uštepēl	—

	Participle	Inf/V. Adj	Stative
G Strong	mušqammimum	šuqammumum	šuqammum
G III e	mušpē/īlum	šupêlum	—
Gt	—	—	—
Gt III e	—	—	—

2. The N-stem Group

The 2nd radical is always *l* or *r*.

	Durative	Perfect	Preterite	Impv
N Strong	ibbalakkat/it	ittabalkat/it	ibbalkit	nabalkit
N IV u	ipparakku	ittaparku	ipparki	naparki
N IV e	iḫḫeleṣṣi	itteḫelṣe	iḫḫelṣi	neḫelṣi
Ntn	ittanablakkat	ittatablakkat	ittabalakkat	—
Š Strong	ušbalakkat	uštabalkit	ušbalkit	šubalkit
Š IV u	ušparakka	uštaparki	ušparki	šuparki
Š IV e	ušḫeleṣṣe	ušteḫelṣi	ušḫelṣi	šuḫelṣi
Št	uštabalkat	uštatabalkit	uštabalkit	—
Štn	uštanablakkat	uštatablakkit	uštablakkit	—

	Participle	Inf/V. Adj	Stative
N Strong	mubbalkitum	nabalkutum	nabalkut
N IV u	mupparkûm > ium	naparkûm	naparku
N IV e	muḫḫelṣûm	neḫelṣûm	neḫelṣu
Ntn	muttablakkitum	itablakkutum	—
Š Strong	mušbalkitum	šubalkutum	šubalkut
Š IV u	mušparkûm	šuparkûm	šuparku
Š IV e	mušḫelṣûm	šuḫelṣûm	šuḫelṣu
Št	muštabalkitum	šutabalkutum	—
Štn	muštablakkitum	šutablakkutum	—

Irregular N

These have identical second and third radicals. Plural forms are indicated in parentheses.

	Durative	Perfect	Preterite	Impv
N	iššallal(lū)	ittašlal(lū)	iššalil(lū)	—
Ntn	ittanašlal(lū)	ittatašlal(lū)	—	—

	Participle	Inf/V. Adj	Stative
N	muššalillum	našallulum	našallul(ū)
Ntn	muttašlillum	itašlullum	—

Izuzzum *to stand* (irregular)

All forms double the final consonant before a vocalic ending, except for the G participle.

	Durative	Perfect	Preterite	Imperative sg., pl.
G	izzaz	ittaziz	izziz	iziz, izizzā
Gt	ittazzaz	—	ittazaz	—
Gtn	ittanazzaz	—	ittazzaz	itazzaz, itazzazzā
Š	ušzaz	uštaziz	ušziz	šuziz, šuzizzā
Štn	uštanazzaz	—	uštazziz	—

	Participle	Inf/V. Adj	Stative
G	muzzi/azum	i/uzuzzum	nazuz
Gt	—	—	—
Gtn	muttazzizzum	itazzuzzum	—
Š	mušzizzum	šuzuzzum	šuzuz
Štn	—	—	—

Synopsis of the Strong Verb

Stem	Durative	Perfect	Preterite	Imper
G	iparras	iptaras	iprus	purus
	ilabbaš	iltabaš	ilbaš	labaš
	ipaqqid	iptaqid	ipqid	piqid
	irappud	irtapud	irpud	rupud
Gt	ip**t**arras	ip**ta**tras	ip**t**aras	pi**t**ras
	im**t**allik	im**ta**tlik	im**t**alik	mi**t**lik
	ir**t**aggum	ir**ta**tgum	ir**t**agum	ri**t**gum
Gtn	ip**tan**arras	ipta**tar**ras	ip**tar**ras	pi**tar**ras
	im**tan**allik	imta**tal**lik	im**tal**lik	mi**tal**lik
	ir**tan**aggum	irta**tag**gum	ir**tag**gum	ri**tag**gum
D	upa**rr**as	upta**rr**is	upa**rr**is	pu**rr**is
Dt	up**t**arras	up**ta**tarris	up**t**arris	pu**ta**rris
Dtn	up**tan**arras	up**ta**tarris	up**t**arris	pu**ta**rris
Š	u**š**apras	u**š**tapris	u**š**apris	**š**upris
Št[1]	**ušt**apras	uš**ta**tapris	uš**t**apris	šu**ta**pris
Št[2]	**ušt**apa**rr**as	uš**ta**tapris	uš**t**apris	šu**ta**pris
Štn	uš**tan**apras	uš**ta**tapris	uš**t**apris	šu**ta**pris
ŠD	u**š**parras	u**š**tapa**rr**is	u**š**pa**rr**is	**š**upa**rr**is
N	i**p**parras	i**t**tapras	i**p**paris	**na**pris
	i**p**paqqid	i**t**tapqid	i**p**paqid	**na**pqid
	i**m**maggur	i**t**tamgur	i**m**magur	—
Ntn	it**tan**apras	it**ta**tapras	it**ta**pras	i**ta**pras
	it**tan**apqid	itta**ta**pqid	it**ta**pqid	i**ta**pqid
R	upa**ra**rras	—	upa**ra**rris	—
Rt	up**tara**rras	—	up**tara**rris	pu**tara**rris

Synopsis of I-w Verbs

Stem	Durative	Perfect	Preterite	Imper
G	ubbal	ittabal	ūbil	bil
		itbal (OB)		
	uššab	ittašab	ūšib	šib, tišab
Gt	ittabbal	ittatbal	itbal	tabal
Gtn	ittanabbal	ittatabbal	ittabbal	itabbal
D	uwattar	ūtatter	uwatter	(w)utter
Dt	ūtaššar	ūtataššer	ūtaššer	utaššer
Dtn	ūtanaššar	ūtataššer	ūtaššer	utaššer
Š	ušabbal	uštābil	ušābil	šūbil
Št	uštabbal	uštatābil	uštābil	šutābil
Štn	uštanabbal	uštatabbil	uštabbil	šutabbil
N	iwwallad	ittawlad	iwwalid	nawlid

Synopsis of the Strong Verb

Participle	Infinitive	Verb Adj	Stative	Class
pārisum	parāsum	parsum	paris	a/u
lābišum	labāšum	labšum	labaš	a/a
pāqidum	paqādum	paqdum	paqid	i/i
rāpidum	rapādum	rapdum	—	u/u
mup**t**arsum	pi**t**rusum	pi**t**rusum	pi**t**rus	a
mum**t**alkum	mi**t**lukum	mi**t**lukum	mi**t**luk	i
mur**t**agmum	ri**t**gumum	ri**t**gumum	ri**t**gum	u
mup**tar**risum	pi**tar**rusum	pi**tar**rusum	pi**tar**rus	a
mum**tal**likum	mi**tal**lukum	mi**tal**lukum	mi**tal**luk	i
mur**tag**gimum	ri**tag**gumum	ri**tag**gumum	ri**tag**gum	u
mupa**rr**isum	pu**rr**usum	pu**rr**usum	pu**rr**us	all
mup**t**arrisum	pu**ta**rrusum	pu**ta**rrusum	pu**ta**rrus	all
mup**t**arrisum	pu**ta**rrusum	pu**ta**rrusum	pu**ta**rrus	all
mu**š**aprisum	**š**uprusum	**š**uprusum	**š**uprus	all
muš**t**aprisum	šu**ta**prusum	šu**ta**prusum	šu**ta**prus	all
muš**t**aprisum	šu**ta**prusum	šu**ta**prusum	šu**ta**prus	
muš**t**aprisum	šu**ta**prusum	šu**ta**prusum	šu**ta**prus	all
mu**š**pa**rr**isum	**š**upa**rr**usum			
mu**p**parsum	**na**prusum	**na**prusum	**na**prus	a
mu**p**paqdum	**na**pqudum	**na**pqudum	**na**pqud	i
mu**m**magrum	**na**mgurum	**na**mgurum	**na**mgur	u
mut**ta**prisum	i**ta**prusum	i**ta**prusum	i**ta**prus	a
mut**ta**pqidum	i**ta**pqudum	—	i**ta**pqud	i
—	—	—	—	
mup**t**a**ra**rrisum	pu**t**a**ra**rrusum	—	—	

Synopsis of I-w Verbs

Participle	Infinitive	Verb Adj	Stative	Class
bābilum	babālum	bablum	babil	a/i
(w)āšibum	(w)ašābum	(w)ašbum	(w)ašib	a/i
muttablum	itbulum	itbulum	itbul	a
muttabbilum	itabbulum	itabbulum	itabbul	a
muwatterum	(w)utturum	(w)utturum	(w)uttur	all
mūtaššerum	utaššurum	utaššurum	utaššur	all
mūtašširum	utaššurum	utaššurum	utaššur	all
mušābilum	šūbulum	šūbulum	šūbul	all
muštābilum	šutābulum	šutābulum	šutābul	all
muštabbilum	šutabbulum	šutabbulum	šutabbul	all
muwwaldum	nawludum	nawludum	nawlud	a

Synopsis of I-aleph Verbs

Stem	Durative	Perfect	Preterite	Imper
G	iḫḫaz	ītaḫaz	īḫuz	aḫuz
	ippeš	ītepeš	īpuš	epuš
	irrub	īterub	īrub	erub
Gt	ītaḫḫaz	ītatḫaz	ītaḫaz	atḫaz
	īteppuš	ītetpuš	ītepuš	etpuš
Gtn	ītanaḫḫaz	ītataḫḫaz	ītaḫḫaz	ataḫḫaz
	īteneppe/uš	īteteppeš	īteppeš	eteppe/uš
D	uḫḫaz	ūtaḫḫiz	uḫḫiz	uḫḫiz
	uppaš	ūteppiš	uppiš	uppiš
Dt	ūtaḫḫaz	ūtataḫḫiz	ūtaḫḫiz	utaḫḫiz
	ūteppeš	ūteteppiš	ūteppiš	uteppiš
Dtn	ūtanaḫḫaz	ūtataḫḫiz	ūtaḫḫiz	utaḫḫiz
	ūteneppeš	ūteteppiš	ūteppiš	uteppiš
Š	ušaḫḫaz	uštāḫiz	ušāḫiz	šūḫiz
	ušeppeš	uštēpiš	ušēpiš	šūpiš
Št	uštaḫḫaz	uštatāḫiz	uštāḫiz	šutāḫiz
	ušteppeš	uštetēpiš	uštēpiš	šutēpiš
Štn	uštanaḫḫaz	uštataḫḫiz	uštaḫḫiz	šutaḫḫiz
	ušteneppeš	ušteteppiš	ušteppiš	šuteppiš
N	innaḫḫaz	ittanḫaz	innaḫiz	nanḫiz
	inneppeš	ittenpeš	innepiš	nenpiš
Ntn	ittanaḫḫaz	—	ittaḫḫaz	—
	itteneppeš	—	itteppeš	—

Synopsis of I-y Verbs

Stem	Durative	Perfect	Preterite	Imper
G	itter	īteter	īter	eter
Gt	ītetter	ītetter	īteter	etter
Gtn	ītenetter	ītetetter	ītetter	itetter
D	ussaq	ūtessiq	ussiq	ussiq
Dt	ūtesseq	ūtetessiq	ūtessiq	utessiq
Dtn	ūtenesseq	ūtetessiq	ūtessiq	utessiq
Š	ušeššeb	uštēšib	ušēšib	šūšib
Št	ušteššeb	uštetēšib	uštēšib	šutēšib
Štn	uštēnnebel	uštetebbil	uštebbil	šutebbil
N	innesser	ittenser	inneser	nēser
Ntn	ittenesser	—	ittesser	—

Synopsis of I-aleph Verbs

Participle	Infinitive	Verb Adj	Stative	Class
āḫizum	aḫāzum	aḫzum	aḫiz	a+a/u
ēpišum	epēšum	epšum	epiš	e+a/u
ēribum	erēbum	erbum	erib	e+u/u
mūtaḫzum	atḫuzum	atḫuzum	atḫuz	a+a/u
mūtepšum	etpušum	etpušum	etpuš	e+u/u
mūtaḫḫizum	ataḫḫuzum	ataḫḫuzum	ataḫḫuz	a+a/u
mūteppišum	ettepušum	ettepušum	eteppuš	e+a/u
muḫḫizum	uḫḫuzum	uḫḫuzum	uḫḫuz	a
muppišum	uppušum	uppušum	uppuš	e
mūtaḫḫizum	utaḫḫuzum	utaḫḫuzum	utaḫḫuz	a
mūteppišum	uteppušum	uteppušum	uteppuš	e
mūtaḫḫizum	utaḫḫuzum	utaḫḫuzum	utaḫḫuz	a
mūteppišum	uteppušum	uteppušum	uteppuš	e
mušāḫizum	šūḫuzum	šūḫuzum	šūḫuz	a
mušēpišum	šūpušum	šūpušum	šūpuš	e
muštāḫizum	šutāḫuzum	šutāḫuzum	šutāḫuz	a
muštēpišum	šutēpišum	šutēpišum	šutēpus	e
muštaḫḫizum	šutaḫḫuzum	šutaḫḫuzum	šutaḫḫuz	a
mušteppišum	šuteppušum	šuteppušum	šuteppuš	e
munnaḫzum	nanḫuzum	nanḫuzum	nanḫuz	a+a
munnepšum	nenpušum	nenpušum	nenpuš	e+a
—	—	—	—	a+a
—	—	—	—	e+a

Synopsis of I-y Verbs

Participle	Infinitive	Verb Adj	Stative	Class
ēterum	etērum	etrum	eter	all
mūtetrum	ītturum	ītturum	itrum	all
mūtetterum	etetturum	etetturum	etettur	all
mussiqum	ussuqum	ussuqum	ussuq	all
mūtessiqum	utessuqum	utessuqum	utessuq	all
mūtessiqum	utessuqum	utessuqum	utessuq	all
mušēšibum	šūšubum	šūšubum	šūšub	all
muštēšibum	šutēšubum	šutēšubum	šutēšub	all
muštebbilum	šutebbulum	šutebbulum	šutebbul	all
munnesrum	nēsurum	nēsurum	nēsur	all
muttessirum	—	—	—	all

Synopsis of I-n Verbs

Stem	Durative	Perfect	Preterite	Imper
G	inaqqar	ittaqar	iqqur	uqur
	inakkis	ittakis	ikkis	ikis
	inabbuḫ	ittabuḫ	ibbuḫ	ubuḫ
Gt	ittaqqar	ittatqar	ittaqar	itqar
	ittakkis	ittatkis	ittakis	itkis
Gtn	ittanaqqar	ittataqqar	ittaqqar	itaqqar
	ittanakkis	ittatakkis	ittakkis	itakkis
	ittanabbuḫ	ittatabbuḫ	ittabbuḫ	itabbuḫ
D	unaqqar	uttaqqer	unaqqer	nuqqer
Dt	uttaqqar	uttataqqer	uttaqqer	utaqqer
Dtn	uttanaqqar	uttataqqer	uttaqqer	utaqqer
Š	ušaqqar	uštaqqer	ušaqqer	šuqqer
Št^1	uštaqqar	uštataqqer	uštaqqer	šutaqqer
Št^2	uštanaqqar	uštataqqer	uštaqqer	šutaqqer
Štn	uštanaqqar	uštataqqer	uštaqqer	šutaqqer
N	innaqqar	ittanqar	innaqer	naqqer
	innakkis	ittankis	innakis	nakkis
Ntn	ittananqar	ittatanqar	ittanqar	itanqar
	ittanankis	ittatankis	ittankis	itankis

Synopsis of II-weak Verbs

Stem	Durative	Perfect	Preterite	Imper
G	ibâš	ibtāš	ibāš	bāš
	ibêl	ibtēl	ibēl	bēl
	iqīa/âš	iqtīš	iqīš	qīš
	ikân	iktūn	ikūn	kūn
	iraᵓᵓub	irtaᵓub	irᵓub	ruᵓub
Gt	ištâl	ištatāl	ištāl	šitāl
	ištīam	ištatīm	ištīm	šitīm
	iktân	iktatūn	iktūn	kitūn
Gtn	ibtanâš	—	ibtāš	—
	ištanâm	—	ištayyim	šitayyam
	iktanân	—	iktūn	—
D	ukān	uktīn	ukīn	kīn
	ušaᵓᵓal	uštaᵓᵓil	ušaᵓᵓil	šuᵓᵓil
Dt	uktān	uktatīn	uktīn	kutīn
Dtn	uktanān	uktatīn	uktīn	kutīn
Š	ušdāk	uštadīk	ušdīk	šudīk
Št	uštadāk	uštatadīk	uštadīk	šutadīk
N	iššâm	—	iššām	—
	innêr	—	innēr	—
	iqqīa/âš	—	iqqīš	—
	iddâk	—	iddīk	—

Synopsis of I-n Verbs

Participle	Infinitive	Verb Adj	Stative	Class
nāqirum	naqārum	naqrum	naqer	a/u
nākisum	nakāsum	naksum	nakis	i/i
nābiḫum	nabāḫum	nabḫum	nabiḫ	u/u
muttaqrum	itqurum	itqurum	itqur	a
muttaksum	itkusum	itkusum	itkus	i
muttaqqirum	itaqqurum	itaqqurum	itaqqur	a
muttakkisum	itakkusum	itakkusum	itakkus	i
muttabbiḫum	itabbuḫum	itabbuḫum	itabbuḫ	u
munaqqirum	nuqqurum	nuqqurum	nuqqur	all
muttaqqirum	(n)utaqqurum	utaqqurum	utaqqur	all
muttaqqirum	(n)utaqqurum	utaqqurum	utaqqur	all
mušāqqirum	šūqqurum	šūqqurum	šūqur	all
muštaqqirum	šutaqqurum	šutaqqurum	šutaqqur	all
muštaqqirum	šutaqqurum	šutaqqurum	šutaqqur	all
muštabbilum	šutabbulum	šutabbulum	šutabbul	all
munnaqrum	nanqurum	nanqurum	nanqur	a
munnaksum	nankusum	nankusum	nankus	i
muttanqerum	itanqurum	itanqurum	itanqun	a
muttankisum	itankusum	itankusum	itankus	i

Synopsis of II-weak Verbs

Participle	Infinitive	Verb Adj	Stative	Class
bāʾišum	bâšum	bāṣum	bāš	ā
bēʾilum	bêlum	bēlum	bēl	ē
qāʾišum	qiāšum	qīšum	qīš	ī
dāʾikum	kânum	kīnum	kīn	ū
rāʾibum	raʾābum	raʾbum	raʾib	ū
muštālum	šitūlum	šitūlum	šitūl	ā
muštīmum	šitūmum	šitūmum	šitūm	ī
muktīnum	kitūnum	kitūnum	kitūn	ū
—	—	—	—	ā
—	šitayyumum	šitayyumum	šitayyum	ī
—	kitayyunum	kitayyunum	kitayyun	ū
mukinnum	kunnum	kunnum	kūn	all
mušaʾʾilum	šuʾʾulum	šuʾʾulum	šuʾʾul	ʾ
muktinnum	kutunnum	kutunnum	kutūn	all
muktinnum	kutunnum	kutunnum	kutūn	all
mušdīkum	šudūkum	šudūkum	šudūk	all
muštadīkum	šutadūkum	šutadūkum	šutadūk	all
—	—	—	—	ā
—	—	—	—	ē
—	—	—	—	ī
muddīkum	nadūkum	nadūkum	nadūk	ū

Synopsis of III-weak Verbs

Stem	Durative	Perfect	Preterite	Imper
G	ikalla	iktala	ikla	kila
	išemme	išteme	išme	ši/eme
	ibanni	ibtani	ibni	bini
	imannu	imtanu	imnu	munu
Gt	ištemme	ištetme	išteme	šitmi
	ibtanni	ibtatni	ibtani	bitni
Gtn	ištenemme	ištetemme	ištemme	šitemme
	ibtananni	ibtatanni	ibtanni	bitanni
D	ušemme	uštemmi/e	ušemmi	šummi/e
	ubanna	ubtanni	ubanni	bunni
Dt	uštemme	uštetemmi/e	uštemmi/e	šutemmi
	ubtanna	ubtatanni	ubtanni	butanni
Dtn	uštenemme	uštetemmi/e	uštemmi/e	šutemmi/e
	ubtananna	ubtatanni	ubtanni	butanni
Š	ušepte	uštepti/e	ušepti/e	šupti/e
	ušabna	uštabni	ušabni	šubni
Št[1]	uštepte	uštetepti/e	uštepti/e	šutepti/e
	uštabna	uštatabni	uštabni	šutabni
Št[2]	uštabanna	uštatabni	uštabni	šutabni
Štn	uštenepte	uštetepti/e	uštepti/e	šutepti/e
	uštanabna	uštatabni	uštabni	šutabni
ŠD	ušmalla	—	ušmalli	—
N	ikkalla	ittakla	ikkali	nakli
	ippette	ittepte	ippeti	nepti
	ibbanni	ittabni	ibbani	nabni
	immannu	ittamnu	immani	namni
Ntn	ittenepte	ittetepte	ittepte	itepte
	ittanabni	ittatabni	ittabni	itabni

Synopsis of III-weak Verbs

Participle	Infinitive	Verb Adj	Stative	Class
kālûm	kalûm	kalûm	kali	ā
šēmûm	šemûm	šemûm	šemi	ē
bānûm	banûm	banûm	bani	ī
mānûm	manûm	manûm	manu	ū
muštemûm	šitmûm	šitmûm	šitmu	ē
mubtanûm	bitnûm	bitnûm	bitni	ī
muštemmûm	šitemmûm	šitemmûm	šitemmu	ē
mubtannûm	bitannûm	bitannûm	bitannu	ī
mušemmûm	šuttû	šuttû	šuttu	ē
mubannûm	bunnû	bunnû	bunnu	ī
muštemmûm	šutemmûm	šutemmûm	šutemmu	ē
mubtannûm	butannûm	butannûm	butannu	ī
muštemmûm	šutemmûm	šutemmûm	šutemmu	ē
mubtannûm	butannûm	butannûm	butannu	ī
mušeptûm	šuptûm	šuptûm	šuptu	ē
mušabnûm	šubnûm	šubnûm	šubnu	ī
mušteptûm	šuteptûm	šuteptûm	šutepnu	ē
muštabnûm	šutabnûm	šutabnûm	šutabnu	ī
muštabnûm	šutabnûm	šutabnûm	šutabnu	ī
mušteptûm	šuteptûm	šuteptûm	šutepnu	ē
muštabnûm	šutabnûm	šutabnûm	šutabnu	ī
—	—	—	—	ā
mukkalûm	naklûm	naklûm	naklu	ā
muppetûm	neptûm	neptûm	neptu	ē
mubbanûm	nabnûm	nabnûm	nabni	ī
mummanûm	namnûm	namnûm	namnu	ū
mutteptûm	iteptûm	iteptûm	iteptu	ē
muttabnûm	itabnûm	itabnûm	itabnu	ī

Synopsis of Doubly Weak Verbs: G Stem

Durative	Perfect	Preterite	Imper
iʾʾil	—	īʾil	eʾil
—	—	īde	—
illi	īteli	īli	eli
iʾêr	—	iʾēr	ēr
—	—	īšu	—
ileʾʾi	ilteʾi	ilʾe, ilē	—
inaʾʾid	ittaʾid	iʾʾid	iʾid
inaddi	ittadi	iddi	idi
inâḫ	ittūḫ	inūḫ	nūḫ
inawwer	ittawer	iwwer	iwer
inêr	ittēr	inēr	nēr
inesse	ittese	isse	ise
inīal	ittīl	inīl	nīl
uṣṣi	ittaṣi	ūṣi	ṣī
i(w)âr	—	iwēr	iʾer
iwīaṣ	—	iwīṣ	—

Synopsis of Doubly Weak Verbs: G Stem

Participle	Infinitive	Verb Adj	Stative
—	eʾēlum	eʾlum	eʾil
mūdûm	edûm	—	—
ēlûm	elûm	elûm	eli
—	êrum	ērum	ēr
—	išûm	—	—
lēʾûm	leʾûm	leʾûm	leʾi
nāʾidum	naʾādum	naʾdum	naʾid
nādûm	nadûm	nadûm	nadi
—	nâḫum	nēḫum	nēḫ
nāwerum	nawārum	nawerum	nawer
nēʾirum	nêrum	nērum	nēr
—	nesûm	nesûm	nesi
—	niālum	nīlum	nīl
wāṣûm	waṣûm	waṣûm	waṣi
—	wiā/ârum	—	—
—	wiāṣum	(w)īṣum	(w)īṣ

Part Two: Helps

Introduction

This section contains a variety of helps, as follows:

2.1 the order of the Akkadian alphabet
2.2 the seven "alephs"
2.3 equivalents between the two common notation schemes for verbal stems
2.4 correspondences among English, German, and French nomenclature for Akkadian, Assyrian, and Babylonian dialect periods
2.5 numbers and their signs
2.6 conjunctions
2.7 prepositions
2.8 common abbreviations used in lexical and grammatical tools

The listings of numbers, conjunctions, and prepositions are extensive and are intended to provide assistance even beyond an initial acquaintance with the language. The most common lexemes of the latter two groups are noted with an asterisk (*).

2.1 Alphabetical Order

ʾ a b d e g ḫ i y (j) k l m n p q r s ṣ š t ṭ u w z

2.2 "Alephs" (with Proto-Semitic equivalent)

1 ʾ 2 h 3 ḥ 4 ʿ 5 ǵ 6 w 7 y

2.3 Notations for Verbs

(Sometimes I is written as I/1, II as II/1, etc.)

I = G	I/2 = Gt	I/3 = Gtn	I/4 = Gtt
II = D	II/2 = Dt	II/3 = Dtn	II/4 = Dtt
III = Š	III/2 = Št	III/3 = Štn	III/4 = Štt
III/II = ŠD	III/II/2 = ŠDt		
IV = N	IV/2 = Nt	IV/3 = Ntn	IV/4 = Ntt

2.4 Dialect Periods

	English		*German*	*Time* B.C.E.	*French*
(OAkk)	Old Akkadian	(aAK)	altakkadisch	(2500–1950)	vieil-akkadien
(OA)	Old Assyrian	(aA)	altassyrisch	(1950–1750)	ancien assyrien
(MA)	Middle Assyrian	(mA)	mittelassyrisch	(1500–1000)	moyen assyrien
(NA)	Neo-Assyrian	(nA)	neuassyrisch	(1000–600)	néo-assyrien
(OB)	Old Babylonian	(aB)	altbabylonisch	(1950–1600)	ancien babylonien
(MB)	Middle Babylonian	(mB)	mittelbabylonisch	(1600–1000)	moyen babylonien
(NB)	Neo-Babylonian	(nB)	neubabylonisch	(1000–625)	néo-babylonien
(LB)	Late Babylonian	(spB)	spätbabylonisch	(625–)	
(SB)	Standard Babylonian	(jB)	jungbabylonisch	(1500–)	

2.5 Numbers

Numbers in parentheses are sign numbers.

2.51 Fractions

A. The fem. forms of the ordinal, e.g.,
šaluštu = $\frac{1}{3}$ *rebûtu* = $\frac{1}{4}$
NOTE: the dual *šittān*, oblique *šittīn* = $\frac{2}{3}$

B. The Sumerian phrase IGI.X̲.GÁL, e.g.,
IGI.8.GÁL = $\frac{1}{8}$

C. Lexemes and signs:

$\frac{1}{60}$	*šūšu*ʾ*û*
$\frac{2}{60}$	(570)
$\frac{1}{36}$	(7)
$\frac{1}{30}$	*šalāšā*ʾ*û*
$\frac{1}{18}$	*samāššerû*
$\frac{1}{13}$	*šalāšseritu*
$\frac{1}{12}$	*šinšarû*
$\frac{1}{10}$	(411+318) *eširtu, ešrētu*
$\frac{1}{9}$	*tišât, tišû*
$\frac{1}{8}$	*samānû, samuntu*
$\frac{1}{7}$	*sebû, sebītu*
$\frac{1}{6}$	(395a,411,536,545,598b) *šuššu, šeššu, šīšātu*
$\frac{1}{5}$	*ḫamuštu, ḫanšu, ḫammušu*
$\frac{1}{4}$	(378a) *rabât*
$\frac{1}{3}$	(571) *šuššān* (dual of *šuššu*), *šalšu, šaluštu*
$\frac{1}{2}$	(74) *aḫu, bamtu, bû, ḫupû, muttatu, zû*
$\frac{2}{3}$	(572) *šīnipu*
$\frac{5}{6}$	(573) *parasrab*

2.52 Cardinal Numbers

A. Generally stand before the thing enumerated; come after it for special emphasis.

B. Only 1 and 2 agree in gender with the thing enumerated; 3 to 19 use a masc. form with a fem. substantive and vice versa, a phenomenon commonly called "agreement polarity."

C. 1 occurs in the singular, 2 masc. in the dual, 2 fem. in the plural, 3 and higher numbers generally take the plural.

D. Sign sequences

1. Before 100, numbers are simply added
2. After 100, values < 10 before the 100 sign are multipliers
3. After 1000, values < 1000 occurring before the thousand sign are multipliers.

E. Numbers sometimes are used as substantives.

F. Multiples, e.g., three times X:

1. take *-iš* + case vowel
2. can be used with *ana* or *adi*

G. Often followed by KAM (406)

	masc		**fem**	
	st. rect.	st. abs.	st. rect.	st. abs.
1.	*ištēnu* (1, 480)	*ištēn*	*ištētu*	*ištiat, ištēt*
2.	*šina* (124, 570)	*šina, šena*	*šitta*	*šitta*
3.	*šalāšu* (2a, 124a, 325a, 593)	*šalāš*	*šalāštu*	*šalāšat*
4.	*erbû, arbaʾu* (124b[+5], 325b, 473, 586, 597)	*erbe*	*erbettu*	*erbet*
5.	*ḫamšu* (125b, 329a, 598a)	*ḫamiš*	*ḫamištu*	*ḫamšat*
6.	*šeššu* (125c, 331a, 598b)	—	*šedištu*	*šeššet*
7.	*sebû* (125d, 331b, 598c)	*sebe*	*sebettu*	*sebet*
8.	*samānu* (125e, 331c, 598d)	*samāne*	*samāntu*	*samānat*
9.	*tišû* (125f, 331d, 363, 598e)	*tiše*	*ti/ešītu*	*tišīt, teltu*
10.	*ešru* (411)	*ešer, ešir*	*ešertu*	*ešeret*

11. *ištēnešret*
12. *šinšeret* (411+570)
15. *ḫamiššerit* (470)
17. *sebêšer*
20. *ešrā* (471)
30. *šalāšā* (472)
40. *erbā* (473)
50. *ḫanšā* (475)
60. *šuššu* (211,480,536)
70. (480+411)
100. *meʾat* (532)
120. (570)
150. (578a)
200. (593a, 570+532)
300. (598a)
360. (598b)
420. (598c)
480. (598d)
540. (598e)
600. *nēru* (480+411)
670. (480+411+480+411)
1,000. *līmu* (449)
2,000. (570+449)
3,600. *šāru* (396)
10,000. *nubi* (351)
36,000. (409)
216,000. *šuššar* (396 × 480, 396 × 343)

2.53. Ordinal Numbers

A. Treated like adjectives, in *parus* form
B. Usually precede the substantive:
rebû bābu, the fourth gate
but: *ina ṣēlim rebîm*, on the fourth rib
C. Often followed by KAM (406) or KÁM (143).
D. Unlike with cardinals, there is no gender polarity with ordinals.

	masc	**fem**
1st	*pānû, maḫrû, ištēn*	*pānītu, maḫrītu, ištêt*
2nd	*šanû* (570+579+406)	*šanītu*
3rd	*šalšu, šalāšiu* (593+406)	*šaluštu*
4th	*rebû*	*rebūtu*
5th	*ḫamšu, ḫamišiu* (598a)	*ḫamuštu*
6th	*šeššu, šadāšiu* (598b+406)	*šeduštu*
7th	*sebû* (598c+406)	*sebūtu*
8th	*samnu, samānû* (598d+406)	*samuntu, samānītu*
9th	*tišû* (598e+406)	*tišūtu*
10th	*ešru* (411+318)	*ešurtu*
11th	*ištēnšerû*	
12th	*šinšarû*	
13th	*šalāššerû*	
14th	*erbêšerû*	

2.6. Conjunctions

The most common and important conjunctions are marked with *.

2.61. Coordinating

*1. *u* = particle of simple coordination "and"
*2. *ū* = "or"
*3. *lū* = "either"; *lū* . . . *lū* "either . . . or"
*4. *-ma* = enclitic particle which implies a temporal or logical sequence between the two clauses "and" "and then"
*5. *-ma* + *u* = and also, and yet
*6. asyndeton

2.62. Subordinating (verbs in subjunctive mood)

*1.	*adi*	as long as, while, until; with neg., before
2.	*adīma*	until
3.	*anāma*	as soon as
4.	*appiš*	since, because of the fact that
*5.	*ašar*	where; as soon as, while; if, in case; what
6.	*ašša*	as soon as, because
*7.	*aššum*	because; so that; that
8.	*balāt*	apart from
9.	*balu*	without
10.	*bīt*	when, where, what
11.	*ēma*	wherever, whither
12.	*ezib*	apart from the fact that
13.	*gadu*	until
14.	*ilti*	(see *ištu*)
15.	*innanu*	when, after
16.	*innu*	there
17.	*īnu*	when
*18.	*inūma/i*	when, after, while; that
19.	*inumti*	(see *inūma/i*)
20.	*iššā*	whereas, although
*21.	*ištu*	after, since, as soon as
22.	*ištuma*	if indeed
*23.	*kî*	as soon as; because; LB if, in case; MA, NA that
*24.	*kīma*	as soon as; if; when; so that; according to
25.	*kīmū*	(see *kīma*)
26.	*kūm*	because, otherwise
*27.	*lāma*	before
28.	*mal*	(see *mala/i*)

*29.	*mala/i*	as many as, as much as, as large as; everything that, everyone who
30.	*maṣi*	as much as, according to
*31.	*mati*	as soon as, when, whenever
32.	*matimê*	(see *mati*)
33.	*nēmel*	because
34.	*nirit*	because
*35.	*qadu*	because, since
36.	*qannu*	outside
37.	*ṣēru*	over, above, upon, in addition
*38.	*šumma*	if, when
*39.	(*w*)*arki*	after
40.	*warkat*	(see (*w*)*arki*)

2.7 Prepositions

The most common and important prepositions are marked with *.

*1.	*adi*	up to (spatial), until (temporal), concerning; together with
2.	*akkâša*	to you
3.	*akla*	apart from
4.	*alān*	other than, more than
5.	*alla*	over, beyond; more or less than; w/neg, only, not more than, nothing but
*6.	*an*(*a*)	to, for, up to, for the purpose of
*7.	*arki*	behind; after
*8.	*ašar*	with, before, from, instead of
*9.	*aššum/t*	with regard to, so that, because of, related to
10.	*balāt*	without
11.	*balu*(*t*)	without, apart from
*12.	*biri*	midst, between, in common
13.	*daiš*	toward, to the side
14.	*dāt*	after
15.	*ebar*	beyond
16.	*el*	on, above, beyond
17.	*ela*(*t*)	besides, apart from
*18.	*elēn*	above, upward; apart from, in addition to
*19.	*eli*	upon, towards, against, more than
20.	*ēma*	wherever, whenever
21.	*ezib*	apart from
22.	*gadu*	(see *qadu*)

*23.	*idi*	beside, near
24.	*idāt*	around, beside
25.	*illa*	without
*26.	*in*(*a*)	in, among, from, within, through (instrum.), on, with
*27.	*īnu*(*ma*)	at the time of
28.	*issi*	(see *ište*)
29.	*iš*	for, to
*30.	*ište*	with
*31.	*ištu*	from; out of; since, after
*32.	*itâti*	alongside, around, next to
*33.	*itti*	with
34.	*itu*	with, beside
35.	*itû*	adjacent to, alongside
*36.	*kî*	like, according to, instead of
37.	*kīka*	like
*38.	*kīma/ū*	as, like, instead of
39.	*kūm*	instead of
40.	*kutallu*	behind
*41.	*la*	from, out of; for; before; NB, NA to
*42.	*lāma*	before
*43.	*lapan*(*i*)	before, from, because of, in front of
*44.	*libbu*	in, among, from, belonging to, like, instead of, according to
*45.	*maḫru*	with, in front of, under the responsibility of
46.	*mala*	to the same amount, as large as
47.	*miḫirtu*	in front of, opposite
48.	*muḫḫu*	upon, over
*49.	*qadi*	with, together with, including
50.	*qannu*	outside
51.	*qudmu*	front
52.	*ṣabat*	reckoned from, beginning with
53.	*ṣēriš*	towards, against
54.	*ṣēru*	over, above, towards
55.	*šalānu*	without
56.	*šaplān*	under, below
57.	*šaplu*	(see *šaplān*)
*58.	*ṭeḫi*	close by, near
*59.	*ullâ*	from
*60.	*ullânu*(*mma*)	before, since, from
61.	*ullîš*	before
*62.	*ultu*	from, since
63.	*warki*	(see *arki*)

2.8 Common Abbreviations

aA	Old Assyrian
aAK	Old Akkadian
aB	Old Babylonian
abbr.	abbreviated, abbreviation
Abl.	Ableitung (derivation)
abs.	absolute
acc.	accusative
add.	addition(al)
adj.	adjective
adm.	administrative texts
adv.	adverb
äg.	Egyptian
AHw	*Akkadisches Handwörterbuch*, W. von Soden (1959–1981)
Akk.	Akkadian
Alal.	Alalaḫ (Alalakh)
altaram.	Old Aramaic
alw. pl.	plurale tantum
Am.	Amarna
ar.	Arabic
arab	Arabic
aram.	Aramaic
Aram.	Aramaic
asa.	Old South Arabic
Ass.	Assyrian
astr.	astronomical (texts)
astrol.	astrological texts
astron.	astronomical texts
äth.	Ethiopic
bab.	Babylonian
Babyl.	Babylonian
b.-aram.	biblical Aramaic
bes.	besonders (especially)
bil.	bilingual
BN	mountain name
Bo.	Boğazköy
Bogh.	Boğazköy
Br.	letter
ca.	circa
CAD	*The Assyrian Dictionary of the Oriental Institute of the University of Chicago* (1956–)
cal.	calendar
chem.	chemical texts
chron.	chronicle
churr.	Hurrian
conj.	conjunction
dat.	dative
DatSuff.	dative suffix
dei.	deity
dem.	demonstrative
denom.	denominative
det.	determinative
diagn.	diagnostic texts
disc.	discussion
DN	divine name
Du.	dual
EA	El-Amarna
econ.	economic texts
Elam.	Elamite
enklit.	enclitic
eth	Ethiopic
F., f.	feminine
fact.	factitive
FamN	family name
fem.	feminine
FN	river name
Fw.	foreign word
GAG	*Grundriss der akkadischen Grammatik*, W. von Soden (1969)
Gen.	genitive
geo	geographical location
Ggst.	an object
Gk.	Greek
gloss.	glossary
GN	divine name (AHw)
GN	geographical name (CAD)

gr.	Greek	math.	mathematical texts
gramm.	grammatical texts	mB	Middle Babylonian
he.	Hebrew	MB	Middle Babylonian
Heb	Hebrew	med.	medical texts
heth.	Hittite	meteor.	meteorology, meteoro-logical texts
Hitt.	Hittite		
Hurr.	Hurrian	meteorol.	meteorology, meteoro-logical texts
imp.	imperative		
Impf.	imperfect	mhe.	middle Hebrew
Ind.	indicative	MN	month name
indecl.	indeclinable	mng.	meaning
indir.	indirect	nA	Neo-Assyrian
inf.	infinitive	NA	Neo-Assyrian
interj.	interjection	nab.	Nabatean
interr.	interrogative	nB	Neo-Babylonian
intr.	intransitive	NB	Neo-Babylonian
intrans.	intransitive	neusum.	Neo-Sumerian
iran	Iranian	nom.	nominative
It.	iterative	npers.	neo-Persian
i.w.	repeatedly	num.	numeral
jaram.	Jewish Aramaic	o.	often
jB	Standard Babylonian	o.ä.	or similar to
kan.	Canaanite	OA	Old Assyrian
kass.	Cassite	OAkk.	Old Akkadian
Kaus.	causative	OB	Old Babylonian
KN	royal name	Obj.	object
Koh.	cohortative	od	or
konstr.	construct	Old Pers.	Old Persian
kopt.	Coptic	ON	place name
LB	Late Babylonian	p.	page(s)
leg.	legal texts	palm.	Palmyrene
let.	letter	Palmyr.	Palmyrene
lex.	lexical texts	part.	participle (CAD)
lit.	literally, literary texts	Part.	particle (AHw)
LL	lexical lists	Pass.	passive
LN	land name	Pf.	perfect
log.	logogram, logographic	PfL	plant lists
lw.	loan word	PfN	plant name
M., m.	masculine	pharm.	pharmaceutical texts
mA	Middle Assyrian	phon.	phonetic
MA	Middle Assyrian	physiogn.	physiognomic (omens)
mand.	Mandaic	pl.	plural, plate
masc.	masculine	Pl.t.	plurale tantum

PN	personal name	Suff.	suffix
PossPr.	possessive pronoun	syn.	synonym(ous)
prep.	preposition	SynL	SB Akkadian synonym lists
pres.	present		
pret.	preterite	Syr	Syria
pron.	pronoun, pronominal	syr	Syrian
prop	misc. proper names	TN	temple name
Prp.	preposition	trans.	transitive
PrSuff.	pronominal suffix	u	and
Prt.	preterite	ug.	Ugaritic
PsPron.	personal pronoun	Ugar.	Ugaritic
Pt.	participle	u.H.	origin unknown
Q.	Qatna	uncert.	uncertain
rel.	religious texts	unkl.	unclear
RelPron.	relative pronoun	unkn.	unknown
rit.	ritual texts	v	of
RN	royal name	v.	verb
RS	Raš Šamra (Ugarit)	Vent.	ventive
s.	substantive	VerbAdj.	verbal adjective
SB	Standard Babylonian	Vet.	vetitive
Sem.	Semitic	Vok.	vocative
sing.	singular	wr.	written form of word, esp. logograms
Skt.	Sanskrit		
spB	Late Babylonian	WSem.	West Semitic
Sum.	Sumerian	Wz	logogram

Part Three: Glossary of Proper Names

Introduction

The glossary contains proper names according to the following categories: astr (astronomy), cal (calendar), dei (deity), geo (geography), and prop (persons and misc.). In the case of locations and human beings, entries are included which are most likely to be of help to the beginning student. Somewhat more extensive listings are given of months, deities, and astronomical phenomena. For additional, consult the bibliography. Most entries are written syllabically. Often a sample of logographic representations is also given. Determinatives are generally not indicated.

Glossary

Ab šarrāni (Abu šarrāni, Ap šarrāni, Apu šarrāni) (cal) *"father of kings,"* Assyrian month name—OA, MA; wr. syll. (OA) and a-bu LUGAL^{meš}, or with MAN as the second element (MA).

Abba (Aba) (dei) (1) *a Babylonian goddess*; (2) *in Sumerian myth a god created by Ninḫursag.*

Abiḫ (dei) *deified mountain*—OAkk; wr. EN.TI.

Abirtum see **Ebirtum**.

Abra (dei) *a god.*

Absinnu (astr) *a star of Virgo*—wr. KI, AB.SIN$_2$.

Abu (cal, dei) (1) *the fifth Babylonian month, July–August, month of torches*; (2) *"father of vegetation," a god, son of Enlil and Ninḫursag*—from OAkk on; wr. NE, NE.NE.GAR.

Abšarrāni, Abu šarrāni see **Ab šarrāni**.

AD$_5$ (astr) *a star.*

Adab (geo) *a city*—wr. ADAB (=UD.NUN.KI).

Adad (Addu, Adda, Anda, Ḫadad) (dei) *the weather (storm) god*—wr. DARA$_3$, IŠKUR, LUGAL, U.

Adad-idri (Adad-ʾidri, BIR-^{d}Dadda, apil-^{d}Adad) (prop) (1) *Ben-hadad I, son of Tabrimmon, king of Damascus 885–870 B.C.E.*; (2) *Ben-hadad II,* *possibly a usurper, king of Damascus 870–842* B.C.E.; (3) *Ben-hadad III, son of Hazael, who succeeded his father as king of Damascus ca. 798* B.C.E.

Adad-nērārī (prop) (1) *Adad-nirari I, king of Assyria 1296–1264* B.C.E.; (2) *Adad-nirari II, king of Assyria 912–892* B.C.E.; (3) *Adad-nirari III, king of Assyria 811–784, father of Tiglath-pileser III.*

Adapa (prop) *hero of Babylonian myth which depicts human beings squandering the hope for immortality; first extant in the Amarna period, 14th century* B.C.E.

Adaru see **Addaru**.

Adda see **Adad**.

Addaru (**Adaru**) (cal) *Adar, the twelfth Babylonian month, February-March, month of the threshing floor*—from OAkk on; wr. syll. (OAkk only) and ŠE, ŠE.KIN.KUD (KUD = KU_5); intercalary month wr. ŠE.DIRI, ŠE.KIN.KUD.DIRI.

Addu see **Adad**.

Admu (dei) *an Akkadian god.*

Agade (geo) *A city in northern Babylonia, the capital of Sargon's empire, ca. 2334–2279* B.C.E.*; as yet not found, but probably near modern Baghdad.*

Agru (astr) *the constellation Aries (the Ram)*—from OA, OB on; wr. LU_2.ḪUN.GA_2, $ERIN_2$.ḪUN.GA_2.

Aia see **Aya**.

Aiaru see **Ayaru**.

Aya (**Aia, Ayya**) (dei) *a goddess, spouse of Šamaš*—wr. GAL, A.A (cf. **Ea**).

Ayaru (**Ayyaru, Aiaru, Yeru**) (cal) *the second Babylonian month, April–May, procession month*—from OB on; wr. GU_4, GU_4.SI.SA_2, GU_4.SI.SU.

Ayaʾūtu (**Ayûtu**) (prop) *rank, position or quality of the goddess Aya*—SB.

Ayya see **Aya**.

Ayyale (geo) *a place in Urartu.*

Ayyaru see **Ayaru**.

Ayûtu see **Ayaʾūtu**.

Akka (geo) *the city Akko.*

Akkad (geo) *in the Ur III period, the name of the northern region, as opposed to the southern, called Sumer; in later texts anachronistically indicates Babylonia as a whole*—wr. URI, UR_5.RA.

Akkadû (adj) *Akkadian*—from OAkk on; wr. URI^{ki}; fem. **Akkadītu**.

Akkû (geo) *the city Akko.*

Akkuddu (geo) *a city of the Ellipi.*

Akšak (geo) *a city*—wr. AKŠAK (= $UḪ_2$.KI), U_4.$KUŠU_2$.KI.

Akzibi (geo) *the city Akzib.*

Alala (dei) *a fertility god.*

Alammuš (dei) *a god*—wr. LAL$_3$.

Alap šamê (astr) *the constellation Taurus (the Bull)*—wr. GU, GU.AN.NA.

Alla (dei) *an epithet of Anšar*—wr. ALLA.

Allānātu (cal) *"acorn month," an Assyrian month name*—OA, MA.

Allattu(m) (**Allatu**) (dei) *a netherworld goddess.*

Alluttu (**Alluʾu**) (astr) (1) *the constellation Cancer (the Crab)*; (2) *a star*—SB, NA; wr. AL.LUL, in mng. 1 KUŠU$_2$ in LB.

Altaqû (geo) *the city Eltekeh.*

Alû (dei) *an individualized demonic power, a ghost*—Bogh., SB, NA; wr. A.LA$_2$, GIŠGAL.LU (=U$_{17}$.LU, Labat; U$_{18}$.LU, Borger).

Ālum (geo) *"the city," a place on which the Assyrian commercial colonies in Asia Minor were dependent (probably Aššur).*

Aluḫappu (dei) *a demon*—wr. AL.ḪAB.

Amanum (geo) *Amanus.*

Amar-^{d}Suenna (prop) *Amar-Sin, king of Third Dynasty of Ur (Sumerian) 2045–2037 B.C.E.*

Amba (dei) *a god*—wr. A.BA$_4$.

Amēl-Marduk (prop) *"man of Marduk," king of Babylon 562–560 B.C.E., son of Nebuchadrezzar II, biblical Evil-merodach.*

Ammīditana (prop) (West-Semitic) *king of Babylon 1683–1647 B.C.E.*

Ammīṣaduqa (prop) (West-Semitic) *king of Babylon 1646–1626 B.C.E.*

Amqarruna (geo) *Ekron, the northernmost of the five principal cities of the Philistines, nine miles (15 km.) east of the Mediterranean, probably modern Khirbet el-Muqanna.*

Amurru (geo, dei, astr) (1) *country of the Amorites, west of Mesopotamia* (wr. MAR.TU); (2) *god of the western nomadic people whose home was in the Jebel Bishri region* (wr. MAR.TU, GU$_4$, GU$_4$.AN.NA, KUR.GAL); (3) *Perseus, the west star* (wr. IM.MAR.TU, ^{d}MAR.TU, IM$_4$)—Nuzi, SB, MB, NB.

Anat see **Antu(m)**.

Anda see **Adad**.

Angubbû (or **Dingirgubbû**) (astr) *a group of stars*—Mari, SB; wr. AN.GUB.BA.

Ankurû (or **Dingirkurû**) (dei, astr) (1) *a protective deity;* (2) *a designation of stars*—SB; wr. AN.KU.A.MEŠ.

Annum see **Anu**.

Annunītu(m) (**Anunītu(m)**) (dei, astr) (1) *epithet of Ištar, became an independent Akkadian goddess*; (2) *the constellation Pisces (the Fish)*; (3) *pseudonym(?) for the planet Venus.*

Anšar (dei) *primeval deity, father of Anu the sky god; equated with Aššur in late Assyrian texts*—wr. AN.ŠAR$_2$.

Antu(m) (**Anat**) (dei) *West-Semitic warrior goddess, spouse of Anu.*

Anu (OB usu. **Annum**) (dei) *sky god, supreme god of the pantheon, spouse of Antu, father of Adad, Enlil, Ištar (in some traditions), and Nisaba; principle temple at Uruk*—SB; wr. AN, AN-num, 21, 60.

Anukku see **Anunnaku**.

Anunītu(m) see **Annunītu(m)**.

Anunnaku (**Anukku, Enunnaku**) (dei) *initially, a designation for all the deities of heaven and earth; later, especially for gods of the earth and the netherworld*—wr. A.NUN.NA, GIŠ$_2$.U, DIŠ+U.

Anūtu (prop) *function or rank of Anu, the highest god*—SB, NB; wr. syll. (with DINGIR) or ^{d}DIŠ with phon. complement.

Anzū (dei, astr) (1) *a god, in the shape of a lion-headed eagle*; (2) *a star*—from OB on; wr. AN.IM.DUGUD, AN.IM.DUGUD.MUŠEN.

Ap šarrāni, Apu šarrāni see **Ab šarrrāni**.

apil-^{d}Adad see **Adad-idri**.

Apišal (geo) *a city, probably in the upper Euphrates area.*

Apladad (dei) *a West-Semitic god*—NA; wr. IBILA.DINGIR.IM.

Apsû (geo, dei) *a region of fresh water under the earth, domain of Ea/ Enki; personified as an ancient god of the fresh underground waters, spouse of Tiamat*—wr. ABZU (= ZU+AB).

Ara see **Usmû**

Araḫsamnu (**Araḫsamna**) (cal) *the eighth Babylonian month, October–November*—from OB on; wr. APIN, APIN.DU$_8$.A.

Araḫtu (geo) *a large canal in northern Babylon*—LB, SB.

Aramu (geo) *Aram, an indefinite location indicating a concentration of Aramean population, roughly north and east of Palestine.*

Aramû (prop) *Aramaeans.*

Aratta (geo) *a city*—wr. ARATTA, ARATTA$_2$.

Arbela (geo) *important Assyrian city and cult center of Ištar, modern Irbil*—wr. LIMMU$_2$.DINGIR.

Arbu (geo) *a place in Urartu.*

Ardat ilî (**Ardat lilî**) (dei) *a female night demon*—SB; wr. KI.SIKIL.LIL$_2$.LA$_2$, KI.SIKIL.LIL$_2$.LA$_2$.EN.NA, KI.SIKIL.UD.DA.KAR.RA, LIL$_2$.LA$_2$ (cf. **Lilītu**).

Āribu (**Ēribu, Ḫērebu** or **Arību, Erēbu, Ḫerēbu**) (astr) *the star Corvus*—from OB on; wr. syll. (**Ḫerēbu** OB lex.) and UGA, BURU$_5$.MUŠEN, BURU$_5$.

Arītu (astr) *a name of the planet Venus*—from OA, MB on.

Arkaītu (**Arkâtu, Arkayītu, Arkāʾītu, Aškaītu, Aškāʾītu, Urukaītu, Urkītu**) (dei) *Ištar of Uruk*—OB, NA, SB, NB; wr. UNU.KI-i-tu (= UNUG.KI-i-tu).

Arkuzzi (cal) *second(?) month in Nuzi*—Hurr. word.

Armanum (geo) *a city, probably in the upper Euphrates district.*

Armatalli (geo) *a district in Urartu.*

Arna (geo) *a place in Urartu.*

Arrapḫa (geo) *a city*—wr. LIMMU$_2$.ḪA.

Arud (prop) *the city Arvad.*

Asakku (**Ašakku**) (dei) *"the one who strikes the arm," a Mesopotamian demon and the diseases it causes*—OB, SB; wr. A$_2$.SAG$_3$.

Asalluḫi (dei) *son of Ea/Enki, god of incantations, often synonymous with Marduk.*

Asdūdu (geo) *Ashdod, one of the five principal cities of the Philistines, inland three miles (5 km.), ten miles (17 km.) north of Ashkelon.*

Asqaluna see **Ašqaluna**.

Ašakku see **Asakku**.

Ašgi (dei) *a Sumerian deity.*

Aškaītu, Aškāʾītu see **Arkaītu**.

Ašnan (dei) *a grain god*—wr. AŠNAN (= ŠE.TIR).

Ašqaluna (**Asqaluna, Isqiluna, Išqalluna**) (geo) *Ashkelon, one of the five principal Philistine cities (the only one located on the seacoast), twelve miles (20 km.) north of Gaza.*

Ašratu (dei) *West-Semitic fertility goddess, wife of Amurru.*

Aššur (geo) (1) *the city Assyria on the Tigris, capital of the empire until 883 B.C.E., modern Qalaᶜat Sharqat* (wr. A.USAR, BAL.TIL, BAL.TIL.LA, BAL.TI.LA, AN.ŠAR$_2$, ŠA$_3$.URU); (2) (with DINGIR) *patron god of Assyria; his wife is Ninlil* (from the time of Sennacherib), *but also Ištar* (wr. AŠ, AN.ŠAR$_2$, A.USAR).

Aššur-aḫa-iddin(a) (prop) *Esarhaddon, king of Assyria and Babylonia 681–669 B.C.E., son of Sennacherib, father of Ashurbanipal*—NA.

Aššur-bāni-apli (prop) *Ashurbanipal, king of Assyria 668–629 B.C.E., son of Esarhaddon*—NA.

Aššurītu (dei) *the Assyrian Ištar.*

Aššur-nāṣir-apli (prop) *Ashurnasirpal II, king of Assyria 884–860 B.C.E.*

Aššur-nērārī (prop) *Aššur-nirari V, king of Assyria 753–746 B.C.E.*

Aššur-uballiṭ (prop) *Aššur-uballiṭ I, king of Assyria 1354–1318 B.C.E.*

Atraḫasis (prop) *"Super-wise," Atrahasis, Mesopotamian flood hero* (see Utanapištim).

Azappu see **Zappu**.

Azūru (geo) *a city.*

Azzati see **Ḫazzatu**.

Baba (dei) *an ancient Sumerian mother and fertility goddess, wife of Ningirsu; her temple was Eurukuga at Lagaš; also considered daughter of Anu and the planet Venus*—wr. BA.BA, BA.BA$_6$, BA.BU.

Bābilim, Bābilīm (geo) *"the gate of the god(s)" (folk etymology), the city Babylon on the Euphrates near modern Hilla southwest of Bagh-*

dad (also the name of the country from the OB period), replacing "Sumer" and "Akkad" in distinction to Assyria—wr. E.KI, KA_2.DINGIR, KA_2.DINGIR.RA, KA_2.DINGIR, KA_2. DINGIR.MEŠ (pl. Bābilīm), KA_2.DIŠ, KA_2.DIŠ.DIŠ, NUN, ŠU.AN.NA, TIN.TIR, UD.KIB.NUN, KIB. NUN.

Bad-tibira (geo) *a city*—wr. BAD_3.TIBIRA.

Baḫir (cal) *month name in Lagaš, Nippur, Adab, and Ešnunna*—OAkk.

Baliḫ (geo, dei) *a subterranean river and deity associated with it*—wr. BALIḪA (= KASKAL.KUR), KASKAL.KUR.A, KASKAL.KUR.RA.

Baltil (geo) *a district of the city Aššur, sometimes used of the city itself.*

Bālu (Ballu) (astr) *nothingness (a designation of the planet Mars).*

Banāyabarqa (geo) *the city Banai-barqa.*

Banītu (geo) *Banitu canal.*

Bānītu (dei) *a god*—wr. DU_3.

Barbaru (astr) *the star Lyra*—from OAkk., OB on; wr. UR.BAR.RA.

Barḫalzi (geo) *a district in upper Mesopotamia.*

Barsipa (geo) *the city Borsippa, south of Babylon, cult center of Nabû; modern Bars Nimrud; many legal and literary tablets found here*—wr. BAR_2.ZI.BA, BAR_2.SIB_2, BAD_3.SI.AB.BA.

Bašmu (astr) *the constellation Hydra (the Snake)*—OB, SB; wr. MUŠ.$ŠA_3$.TUR_3.

Bāštu (astr) *Corona Borealis (the Northern Crown)*—wr. BAL.$TEŠ_2$.A.

Bau (Babu) (dei) *city-state goddess of Lagaš, goddess of vegetation and birth, daughter of Anu, mother of Abu*—wr. KA_2

Bēl (dei) *a title for various gods, later became synonymous with Marduk*—wr. EN, IDIM.

Bēl-labrē (Bēl-libria, Bēl-ibria) (dei) *an epithet of Enlil*—wr. EN.LIBIR.RA.

Bēl-ṣarbi (dei) *"lord of the mulberry trees," an epithet of Nergal*—wr. EN.$ASAL_2$.

Bēlet see **Bēltu**

Bēlet-ekallim (dei) *Babylonian goddess, "lady of the Great House," spouse of Uraš; temples at Mari, Larsa, Ur and Qatna*—wr. NIN.E_2.GAL.

Bēlet-erum (dei) *a goddess*—wr. NIN.$ERIM_2$.

Bēlet-ilī (dei) *"lady of the gods," an appellative of various goddesses*—wr. MAḪ.

Bēlet-muballiṭat-mīti (dei) *"lady who brings to life the dead," the goddess Gula*—wr. NIN.TIN.UG_5.GA, ME.ME.

Bēlet-napḫa (dei) *a goddess*—wr. GAŠAN.KUR-ḫa.

Bēlet-ṣēri (dei) *Babylonian goddess, "lady of the Steppe," wife of Amurru, scribe in the netherworld.*

Bēltu (dei) *"Lady" (title for various goddesses)*—wr. GAŠAN

Bērutu (geo) *the city Beirut*—wr. PU_2.$ḪA_2$.

Bibbu (astr) *a planet (Mercury, Mars, Saturn), star, comet(?)*—OB, SB, NA; wr. ^{d}UDU.IDIM, UDU.IDIM.GU$_4$.UD, UDU.IDIM, DAḪ, ELLAG.
BIR-**^{d}Dadda** see **Adad-idri**.
Bīt Amman (geo) *the city Beth Ammon.*
Bīt Barrû (geo) *region of the Ellipi.*
Bīt Daganna (geo) *the city Beth Dagan.*
Bīt Kilamzaḫ (geo) *a city of the Kassites.*
Bīt Kubatti (geo) *a city of the Kassites.*
Bīt Zitti (geo) *the city Beth Zitti.*
Bubuzi (geo) *a place in Urartu.*
BUN$_x$ (astr) *Aldebaran, a double star in the constellation Taurus*—BUN$_x$ is sign 22.
Bunene (dei) (1) *courier and chariot driver of Šamaš;* (2) *an epithet of various deities including Aya and Šamaš*—wr. GADIBDIM (= SAGGAR$_2$).
Burraburiyaš (prop) (Kassite) *king of Babylon 1375–1347 B.C.E.*
Burušḫanda (geo) *Burušḫanda, a city in Anatolia famous for wealth and commerce.*

Daban (**Ṭaban**) (geo, dei) (1) *a river lying south of the Diyala, probably modern Abi-Neft or Abi-Gangir*; (2) *a city*; (3) *deified river.*
Dābinu see **Dāpinu**.
Dagan (dei) *Amorite and West-Semitic deity*—wr. KUR.
Dayyanū (dei) *a god*—wr. DI.KU$_5$., DI.TAR.
Damkina (**Damgal, Damgalnunna, Ninmaḫ**) (dei) *"the rightful wife," a Sumerian goddess, consort of Ea; name used synonymously with Ninḫursag in the story of Enki and Ninḫursag; also wife of Ea/Enki, and mother of Marduk.*
Damru (geo) *a city*—wr. DU$_{10}$.GAR.
Damu (dei) *Sumerian god of well-being, son of Ninisina.*
Dāpinu (**Dābinu, Dapnu, Dappinu**) (astr) *a name of the planet Jupiter*—OB, SB, NB; wr. AL.TAR, ^{d}UD.AL.TAR, and U$_4$.AL.TAR.
Dēr (geo) *a city in the East Tigris region, cult center of Ištarān*—wr. BAD$_3$.DINGIR.
Diyālā (geo) *river which joins the Tigris south of Baghdad*—wr. DUR.UL$_3$.
Dilbat (geo) *a city*—wr. DILI.BAD.
Dilmun (geo) *the island Bahrein, important commercial center, sometimes portrayed in Sumerian texts as a paradise*—wr. DILMUN (= NI.TUK).
Dingirgubbû see **Angubbû**.
Dingirkurû see **Ankurû**.
Dumuzi (dei, astr) (1) *antediluvian ruler in Bad-tibira*; (2) *postdiluvian king of Uruk*; (3) *Sumerian shepherd god, lover of Inanna, often taken*

as archetypal dying/rising god of the netherworld; his name was annually mourned; "Tammuz" in Hebrew and Aramaic (wr. DUMU.ZI).

Dumuziabzu (dei) *Sumerian goddess known as a male deity around Eridu.*

Dunnu (geo) *a small city in Babylonia.*

Dūr-kurigalzu (geo) *capital city of Babylon under the Kassites*—wr. BAD_3.ESA.

Durul (geo, dei) (1) *a river*; (2) *deification of the river*—Ur III and later; wr. syll.

Dûzu (**Duʾūzu**) (cal) *the fourth Babylonian month, June–July, month of Dumuzi (Tammuz) the god of fertility*—from OB on; wr. ŠU, ŠU.NUMUN.NA, ŠU.NUMUN.A.

Ea (**Aya, Ayya**) (dei) *also Enki; father of Marduk, god of wisdom, also associated with water and creation, patron of artisans, protector of the persecuted*—wr. $BAḪAR_2$, $DARA_3$, DIŠ, EN.TI, MUŠDA, $NU.DIM_2$.MUD, 40, IDIM, EN.AN.KI (cf. **Aya**).

Eabzu (geo) *a temple*—wr. E_2.ABZU.

Eanatum (prop) *Sumerian ruler of Lagaš, grandson of Urnanshe (25th century B.C.E.).*

Eanna (geo) *"house of heaven," Inanna's main temple in Uruk*—wr. E_2.AN.NA, E_2.AN.NAK.

Eannākum (geo) *Sumerian temple name*—OAkk.

Ebabbar (geo) *"white house," temple of Utu (Šamaš) at Sippar*—wr. E_2.BABBAR.

Eber nāri (geo) *the region west of the Euphrates, Syria*—NA, NB, LB.

Ebiḫ (geo) *a mountain*—wr. EN.TI.

Ebirtum (**Abirtum, Ḫebirtum, Ḫibirtum**) (cal) *a month name in Mari*—OAkk, OB.

Ebla (geo) *a city in northern Syria.*

Edammītu (dei) *an Ištar*—SB.

Ēdu(m) see **Wēdu(m)**.

Eengurra (geo) *temple of Ea/Enki in Eridu.*

Egalgina (geo) *"palace of justice," a place.*

Egalmaḫ (geo) *temple of Gula at Isin*

Ekarzida (geo) *temple of Ningal at Ur.*

Ekišnugal (geo) *temple of Sîn at Ur.*

Ekkena (cal) *a month name in Alal.*

Ekur (geo) (1) *temple of Enlil in Nippur*; (2) *a general term for "temple"*; (3) *a place of demons in the netherworld*—SB.

Elamatu(m) (**Elamattu(m)**) (astr) *Ištar of Elam, as designation of Canus Major (the Big Dog) without Sirius(?).*

Elamtu (geo) *the land of Elam, covering the territory of the Zagros Mountain range and of modern Luristan and Khuzistan; potrayed in Akkadian literary texts as hostile to Babylonia*—wr. ELAM, ELAM.MA.
Elenzaš (geo) *a city of the Ellipi.*
Ellil see **Enlil**.
Ellilatu, Ellilītu see **Illilatu**.
Ellilūtu see **Illilūtu**.
Ellipu (geo) *land of the Ellipi.*
Elūlu, Elūnu see **Ulūlu**.
Emaḫtila (geo) *part of the temple of Ezida in Borsippa.*
Emar (**Imar**) (geo) *a city in northern Mesopotamia.*
Emašmaš (geo) *a temple of Ištar at Nineveh.*
Emeslam (geo) *a temple of Nergal at Kutha.*
Emutbal (geo) *a country*—wr. GI.IN.SAG.6.
Enbilulu (dei) *Sumerian agricultural deity, son of Ea, used as a name of Marduk in the Creation Epic.*
Enḫeduanna (prop) *daughter of Sargon of Akkad (Agade), ca. 2334–2279 B.C.E., priestess of the moon god Nanna at Ur, noted as composer of temple hymns.*
Eninnu (geo) *temple of Ningirsu.*
Enki (dei) also Ea; *Sumerian god, associated with water, especially the Apsû; also the god of wisdom, one of the chief gods of the pantheon*—wr. EN.KI, NUN.GAL.
Enkidu (prop) *"lord of the good place," hero and friend of Gilgamesh; archetypal non-civilized wild man*—wr. EN.KI.DU_3.
Enkimdu (dei) *Sumerian agricultural god.*
Enlil (Akk. **Ellil, Illil**) (dei) *"lord wind," chief god of Sumerian pantheon, city god of Nippur, son of Anu; conferred Ellil-ship onto other gods, as did Anu*—wr. AB, EN.LIL_2, EN.LIL_2.LA_2, KUR.GAL, 50 (see **Illilu**).
Enmeduranki (prop) *antediluvian king of Sippar.*
Ennugi (dei) *a netherworld deity.*
Entemenanki (dei) *"lord of the foundation of heaven and earth," name of Marduk at Babylon.*
Enunnaku see **Anunnaku**.
Enzu (**Ezzu, Inzu**) (astr) *the constellation Lyra (the Lyre)*—from OB on; wr. UZ_3, UDU.UZ_3.
Epennu (**Epinnu**) (astr) (1) *the constellation Andromeda*; (2) *the constellation Cassiopeia*—wr. APIN.
Era see **Erra**.
Ereš (geo) *a city*—wr. $EREŠ_2$.
Ereškigal (dei) *"lady of the big place," queen of the netherworld, wife of Nergal*—wr. EREŠ.KI.GAL.
Erēbu, Ēribu see **Āribu**.

Eridu(m) (geo) *a Sumerian city on the old coast of the Persian sea, cult center of Ea/Enki, sometimes portrayed as the primeval city of Mesopotamia; modern Abu Shahrein*—wr. $ERI_4.DU_{10}$, $ERI_4.DU_{10}.GA$, NUN.KI, NUN.KI.GA.

Eriqqu (astr) *the constellation Ursa Major or Big Dipper*—from OA, OB on; wr. GIŠ.MAR.GID_2.DA, MAR.GID_2.DA.

Erra (dei) *Akkadian warrior god, associated with the netherworld, spouse of Ereškigal, son of Anu*—wr. IR_3, IR_3.RA.

Errakal (geo) *a name for Nergal.*

Erṣetu (geo) *the netherworld*—wr. KI.

Erû (astr) *the constellation Aquila (the Eagle)*—wr. TE_8.

Erua (dei) *goddess, spouse of Marduk (equivalent to Ṣarpanītum)*—wr. $E_4.RU_6$-ú-a.

Esagil (**Esagila**) (geo) *temple of Marduk in Babylon*—wr. E_2.SAG.IL_2.

Esikil (geo) *temple of Ninazu in Eshnunna.*

Ešarra (geo) (1) *region in heaven*; (2) *temple of Aššur in the city Aššur*; (3) *name for the temple of Enlil in Nippur.*

Ešartu (dei) *a goddess*—wr. U-te.

Ešnunna (geo) *capital of a small kingdom in the East Tigris area which flourished during the OB period, modern Tell Asmar*—wr. $EŠ_3$.NUN.NA.

Etemenanki (geo) *part of Marduk's temple complex at Babylon.*

Eulmaš (geo) (1) *the temple of Ištar in Akkad*; (2) *the temple of Annunītu(m) in Sippar*; (3) *(possibly) the temple of Antu in Uruk.*

Eunir (geo) *temple of Enki at Eridu.*

Ezida (geo) *temple of Marduk in Borsippa*—wr. E_2.ZI.DA.

Ezzu see **Enzu**.

Gallû (**Galla**) (dei) *ruthless demons of the netherworld*—SB; wr. $GAL_5.LA_2$, ḪUL.

Gamlu (astr) (1) *the planet Jupiter*; (2) *the constellation Auriga (the Charioteer)*—wr. ZUBI.

Gasur (**Gazur**) (geo) *the Old Akkadian name for Nuzi, modern Yorgan Tepe near Kirkuk.*

Gašrānu (dei) *"giant," name of a god*—MA, NA, SB.

Geštinanna (dei) *Sumerian goddess, "lady of the grape-vine," part of the city pantheon of Lagaš, scribe of the netherworld.*

Gibil see **Girru**.

Gilgameš (dei) *Gilgamesh, son of the goddess Ninsun, a Sumerian king of Early Dynastic Uruk; later deified and made an epic hero*—wr. GIŠ, GIŠ.GIN_2.MAŠ, GIŠ.GIN_2.MEZ, GIŠ.BIL_2.GA.MEŠ.

Gimtu (**Ginti**) (geo) *Gath, one of the five principal cities of the Philistines, south and east of Ekron.*

Girru (Sum. **Gibil**) (dei) *Sumerian god of fire, son of Enki*—from OB on; wr. GIŠ.BAR, BIL.GI, MURGU$_2$.

Girsû (geo) *a district of Lagaš*—wr. GIR$_2$.SU.

Gublu (geo) *Gebal (Greek: Byblos), a Phoenician city between Tripolis and Beirut, modern Jebeil.*

Gudea (prop) *ruler of Lagaš in the Neo-Sumerian period, ca. 2199–2980 B.C.E.*

Gugalanna (dei) *"wild bull of Anu," Sumerian god, husband of Ereš-kigal.*

Gula (dei) *Babylonian goddess of well-being.*

Gunātum (geo) *a place in Babylonia.*

Gurasimmu (geo) *Aramaic tribe of nomads in southern Babylonia.*

Guti (Quti) (prop) *a name used anachronistically for barbarian peoples, especially to the north and east of Mesopotamia; of their country, Gutium.*

Ḫabaṣīrānu (**Ḫaṣīrānu**) (astr) *a star*—SB; wr. EN.TE.NA.BAR.LUM, EN.TE.NA.BAR.SIG.

Ḫabur see **Ḫubur**.

Ḫadad see **Adad**.

Ḫalaḫḫi (geo) *a place.*

Ḫaldia (**Ḫaldi**) (dei) *national god of the Urarti people.*

Ḫammurapi (prop) (West-Semitic) *the sixth king of the First Dynasty of Babylon 1792–1750 B.C.E., son of Sîn-muballit, father of Samsuiluna; also known as Ḫammurabi.*

Ḫana (geo) *city and country on the middle Euphrates.*

Ḫanīš (dei) *divine servant of Adad, the storm god*—wr. LUGAL.

Ḫararāte (geo) *the city Harrutu.*

Ḫardišpi (geo) *a city of the Kassites.*

Ḫa-a-rim read **Zaḫrim**.

Ḫarḫar (geo) *the city Harhar.*

Ḫarrānu (geo) *a city in northern Mesopotamia about sixty miles (100 kilometers) above the confluence of the Balikh and Euphrates rivers, worship center for the moon god Sîn, biblical Haran*—wr. KASKAL.

Ḫaṣīrānu see **Ḫabaṣīrānu**.

Ḫattu (geo) *Hittite land.*

Ḫazaʾilu (prop) *"God sees," Hazael, usurper king of Damascus ca. 841–798 B.C.E.*

Ḫaziti see **Ḫazzatu**.

Ḫazqiaʾu (**Ḫazqiyaʾu**) (prop) *King Hezekiah of Judea.*

Ḫazzatu (**Azzati, Ḫaziti**) (geo) *Gaza, the southernmost of the five principal cities of the Philistines.*

Ḫegala (astr) *the constellation Coma Berenices ("Berenice's hair")*—wr. ḪE$_2$.GAL$_2$.LA.

Ḫendursanga (dei) *Sumerian god, son of Utu and Ninlil, spouse of Ninmuga*—wr. PA.SAG, PA.SAG.GA.

Ḫērebu, Ḫerēbu see **Āribu**.

Ḫibur see **Ḫubur**.

Ḫinnatuni (geo) *a city in Canaan.*

Ḫirimme (geo) *the city Hirimmu.*

Ḫit (geo) *a city*—wr. I$_7$.KI.

Ḫubur (**Ḫabur, Ḫibur**) (cal, geo) (1) *an Assyrian month name*; (2) *the river of the netherworld*—SB; Sum. lw.

ḪUL (astr) *the planet Mars.*

Ḫultuppu (**Ḫuštuppu, Ḫurteppu**) (dei, cal) (1) *a demon*; (2) *name of a month*—wr. ḪUL.DUB$_2$.

Ḫumban (dei) *a god*—wr. GAL.

Ḫumri (prop) *Omri, sixth king of Israel, ca. 876–869 B.C.E.*

Ḫundur (geo) *a place in Urartu.*

Ḫursagkalamma (geo) *temple of Ištar at Kiš.*

Ḫuršubium (**Ḫuršubûm**) (cal) *a month name in Elam*—OB.

Ḫurteppu see **Ḫultuppu**.

Ḫusarikku see **Kusarikku**.

Ḫuštuppu see **Ḫultuppu**.

Ḫutalše (cal) *a month name in Nuzi.*

Ḫutizzi (cal) *a month name in Alal.*

Ibbi-^{d}Sîn (prop) *"Sîn has named," king of the Third Dynasty of Ur 2027–2003 B.C.E.*

Id (**Ittu**) (dei) *the god "River"*—OB, MA, SB; wr. ID$_2$ (= I$_7$), ID$_2$.LU$_2$.RU.GU$_2$.

Īda-il (dei) *a god*—wr. syll. and with DINGIR for the second element.

Idiglat (geo) *the Tigris river*—wr. ḪAL.ḪAL, IDIGNA.

Igīgū (dei. pl.) *collective name for the major gods of heaven*—wr. I$_2$.GI$_3$.GI$_3$, NUN.GAL, NUN.GAL.MEŠ, DIŠ.U.

Iglanu (prop, geo) (1) *12th century B.C.E. king of Moab*; (2) *a Canaanite royal city, perhaps modern Tell Aitun.*

Iku (astr) *the constellation Pegasus*—wr. AŠ.IKU.

Ikû (astr) *square of the constellation Pegasus*—from OB on; wr. GAN$_2$ (= IKU).

Ikūnum (prop) *father of Sargon I.*

Il-ab (dei) *a god*—wr. DINGIR.A.MAL.

Il-aba (dei) *a god*—wr. DINGIR.AB.

Illat (dei) *a god.*

Illil see **Enlil**.

Illilatu (**Ellilatu, Ellilītu**) (dei) *goddess of the highest rank (said of, e.g., Ištar and Ninlil)*—OB, SB, NB; wr. ^{d}EN.LIL$_2$ with phonetic complement ^{d}NIN.LIL$_2$ (see **Illilu, Illilūtu, Enlil**).

Illilu (dei) *god of the highest rank (said of, e.g., Marduk, Aššur, Nergal, Ninurta)*—OB, SB, NB; wr. ^{d}EN.LIL, ^{d}EN.LIL.LA$_2$ (see **Illilatu, Illilūtu, Enlil**).

Illilūtu (**Ellilūtu**) (prop) *executive power, highest rank (of, e.g., Marduk, Enlil, Aššur, Sîn, Ištar)*—OB, SB; wr. ^{d}EN.LIL$_2$, ^{d}EN.LIL$_2$.LA$_2$, ^{d}BE, with phonetic complement (see **Illilu, Illilatu, Enlil**).

Il-mār (dei) *a god.*

Imar see **Emar**.

Imērišu (geo) (1) *the city Damascus* (wr. ša-ANŠE-šu, ša-ANŠE-šú, ša-DUR$_3$, ša-DUR$_3$.ANŠE-šu); (2) the region of Damascus (wr. KUR.ANŠE-šú).

Inanna (**Innin, Ninni, Ninnin**) (dei) *Sumerian goddess, later identified with the Semitic Ištar, main cult-center was Eanna at Uruk*—wr. MUŠ$_3$, NIN.AN.NA (Emesal, GAŠAN.AN.NA).

Inin (dei) *a (war?) goddess.*

Inšušinak (dei) *a god*—wr. NIN.NINNI.ERIN, MUŠ$_2$.EREN, MUŠ$_2$.ŠEŠ$_2$.

Inzu see **Enzu**.

Irkallu (**Irkalla**) (geo) *the netherworld*—MA, SB; wr. ^{d}IR.KAL.

Irnina (dei) *a name for Ištar.*

Is lê (astr) *Hyades, an asterism of five stars in the constellation Taurus*—SB; wr. GUD.AN.NA, AGA.AN.NA, GIŠ.DA.

Isimmud (dei) *a god*—wr. SIG$_7$.PAB.NUN.

Isin (geo) *ancient Sumerian town, modern Bahriyat*—wr. IN, PA.ŠE.

Ispabāra (prop) *king of the Ellipi.*

Isqiluna see **Ašqaluna**.

Išar (dei) *a god of the netherworld.*

Išḫara (dei) *goddess assimilated to Ištar, a guarantor of oaths, also associated with war.*

Iškur (dei) *Sumerian weather god, son of Enlil or Anu*—wr. IM.

Išme-Dagan (prop) *Išme-Dagan I king of Asyria 1717–1677* B.C.E.*, son of Šamši-Adad I.*

Išqalluna see **Ašqaluna**.

Ištar (dei) *an important goddess of the pantheon, goddess of love and war; associated with the planet Venus*—wr. iš-tar, iš-šar, iš-šár, DILI.BAD, INANNA, INNIN, 15, IŠḪARA$_4$, AN.ZIB$_2$, ZIB$_2$, ZIB$_2$, EŠ$_4$.TAR$_2$.

Ištar-Annunītum (prop) *militant dimension of Ištar.*

Ištarān (dei) *healing deity, city god of Dēr*—wr. GAL, KA.DI.

Ištar-dur (prop) *Sardur II of Urartu, 760–730* B.C.E.

Išum (dei) *a Babylonian herald and counsellor god, the* sukallu *(lieutenant) of Anu*—wr. ALAD$_3$.

Itu (**Iti, Ita**) (geo) *a city*—wr. ID_2.

Itur-Mer (dei) *"Mer has returned," Babylonian god, hypostasis of the weather god Mer, patron deity of Mari.*

Yabliya (geo) *a place.*

Yamutbal see **Emutbal**.

Yappû (geo) *Joppa, a coastal city just south of Tel Aviv.*

Yaratu (cal) *name of a month in Nuzi.*

Yasmaḫ-Adad (prop) *viceroy of Mari, son of Šamši-Adad I.*

Yasubigallu (geo) *a place.*

Yaudāya (prop) *Judean.*

Yeru see **Ayaru**.

Kabbartu (geo) *a city*—wr. NIGIN-tu.

Kabta (dei) *god of brick-making*—wr. ALAMMUŠ, KI.DU_8.MEŠ.

Kadmuru (**Kidimuru, Kidmuru**) (dei) *a god.*

Kadukū (geo) *a district in Mesopotamia.*

Kayyamānu (**Kayamānu**) (astr) *the planet Saturn*—wr. GENNA, LU.LIM, SAG.UŠ, UDU.IDIM.SAG.UŠ.

Kakkabu peṣû (astr) *"the white star"*—wr. BABBAR.

Kalbu (astr) *the constellation Hercules*—from OAkk. on; wr. UR, UR.GI_7.

Kaldu (geo) *the country Chaldea,* **Kaldû**, *Chaldean.*

Kalītu (astr) *a constellation or fixed star*—from OB on; wr. BIR, UZU.BIR.

Kalkal (dei) *servant god to Enlil.*

Kāniš (geo) *a city in Asia Minor, modern Kültepe.*

Kanūnu see **Kinūnu**.

Kanwarta see **Tanwartu**.

Kanzi (geo) *a place in Urartu.*

Kār-^{d}Bēli (geo) *a district in Babylonia.*

Kār-Duniyaš (geo) *Babylonia in the time of the Kassites*—wr. syll. and KUR.KAR_2-^{d}dun-yá-àš.

Kār-Sîn-aḫḫē-erība (geo) *later name for the city of Elenzaš.*

Karkara (geo) *Karkar, a city in western Syria on the Orontes river; Shalmaneser III claimed victory here over a Syrian coalition in 853 B.C.E.*—wr. IM.

Karru (**Karu**) (dei) *an epithet for various deities*—wr. KAR_2, GAR_2.

Kaššû (geo, prop) (1) *land of the Kassites*; (2) *of the Kassites, Kassite, a non-Mesopotamian people who seized power in Babylonia and ruled during the second half of the second millennium B.C.E.*—from OB on; wr. with KUR.LU.

Keš (geo, dei) (1) *a city in middle Babylonia*; (2) *a birth goddess*; (3) *her temple in Sumer*—wr. $KEŠ_3$.

Ki (dei) *Sumerian goddess, "earth."*

Kidimuru, Kidmuru see **Kadmuru**.

Kinaḫḫi (geo) *Canaan.*

Kingu (**Qingu**) (dei) *second spouse of Tiamat, elevated to kingship in the Creation Epic, slain by Marduk.*

Kinku (cal) *a festival and the month in which it is celebrated*—OB (Diyala and Harmal).

Kinūnu (Ass. **Kanūnu**) (cal, dei) (1) *the tenth Assyrian month*; (2) *name of a demon*—from OA, OB on; wr. KI.NE, GENE, KI.NE.NE in RS and NB.

Kipānu see **Qipānu**.

Kirbān (dei) *a god*—wr. MEZ.

Kissilimu (**Kislimu**) (cal) *the ninth Babylonian month, November–December*—wr. GAN.GAN.NA, GAN.GAN.E_3, GAN.

Kiš (geo) *Kish, a Sumerian town near Babylon, modern Tell el Oheimir*—wr. KIŠ, GU_2.DU_8.A.

Kiššītu(m) (dei) *Ištar of Kish*—OB, SB.

Kiti (geo, dei) (1) *a city in or near the Diyala region*; (2) *a god.*

Kullab (geo) *a city*—wr. KUL.ABA_4, KUL.AB.

Kumāru (astr) *a part of the constellation Cygnus*—MA, NA, SB, NB, LB.

Kummaḫlum (geo) *a city of the Ellipi.*

Kurnugi (**Kurnugû**) (geo) *Sumerian term for the netherworld*—lex.; wr. KUR.NU.GI_4.

Kurunītu (dei) *goddess at Dēr*—SB.

Kusarikku (**Kusarakku, Ḫusarikku**, Bogh. **Kušariḫḫu**) (astr) *constellation of the Bison*—OAkk., OB, Bogh., SB; wr. GUD.ALIM (= GU_4.ALIM), GUD.A.LIM.

Kutû (**Kutâ, Kūtuna**) (geo) (1) *Kutha* (*Cutha*), *an ancient northern Babylonian city, modern Tell Ibrahim, a center for the cult of Nergal*; (2) *a name for the netherworld*—wr. GU_2.DU_8.A.

Kūtuna see **Kutû**.

Kutušar (dei) *mother of Nergal and Ninurta.*

Laba (dei) *a divine epithet.*

Labbu (prop) *monstrous creature with leonine and serpent features, created by Enlil to destroy the noisy human race, destroyed by Tišpak(?)*—wr. KAL.BU.

Lagaš (geo) *Lagash, a Sumerian city-state halfway between the Tigris and the Euphrates, incorporating several modern sites*—wr. LAGAS (= ŠIR.BUR.LA).

Laḫamu, Laḫama see **Laḫmu**.

Laḫar (dei) *a god*—wr. LAḪAR.

Laḫḫu (cal) *name of a month*—Ur III, Mari, Elam.

Laḫmu (**Laḫamu**, Sum. **Laḫama**) (dei) *collective name for Mesopotamian gods.*

Lakišu (**Lakisu**) (geo) *the city Lachish, modern Tell ed-Duweir, five miles (8 km.) south of Beit Jibrin*—Amarna.

Lallubû (**Lanlubû, Lullubû**) (cal) *the sixth month in the calendar used in Elam*—Elam, SB.

Lamamāḫu (dei) *a demon*—SB; wr. LAMMA.MAḪ (= LAMA$_2$.MAḪ).

Lamaštu (NA also **Lamassu**) (dei) *Babylonian fever-demoness, daughter of Anu; she threatened infant and child mortality*—from OB on; wr. syll. and DIM$_3$.ME.

Lammu (geo, astr) (1) *a name of the netherworld*; (2) *name of a star*—SB.

Lanlubû see **Lallubû**.

Larsa(m) (geo) *a city in southern Babylonia, modern Senkereh*—wr. LARSA (= UD.UNUG).

Lāsimu (dei) *a god*—wr. KAŠ$_4$.

Latarak (dei) *a manifestation of Sîn*—wr. LU$_2$.LAL$_3$.

Laz (dei) *a name of Ereškigal in the first millennium* B.C.E.

Libittu (dei) *"brick," of Ea*—wr. KULLA, SIG$_4$.

Likkaše (cal) *month name*—OB Alal.

Lilītu (dei) *a demoness, known for attacking women in childbirth, Lilith in Hebrew*—wr. MUNUS.LIL$_2$.LA$_2$ (fem. of **Lilû**, cf. **Ardat ilî**).

Lilû (dei) *a type of demon*—OB, SB; wr. (sometimes with LU$_2$/GURUŠ) LIL$_2$.LA$_2$, LIL$_2$.LA$_2$.EN.NA, LIL$_2$.LA$_2$.EN.NU (see **Lilītu**).

Lisikūtu (dei) *a group of gods*—MA, NA.

Lišān kalbi (astr) *a star*—from MB on; wr. U$_2$.EME.UR.GI$_7$, EME.UR.GI$_7$.

LUGAL.AMAŠ.PA.E$_3$ (dei) *a demon.*

Lugalbanda (dei) *deified Sumerian king and hero, third king of the First Dynasty of Uruk, son of Enmerkar, husband of Ninsun*—wr. LUGAL. BAN$_3$.DA.

Luḫušû (dei) *a name of the god Nergal, "the terrifying one"*—OB, SB; wr. LU$_2$.ḪUŠ.A, LU$_2$.ḪUŠ.

Lulî (prop) *king of Sidon.*

Lulīmu (astr) (1) *a constellation*; (2) *a name of the planet Saturn*—OB, EA, SB; wr. syll. and LU.LIM.

Lullubû see **Lallubû**.

Lumāšu (astr) (1) *one of several stars whose heliacal risings fall at or near the solstices and equinoxes, and which therefore serve to divide the year*; (2) *a zodiacal constellation*—SB, LB; wr. LU.MAŠ LU$_2$.MAŠ-ši.

Lumnu (astr) *a name of the planet Mars*—OB, MB, EA, MA, SB, NA, NB; wr. ḪUL.

Ma'aba (Ma'ab, Mu'aba) (geo) *Moab, a state in Transjordan, east of the Dead Sea and of the south few miles of the Jordan River.*
Madāya (prop) *Mede.*
Madānu (Mandānu) (dei) *a Babylonian judicial god*—OAkk., OB, SB, NB; wr. DI.KUD (= $DI.KU_5$).
Magan (geo) *a coastal region near the Indian Ocean.*
Magmaru (cal) *name of a month in Ugarit*—RS.
Magrānu (cal) *name of a month*—OB.
Magrattu (cal) *name of a month*—OB (Elam, Diyala), Nuzi.
Magurru see **Makurru**.
Maḫalliba (geo) *the city Mahalliba.*
Māḫiru (astr) *the constellation Perseus*—wr. ŠU.GI.
Maliḫu see **Malku**.
Malikatu see **Malkatu**.
Maliku see **Malku**.
Malkānu (cal) *the second month in Mari*—Mari.
Malkatu (Malikatu) (dei) *a title of Ištar*—SB; wr. INNIN.GALGA.SUD.
Malku (Maliku, Maliḫu) (dei) *a god or chthonic demon, perhaps originally an epithet for Dagan*—OAkk., OB, Mari, SB.
Mama, Mami see **Mamma**.
Māmītu (dei) *"oath, curse," Akkadian goddess, a punisher of those who perjure, wife of Nergal or Erra*—wr. $NAM.ERIM_2$.
Mamma (Mama, Mami) (dei) *Akkadian goddess, baby-word for "mother."*
Mammītu (Mammiatu) (cal) *name of a month*—OAkk., OB (Chagar Bazar, Mari, Diyala, exceptionally Babylonia).
$MA.MU_2$ (dei) *gods of dreams.*
Mana (cal) *name of a month in Chagar Bazar and Mari*—OB.
Mandānu see **Madānu**.
Manzât (Manziat, Manzīt) (dei) (1) *the god "Rainbow"*; (2) *a star nebula(?)*—OAkk., OB on; wr. TIR.AN.NA.
Marad (geo) *a city in Central Mesopotamia*—wr. $MAR_2.DA$.
Mār-bīti (dei) *"son of the temples," a Babylonian god of destiny and war*—wr. $A.E_2$, $DUMU.E_2$.
Marduk (dei) *patron god of Babylon, in the Creation Epic he reorganizes the cosmos placing Babylon at the world's center*—wr. AMAR.UTU (= AMAR.UD), $ASAR.LU_2.ḪI$, EN, MEŠ, MEZ, $ŠA_3.ZU$, $ŠU_2$, TU.TU.
Marduk-apla-iddin (prop) *"Marduk has given an heir," Merodachbaladan, twice king of Babylon 721–710* B.C.E., *and leader of the Chaldean tribe Bīt Yakin in southern Babylonia*—wr. DINGIR.MEZ.A.SUM-na.
$MAR.GID_2.DA$ (astr) *the constellation Ursa Major (the Big Bear).*

MAR.GID$_2$.DA.AN.NA (astr) *the constellation Ursa Minor (the Little Bear).*
Mari (geo) *a city in the middle Euphrates region, conquered by Hammurapi in ca. 1765 B.C.E., modern Tell Hariri*—wr. ḪA.NA.
Marubištu (geo) *a city of the Ellipi.*
Massât (dei) *epithet of Ištar, "princess."*
Māšātu (astr) *the constellation Gemini (the Twins)*—wr. MAŠ, MAŠ.TAB.BA.
Māšu (Maššû, Mašû) (astr) (1) *the constellation Gemini*; (2) *a star*—OAkk., OB, SB; wr. MAŠ.TAB.BA, MAŠ.TAB, MAŠ.MAŠ, and MAŠ.
Medûm (geo) *a district in southern Mesopotamia.*
Meluḫḫi (Meluḫḫa) (geo) *Ethiopia (or the western Indus region).*
Meme (dei) *a goddess with healing and fertility characteristics, identified with Ninmug and other goddesses.*
Mera (geo) *archaic name for the city Mari.*
Mersû(tu) (geo) *form of Girsu in Emesal (Sumerian dialect).*
Meslam (geo) *name of a Sumerian temple of the god Meslamtaʾea at Kutha.*
Meslamtaʾea (dei) *"the one who emerges from Meslam," Sumerian god with temple Meslam at Kutha, identified with Nergal by the Ur III period.*
Miṣru (geo) *Egypt.*
Mīšaru (Mēšaru, Mēšeru) (cal) *name of a month in OB Alal.*—from OAkk. on; wr. NIG$_2$.SI.SI$_2$.
Mitinti (geo) *the name of various kings of Ashdod.*
Mitirunnu (cal) *a festival and name of a month*—Nuzi.
Muʾaba see **Maʾaba**.
Muati (dei) *husband of Nanâ, goddess of love.*
MUL.GE$_8$ (astr) *"the black star."*
Mulaḫḫišu (cal) *the god "Whisperer"*—NA.
Mummu (dei) *the craftsman god, vizier of Apsû.*
Munḫiātu (geo) *name of a region*—OB.
Murtaʾimu (dei) *a name of Adad, "thunderer"(?).*
Muṣurāya (prop) *Egyptian.*
Muṣuru (geo) *Egypt.*
Mušīrtu (Mušērtu) (dei) *a demon, "she who leans into the window"*—SB.
Muštarīlu (or **Muštadallu**) (astr) *a name of the planet Mercury.*
Mutir (cal) *name of the sixth month in Adab*—OAkk.
Muṭṭilu (fem. **Muttiltu**) (dei) *a demon*—SB; wr. KIN.GAL.UD.DA.

Nabiu see **Nabû(m)**.
Nabrû (Nabriu, Nabiriu) (cal) (1) *name of a festival*; (2) *name of a month*—used mostly in the pl.

Nabû (Ass. **Nabiu**) (dei) *Babylonian god of wisdom, son of Marduk, patron of scribes, rose to high rank in the NB pantheon after the fall of Assyria*—wr. AK (= NA_3), PA (= MUATI).

Nabû-apla-uṣur (prop) *"Nabû, protect the heir," Nabopolasser, king of Babylonia 626–605 B.C.E., first king of the Neo-Babylonian Dynasty, father of Nebuchadrezzar II.*

Nabû-bēl-šumāti (prop) perhaps *"Nabû is lord of the names" (authority to give names), governor of the city Harrate*—wr. ^{m,d}MUATI.EN.MU.MEŠ.

Nabû-kudurri-uṣur ′ (prop) *"Nabû, protect my boundary stone" (*1) *Nebuchadrezzar I, king of the Second Dynasty of Isin (southern Mesopotamia) 1124–1103 B.C.E.*; (2) *Nebuchadrezzar II, king of Babylonia 605–562 B.C.E., son of Nabopolassar, father of Amēl-Marduk.*

Nabû-naʾid (prop) *"Nabû is awe-inspiring," Nabonidus, the last Neo-Babylonian king, 555–539 B.C.E., father of Belshazzar.*

Nabû-nāṣir (prop) *"Nabû is protector," Nabonassar, king of Babylonia 747–734 B.C.E., contemporary with Tiglath-pileser III.*

Naddullu see **Nattullu**.

Nagurzam (geo) *a place in southern Mesopotamia.*

Namaššû (**ša Adad**) (astr) *the constellation Grus (the Crane)*—wr. NU.MUŠ.DA.

Nammar see **Nimru**.

Nammu (dei) *a Sumerian goddess, personification of the Apsû as the source of water and fertility*—wr. ENGUR.

Namraṣīt (dei) *"brightly-rising-god," epithet of Sîn, the moon-god*—SB; wr. AŠ.IM_2.BABBAR.

Namtaru (dei) *a netherworld demon associated with death by plague*—wr. NAM.TAR.

Namtullu see **Nattullu**.

Nanâ (**Nana**) (dei) *Sumerian goddess of love* (see **Nanāya**).

Nanāya (dei) *Sumerian goddess of love and sensuality, daughter of Anu and sister of Utu (Šamaš), often identified with Ištar, and sometimes impossible to differentiate from Nanâ.*

Nankulu (cal) *name of a constellation*—SB.

Nanna (**Nannar**) (dei) *Sumerian moon god, city god of Ur, son of Ninlil and Enlil, husband of Ningal, father of the sun god Utu*—wr. ŠEŠ.KI, 30.

Nannaru (dei) *luminary, light as poetic term, an epithet of the moon god and Ištar*—OB, Bogh., MB, SB; wr. ŠEŠ.KI, ^{d}ŠEŠ.KI, UD.SAR.

Nanše (dei) *Sumerian goddess, associated with rivers and canals, daughter of Enki*—wr. NANŠE.

Napḫuʾruriya (Egyptian: nfr-ḫpr.w Re) (prop) *Amenophis IV, 1364–1347 B.C.E.*

Narām-^{d}Sîn (prop) *"favorite of Sîn," king of the Dynasty of Akkad 2259–2223 B.C.E.*

Narbātu (cal) *name of the seventh month in Hurr.(?).*

Narkabtu (astr) *the constellation Auriga (the Charioteer)*—from OAkk. on; wr. GIGIR, GIŠ.GIGIR, GIŠ.$GIGIR_2$.

Nāru (dei) *the god "River" (or "Canal"), with judicial and creative traits* (see **Id**).

Naṣrapu (Našrapu) (astr) *a group of stars.*

Našrapu see **Naṣrapu**.

Naššīku see **Niššīku**.

Nattullu (Namtullu, Naddullu) (astr) *part of a constellation*—EA, MB, SB, NB; wr. ŠUDUN.ANŠE.

Nazi (dei) *Sumerian fish goddess who interprets dreams and is concerned with justice*—wr. AB + KU_6.

Nēberu (Nēbaru, Nēperu) (astr) *one of the names of the planet Jupiter*—wr. GIŠ.MA_2.DIRI.GA, SAG.ME.GAR.

Nēltu see **Nēštu**.

Nēperu see **Nēberu**.

Nergal (Nerigal) (dei) *Babylonian god of the netherworld where he is king*—wr. GIR_4.KU_3, MAŠ.MAŠ, NE_3.IRI_{11}.GAL, U.GUR, URI_3.GAL, U_4.U_{17}-lu, GIR_3.UNU.GAL, U.GAR.

Nēša (astr) *the constellation Leo Minor (the Little Lion)*—wr. UR.A.

Nēštu (Nēltu) (astr) *a constellation*—wr. SAL.UR.MAḪ.

Nēšu (astr) *the constellation Leo (the Lion)*—wr. UR.MAḪ, UR.A.

Nidaba see **Nisaba**.

Niggallu (Ningallu) (cal) *name of a month*—wr. URUDU.KIN, URUDU.ŠU.KIN.

Nimru (Nammar) (astr) *a constellation, comprising Cygnus*—wr. PIRIG.TUR.

Nina see **Ninua**.

Ninazu (dei) *Sumerian god, "lord healer"; traditions about him are composite and often contradictory; the old city god of Ešnunna, residing in the temple Esikil.*

Ningal (dei) *Sumerian goddess, "great lady"; consort of the moon god Sîn (Nanna); her temple was Ekarzida at Ur; she was mother of Inanna, and goddess of dream interpretation.*

Ningallu see **Niggallu**.

Ningirin (dei) *Sumerian goddess, "lady of incantations"*—wr. NIN.A.ḪA.KUD.DU.

Ningirsu (dei) *Sumerian vegetation and warrior god, "lord of Girsu," a city in the district of Lagaš; his temple was Eninnu; he was later equated with Ninurta.*

Ningišzida (dei) *Sumerian netherworld god, "lord of the good tree," husband of Geštinanna*—wr. NIN.GIŠ.ZID.DA.

Ningublaga (dei) *a god*—wr. NIN.EZEN×LA.

Ninḫursanga (**Ninḫursag**) (dei) *"the lady of the ḫursag" (stony desert ground), a name for Ninlil.*

Ninisina (**Ninʾinsina**) (dei) *"lady of Isin," Sumerian goddess, tutelary goddess of Isin, daughter of Anu and Uraš.*

Ninkarak (**Ninkara**) (dei) *"lady of the quay(?)," a goddess of healing, later identified with Ninisina.*

Ninlil (dei) *"lady wind," Sumerian mother goddess, spouse of Enlil, goddess of Nippur; originally a grain goddess*—wr. NIN.

Ninmaḫ see **Damkina**.

Ninni, Ninnin see **Inanna**.

Ninpanigingarra (dei) *a name for Ninurta.*

Ninsianna (astr, dei) *Sumerian goddess, personification of the planet Venus, identified with Ištar.*

Ninsunna (dei) *"lady of the irrigation works" (or "lady of the wild cow"), Ninsun, Sumerian goddess, mother and dream interpreter of Gilgamesh*—wr. NIN.SUN_2.NA.

Ninšīku see **Niššīku**.

Ninšubur (dei) *Sumerian god/goddess, messenger (sukkal) of either Anu or Ištar/Inanna*—wr. SUKAL.AN.NA.

Ninšušinak see **Inšušinak**.

Nintinugga (dei) *a healing deity.*

Nintu (**Nintur**) (dei) *"lady who gives birth," Sumerian mother goddess.*

Ninua (Sum. **Nina**, OB **Ninuwa**) (geo) *Nineveh, capital city of Assyria 705–612 B.C.E., near Mossul in modern Iraq*—wr. NINA.KI (NINA = AB + NA).

Ninurta (dei) *"lord earth," Sumerian god of vegetation, later a war god*—wr. MAŠ, PA.BIL, SAG, PA.BIL_2.SAG.

Ninuwa see **Ninua**.

Nippur (geo) *Sumerian city in central Babylonia, sacred to the god Enlil; important cultural and religious center, modern Nuffar*—wr. EN.LIL_2, DUR.AN, NIBRU (**Nippurāya**, *an inhabitant of Nippur*).

Niqmu (cal) *name of a month.*

Niraḫ (dei) *"serpent," a god*—wr. MUŠ.

Nīru (astr) *Arcturus, the brightest star in the constellation Boötes*—wr. GIŠ.ŠUDUN, MU.GID_2, MU.GID_2.$KEŠ_2$.DA.

Nisaba (**Nidaba**) (dei) *Sumerian agricultural goddess, also patron of scribes*—wr. NIDABA, NAGA.

Nisānu (**Nisannu**) (cal) *the first month of the Babylonian calendar, March–April, month of sacrifice*—wr. BAR_2, BAR_2.ZA_3.GAR.

Niššīku (**Naššīku, Ninšīku**) (dei) *"prince," a name and epithet of Ea/Enki*—wr. NIN.ŠI.KU_3.

Niššīkūtu (prop) *rank of the god Ea.*

Nudimmud (dei) *epithet of Ea/Enki.*

Nunamnir (dei) *a name for Enlil.*

Nungal (dei) *Sumerian goddess, "great princess"; daughter of Anu and Ereškigal, wife of Birtum.*

Nūnu (astr, dei) (1) *the constellation Piscis Austrinus (the Southern Fish)*; (2) *a star or constellation*; (3) *a god*—wr. ḪA (= KU_6).

Nusku (dei) *Sumerian god, son of Enlil, god of light and fire, "vizier" of Enlil*—wr. ENŠADA.

Nuzi (geo) *a predominantly Hurrian city, modern Yorgan Tepe, east of the Tigris, southwest of Kirkuk in northern Iraq; it flourished during the middle second millennium* B.C.E.*; important Akkadian texts found there.*

Pabilsag (dei, astr) (1) *Sumerian god of Larag, son of Enlil, equated with Ninurta*; (2) *the constellation Sagittarius (the Archer)*—wr. PA.BIL.SAG, PA.BIL_2.SAG.

Padān (dei) *the god "Road"*—Ur III.

Padî (prop) *king of Ekron.*

Palae (**Palai**) (cal) *a month name in Alal.*

Palil (dei) *"the preceding one," epithet of Ninurta*—wr. IGI.DU.

Papsukal (dei) *"male courier"*—wr. SUKAL (see **Ninšuber**).

Pāšittu (dei) *"the blotting out one," name of a Lamaštu demon*—OB, SB.

Pirizzarru (cal) *a month name in Ḫana*—OB.

Pû-lišāni (dei) *a god*—wr. KA.EME.

Purattu(m) (geo) *the Euphrates river*—wr. BURANUN (= ID_2.UD.KIB.NUN).

Qaltu see **Qaštu**.

Qarrātu (cal) *name of a month and of a festival in Assyria.*

Qaštu (**Qaltu**) (astr) (1) *the constellation Canis Major (the Big Dog)* (wr. BAN); (2) *the planet Venus* (wr. BAN, DILI.BAD)—wr. GIŠ.PAN, PAN.

Qingu see **Kingu**

Qipānu (**Kipānu**) *a place.*

Rābiṣu (dei) *a demon*—wr. MAŠKIM, $MAŠKIM_2$, $MAŠKIM_3$.

Raḫianu (prop) *Rezin, king of Damascus 740–732* B.C.E.

Raʾību (dei) *a name of the Igīgū gods.*

Raman (dei) *a god*—wr. KUR.

Rašap (dei) *the god "Flame," a god of pestilence, identified with Nergal at Ugarit, and with Apollo among the Greeks.*

Rāšîl (dei) *a tutelary deity.*

Riyar (geo) *a place in Urartu.*

Rīmē (dei) *a god*—wr. AN.MEŠ.

Rīmuš (prop) *king of the dynasty of Akkad 2284–2275 B.C.E.*

Rukibti (prop) *king of Ashkelon.*

Sabūtu see **Sibūtu**.

Sagḫulḫazû (or **Sagḫulḫazakku**) (dei) *a demon, "the one who provides evil."*

Saḫarātu (cal) *name of a month.*

Saḫritu (geo) *a place*—wr. NIGIN-tu.

Samerina (geo) *Samaria, capital city of the northern kingdom of Israel, and the region encompassing the central hill country of Palestine.*

Sammena see **Šamme**.

Samsimmuruna (geo) *a place.*

Samsuditana (prop) (West-Semitic) *king of Babylon 1625–1594 B.C.E.*

Samsuiluna (prop) (West-Semitic) *king of Babylon 1749–1712 B.C.E., son of Hammurapi.*

Sangibute (geo) *a district in Urartu.*

Sarni (geo) *a place in Urartu.*

Sarrar (geo) *a city*—wr. KAR.KI.

Sarru (**Sāru**, **Ṣarru**) (astr) *a name of the planet Mars*—from OAkk. on; wr. LUL.

Sataran see **Ištarān**.

Sîʾ see **Sîn**.

Sibbatu see **Zibbatu**.

Sibittû (dei) *Babylonian group of demons, called "the Seven"; the offspring of Anu and the earth, they come in two groups, one good and one evil; Erra is the leader of the latter and they instigate his revolt*—wr. IMIN, IMIN.BI.

Sibūtu (Nuzi **Sabūtu**, Elam **Šebūtu**) (cal) *name of a festival and a month*—OB, Mari, Elam, Nuzi, SB.

Siduri (dei) *Babylonian goddess, "she is my wall/protection"; later assimilates to Ištar, the ale-wife (sābitum) of the Gilgamesh Epic.*

Sililītu (cal) *name of the tenth month in the calender used in Elam*—Elam, SB.

Simānu (**Simannu**) (cal) *the third month of the Babylonian calendar, May–June, fixed season or time of brickmaking*—from OAkk on; wr. SIG$_4$, SIG$_4$.GA, SIG$_4$.GA.SIG and SIG$_4$.SIG.

Simbatu see **Zibbatu**.

Simut (dei) *the god Mars at Elam*—SB.

Sîn (**Sîʾ, Suʾēn**) (dei) (1) *the Babylonian moon god*; (2) MA *the third Assyrian month*—OAkk., MA, NA, OB on; wr. ZU, AŠ.IM$_2$.BABBAR, NANNA (= NANNAR), ZUEN (= EN.ZU), 30.

Sîn-aḫḫē-erība (prop) *"Sîn has replaced the brothers," Sennacherib, king of Assyria 705–681 B.C.E., son of Sargon II, father of Esarhaddon; murdered by two of his other sons*—wr. ^{m,d}EN.ZU.ŠEŠ.MEŠ-eri-ba, ^{m,d}30. PAP.MEŠ.SU.

Sinuntu (**Sinundu, Ṣinundu, Sinūnu**) (astr) *the constellation Aquarius (the Water Bearer)*—OB, MB, SB; wr. syll. and SIM, SIM.MUŠEN, GU.AN.NA, GU, GU.LA, UD.KIB.NUN.KI.

Sippar(um) (geo) *Sippar, a city in central Mesopotamia, north of Babylon, modern Abu Habba*—wr. UD.KIB.NUN, ZIMBIR.

Sippar-Yaḫrurum (geo) *a district in the city Sippar.*

Sirara (geo) *a city*—wr. SIRARA.

Siriš (dei) *goddess of fermentation and beer*—wr. SIRIS.

Sīsāʾu see **Sīsû**.

Sisinnu (astr) *the constellation Virgo (the Virgin)*—wr. AB.SIN$_2$, ERU$_4$.

Sissinnu (**Šissinnu, Šissintu**) (astr) *part of the constellation Coma Berenices*—from OA, OB on; wr. GIŠ.AN.NA.GIŠIMMAR.

Sīsû (**Sīsāʾu**) (astr) *constellation of the Horse*—from OA on; wr. ANŠE.KUR.RA; in NA also abbr. KUR.

Subartu (geo) *third-millennium term for northern Mesopotamia, used in later texts for Assyria*—wr. SUBAR, SU.BIR$_4$.

Suʾēn see **Sîn**.

Suḫurmašû (astr) *the constellation Capricorn (the Goat)*—from MB on; wr. SUḪUR.MAŠ$_2$.KU$_6$, SUḪUR.MAŠ$_2$, MAŠ$_2$.

Sumuqan see **Šakkan.**

Surḫurmāšu (astr) *tail of the constellation Capricorn*—wr. SUḪUR. MAŠ$_2$.

Ṣaʾidunu see **Ṣidunnu**.

Ṣalbatānu (astr) *a name of the planet Mars*—SB; wr. UDU.IDIM.SA$_5$.

Ṣaliltu (cal) *month name*—OAkk.

Ṣalmat qaqqadi (s.) *the "dark-headed," a poetic expression for Mesopotamians as opposed to other peoples—from* OB on; wr. syll. and SAG.GE$_6$.

Ṣalul (cal) *month name*—OAkk.

Ṣarbû (also **Bēl Ṣarbu**) (dei) *an epithet of Nergal*—OB, SB, MA, NA; wr. ASAL$_2$.

Ṣariptu (geo) *the city Zaribtu.*

Ṣāriru (**Zāriru**) (astr) *a star, constellation*—SB, NB; wr. AN.TA.SUR.RA.

Ṣarpānītum (**Zarpānītum**) (dei) *Babylonian goddess, "the one shining bright as silver"; spouse of Marduk*—from OB on.

Ṣarru see **Sarru**.
Ṣerru (astr) *the constellation Hydra (the Snake)*—wr. MUŠ.
Ṣidqa (prop) *king of Ashkelon.*
Ṣidunnu (**Ṣaʾidunu**) (geo) *the ancient Phoenician city Sidon, between Tyre and Beirut, on the east Mediterranean coast; modern Saīda* (**Ṣidunnāya**, *Sidonian*).
Ṣililītu (**Zililītu**) (cal) *month name*—OB Elam.
Ṣinišpala (geo) *a place in Urartu.*
Ṣiniunak (geo) *a place in Urartu.*
Ṣinundu see **Sinuntu**.
Ṣippu (**Ṣipʾu**) (cal) *an Assyrian month name*—OA, MA, NA.
Ṣiṣirtu (geo) *city of the Ellipi.*
Ṣitaš (cal) *a name of the month Simānu*—SB.
Ṣurru (geo) *the Phoenician city Tyre, coastal city forty-five miles (75 km.) south of Beirut.*

Šabāṭu (cal) *the eleventh Babylonian month, January–February, month of storms and rain*—OAkk., OB, MB, SB, NA, NB; wr. ZIZ$_2$, ZIZ$_2$.A.AN, ZIZ$_2$.A.
Šadâna (dei) *a god*—wr. KUR-na.
Šaḫû (astr) *a constellation or star, perhaps the constellation Delphinus*—from OB on; wr. ŠAḪ, ŠAḪ$_2$.
Šakkan (**Šakan**, Akk. **Sumuqan**) (dei) *Sumerian god of the wild animals who live in the steppe, has chthonic aspects*—wr. SAKKAN.
Šala (dei) *wife of Adad or Dagan, mother of Girru.*
Šalim (dei) *a god.*
Šalimtu (dei) *a goddess.*
Šamaš (**Šamšu, Šanšu, Šaššu**) (dei) *Babylonian sun god, probably originally a goddess, patron of truth, justice, and divination; also an epithet of other gods*—from OA, OB on; wr. GIŠ.NU$_{11}$, GIŠ.NU$_{11}$.GAL, UTU, 20, MAN.
Šamme (**Sammena**) (cal) *name of a month*—MB Alal.
Šamšī-Adad (prop) (1) *Shamshi-Adad I, king of Assyria, contemporary and opponent of Hammurapi*; (2) *Shamshi-Adad V, king of Assyria 823–810 B.C.E.*
Šankanum (geo) *a place.*
Šanšu see **Šamšu**.
Šar-kali-šarri (**Šar-kal-šarri**) (prop) *"king of kings," king of the dynasty of Akkad 2217–2193 B.C.E.*
Šar-Marad (dei) *town god of Marad.*
Šara (dei) *Sumerian city god of Umma.*
Šarrabdû (dei) *a netherworld demon*—MB, SB.

Šarrabtu (dei) *a female demon(?)*—SB.
Šarrabu (dei) *a demon*—MB, SB.
Šarru (astr) *Regulus, a bright double star in the constellation Leo*—wr. LUGAL.
Šarru-kīn (prop) *"the king is legitimate,"* (1) *Sargon of Akkad (Agade), ca. 2340–2284 B.C.E., king of Akkad*; (2) *Sargon I, ca. 1850 B.C.E., king of Assyria, son of Ikūnum, father of Puzur-Ashur*; (3) *Sargon II, 722–705 B.C.E., king of Assyria and Babylonia, son of Tiglath-pileser III, father of Sennacherib, brother of Shalmaneser V.*
Šarru-lū-dāri (prop) *"may the king (live) forever," king of Ashkelon.*
Šaššu see **Šamšu**.
Šazu (dei) *"he-who-knows-the-inside (of things)," a name of Marduk.*
Šebūtu see **Sibūtu**.
Šēdu(m) (**Šeddu, Šidum**) (dei) *a demon*—OB, MB, NB, LB, NA; wr. $ALAD_2$, $ALAD_3$.
Šeḫali see **Šeḫli**.
Šeḫli (**Šeḫali**) (cal) *a month name in Nuzi.*
Šēlebu(m) (**Šellebu, Šelibu**) (astr) *a star in Ursa Major*—OB, MB, SB, MA, NA; Ass. **Šēlabu**; wr. KA_5.A.
Šelibu see **Šēlebu**.
Šellebu see **Šēlebu(m)**.
Šeriš (dei) *a god*—wr. GUD.
Šerua (dei) *goddess of dawn*—wr. EDIN.
Šidum see **Šēdu(m)**.
Šiḫṭu (astr) *the planet Mercury*—wr. UDU.IDIM.GU_4.UD.
Šiltāḫu (astr) *the star Sirius*—wr. GAG.SI.SA_2, GAG.BAN, KAK.BAN.
Šinišḫu (geo) *a place*—Nuzi.
Širimtum (geo) *a place.*
Šissinnu, Šissintu see **Sissinnu**.
Šitādālu (astr) *the constellation Orion (the Hunter)*—wr. SIPA.ZI.AN.NA.
Šukūdu(m) (astr) *the star Sirius*—from OB on; wr. GAG.SI.SA_2.
Šulgi (prop) *king of the Third Dynasty of Ur (Sumerian) 2093–2046 B.C.E.*
Šullat (dei) *servant deity of Adad*—wr. PA, ŠU.PA.
Šulmānu (dei) *a god*—wr. SILIM.MA.
Šulmānu-ašarid (prop) *"Šulmānu is a leader," Shalmaneser:* (1) *S. I (1274–1245 B.C.E.), son of Adad-nirari I, whose victories marked the return of Assyria to power*; (2) *S. II (1031–1020 B.C.E.)*; (3) *S. III (858–824 B.C.E.), son of Ashur-nasirpal II, whose numerous campaigns included contact with Israel*; (4) *S. IV (782–772 B.C.E.), son of Adad-nirari III*; (5) *S. V (727–722 B.C.E.), son of Tiglath-pileser III, brother of Sargon II, who ruled in Babylon under the name of Ululai.*

Šulpaʾe (dei) *Sumerian god, "radiantly appearing youth"; husband of Ninḫursag*—wr. ŠUL.PA.E_3.
Šuluḫḫītu (dei) *a god*—SB.
Šumeru(m) (geo) *the country Sumer/Sumeria (and Sumerian), situated on the alluvial plain between the Tigris and Euphrates rivers in the southern part of modern Iraq, an area of approximately 8000 square miles; the first major civilization of the ancient Near East; major Sumerian cities include Ur, Uruk, Lagaš, Nippur, Šuruppak, Eridu, Kiš, and Ešnunna; the Sumerians entered the area ca. 3300* B.C.E.*, displacing the Ubayids; the area, with Akkad to the north, was later known as Babylonia*—SB, NA; wr. EME.GI_7, KI.EN.GI, KI.IN.GI, KALAM.
Šūpû (astr) *Arcturus, the brightest star in the constellation Boötes*—wr. ŠU.PA.
Šuruppak (geo) *Shuruppak, a city twenty miles (33 km.) south of Nippur on the old course of the Euphrates, modern Fara*—wr. ŠURUPPAK.
Šušan (geo) (1) *Susa, capital city of Elam; biblical Shushan*; (2) *a country*—wr. $MUŠ_2$.EREN, $MUŠ_2$.$ŠEŠ_2$, $MUŠ_3$.EREN, $MUŠ_3$.$ŠEŠ_2$.
Šušinak (dei) *a god*—wr. $MUŠ_2$.EREN, $MUŠ_2$.$ŠEŠ_2$, $MUŠ_3$.EREN, $MUŠ_3$.$ŠEŠ_2$.
Šuzianna (dei) *a Sumerian deity.*

Tammuz see **Dumuzi**.
Tamnâ (geo) *the city Timnah.*
Tanbartu see **Tanwartu**.
Tanwartu (**Tanbartu**, OA **Kanwarta**) (cal) *Assyrian month name.*
Tašmētu (OAkk **Tašmaᶜtum**) (dei) *"the granting of requests," Babylonian goddess, associated with protection, merciful mediation, love and potency; spouse of Nabû.*
Tašrītu (cal) *the seventh month of the Babylonian calendar, September–October, month of beginning*—wr. DU_6, DU_6.KU_3; OB, MB, NB, LB, SB, NA.
Tatium (cal) *the name of a month in Elam.*
Tebiltu (geo) *a canal near Nineveh.*
Teliyatu see **Telītu**.
Telītu (**Telētu, Teliyatu**) (dei) *"the exceedingly strong" (or "expert"), an epithet of Ištar*—wr. ZIB_2, AN.ZIB_2.
Tešub (**Tešup**) (dei) *Hurrian weather god*—wr. IŠKUR, U.
Tiamat (dei) *chief goddess of the sea, spouse of Apsû*—wr. TI.$GEME_2$.
Tibar (geo, dei) (1) *a mountain in the Gasur area*; (2) *a god.*
Tilmun see **Dilmun**.
Tiru (dei) *a god.*
Tišpak (dei) *town god of Ešnunna, replaced Ninazu*—wr. TIŠPAK.
Tukultī-apil-Ešarra (prop) *"my trust is the heir of (the temple) Ešarra," Tiglath-pileser III, king of Assyria and Babylonia (under the name*

Pūlu, biblical Pul) 745–727 B.C.E., son of Adad-nirari III, father of Shalmaneser V.

Tukultī-Ninurta (prop) *"my trust is Ninurta," Tukulti-Ninurta I, king of Assyria 1235–1198 B.C.E. who partially destroyed Babylon.*

Turukkūtum (prop) *the Turukki folk, name of a mountain people.*

Tuttul (geo) *a place on the Euphrates, probably modern Hit.*

Tutu (dei) *epithet of Nabû and Marduk.*

Ṭaban see **Daban**.

Ṭebētu (cal) *the tenth month of the Babylonian calendar, December–January, month of plunging (into water)*—from OB on; wr. AB, AB.BA.E_3.

Ubianda (geo) *a mountain in Urartu.*

Ubsaḫarrakku (geo) *a chapel in Babylon*—wr. UB.SAḪAR.RA, UB.SA.ḪA.RI.

U_4.DA.KAR.RA (dei) *a demon.*

UD_5 (astr) *Capella, a double star in the constellation Auriga.*

Udummu (geo) *the land of Edom* (**Udummāya**, *Edomite*).

Ugallu (dei) *a lion demon*—wr. UD.GAL (or $PIRIG_2$.GAL?).

UG_8.GA (astr) (1) *"the black star"*; (2) *the constellations Corvus and Crater.*

Uggae (dei) *god of death.*

Ukadūʾa (astr) *a star*—wr. U_4.KA.DUḪ.A.

Ullisum (geo) *a region probably in Syria.*

Ulūlu (Elūlu, Elūnu) (cal) *the sixth month of the Babylonian calendar, August–September, month of purification*—wr. KIN, KIN^{d}INNIN.NA; intercalary month wr. KIN^{II}KAM, KIN^{II}KAM.MA.

Ūm nāʾiri (astr) *the constellations Cygnus (the Swan or Northern Cross) and Lacerta (the Lizard)*—wr. U_4.KA.DUḪ.A.

Umma (geo) *Sumerian city-state, near Lagaš, its arch-enemy*—wr. $KUSU_2$.

Ummān-manda (OB also **Ummān-madda, Ummān-badda**) (prop) *an undetermined people.*

Ūmu(m) (OA **Umšu**) (dei) (1) *the god "Day"*; (2) *sun and storm demons*—wr. syll. and (def. 2) UD.

Upe (geo) *the city Opis*—wr. UPE (= UD.$KUŠU_2$.KI, $UḪ_2$.KI).

Urāḫum (cal) *a month name*—OB Mari.

Urarṭu (geo) *the country Urartu*—wr. TILLA.

Uraš (dei) *a Babylonian god, spouse of Bēlet-ekallim*—wr. URAŠ (= URTA).

Urgulû (astr) *the constellation Leo (the Lion)*—wr. UR.GU.LA.

Uri (geo) *Ur, a city-state in southern Mesopotamia, modern Tell Muqqayir*—wr. URI$_2$ (= URIM$_2$).
Uridimmû (astr) *the constellation Lupus (the Wolf)*—wr. UR.IDIM.
Urkītu see **Arkaītu**.
Urmašum (dei) *epithet of Zababa.*
UR.SAG (dei) *"heroine," a goddess.*
Ursalimmu (geo) *the city Jerusalem.*
Uruk (geo) *Uruk, a city-state in southern Mesopotamia, cult center of Anu and Ištar; biblical Erech, modern Warka*—wr. UNU.KI (= UNUG.KI).
Urukagina see **Uuinimgina**.
Urukaītu see **Arkaītu**.
Uruttu (1x **Uruntu**) (geo) *a name of the Euphrates river.*
Usab (geo) *a city*—wr. ARAB.
Usmû (also **Ara**) (dei) *"double-sighted," messenger of Ea*—wr. DINGIR.ARA.
Uṣur-amassu (dei) *perhaps a designation of Nanâ of Uruk*—wr. URU$_3$.INIM-su.
Ušû (geo) *the city Ushu.*
Utanapištim (dei) *hero of the Old Babylonian flood epic; variant of Atraḫasis*—wr. ut-ZI.
Utitḫe (cal) *month name in Alal.*
Utnapištim see **Utanapištim**.
Uttu (dei) *Sumerian goddess of vegetation*—wr. UTTU.
Utu (dei) *the Sumerian sun god, temple Ebabbar at Larsa (main sanctuary), son of Nanna, later identified with Šamaš*—wr. UTU.
Utukku(m) (dei) *a malicious demon, or a dead person's spirit*—wr. UDUG.
Uuinimgina (formerly **Urukagina**) (prop) *Sumerian ruler of Lagaš, ca. 25th century* B.C.E., *known for social reforms.*

Wēdu(m) (**Ēdu(m)**) *a star in Hercules*—wr. AŠ.

Zababa (dei) *Sumerian and Akkadian warrior god, city god of Kiš, husband of Inanna or Baba*—wr. ZA.BA$_4$.BA$_4$.
Zabalam (geo) *a city*—wr. ZA.MUŠ$_2$.UNUG, ZA.MUŠ$_3$.UNUG.
Zabbu see **Zappu**.
Zagmukku (**Zammukku**) (cal) *beginning of the year, New Year's festival*—from OB on; wr. ZAG.MUK.
Zaḫrim (dei) *epithet of Marduk.*—wr. ZAḪ$_2$.RIM.
Zammukku see **Zagmukku**.
Zappu (**Zabbu, Azappu**) (astr) *the star cluster Pleiades*—from OA on; wr. MUL.MUL.

Zaqīqu (**Ziqīqu**) (dei) *the god of dreams*—SB, NB; wr. AN.ZAG.GAR, AN.ZAG.GAR.RA, AN.ZA.GAR_3, AN.ZA.GAR.

Zāriru see **Ṣāriru**.

Zarpanītu(m) see **Ṣarpanītum**.

Zibānītu (astr) *the constellation Libra (the Scales)*—MB, SB, NB; wr. ZI.BA.AN.NA).

Zibānû (astr) *the constellation Libra*—NB.

Zibbatu (**Zimbatu, Simbatu, Sibbatu**) (astr) *the constellation Pisces (the Fish)*—from OB on; wr. KUN.MEŠ, ZIB.ME.

Zililītu see **Ṣililītu**.

Zimbatu see **Zibbatu**.

Zimri-lim (prop) *final king of Mari*.

Ziqīqu see **Zaqīqu**.

Zû see **Anzû**.

Zukaqīpu, Zukiqīpu see **Zuqaqīpu**.

Zuqaqīpu (**Zuqaqqīpu, Zukaqīpu, Zuqiqīpu, Zukiqīpu**) (astr) *the constellation Scorpio (the Scorpion)*—from OAkk., OB on; wr. GIR_2.TAB.

Part Four: Logograms

Introduction

The logograms listed here have been chosen because they are commonly found in introductory Akkadian texts. Two listings of logograms and the lexemes that they represent are given. The first (4.1) is of individual logograms, the second (4.2) of composite. Both are organized by sign number, the composite list by the number in boldface type (see the sign list in Part Five). When the sign numbers given by the lists of Labat and Borger disagree, preference has been given to Borger's numbering (also see next section). Numbers of determinatives are given in parentheses. All lexemes are listed without mimation.

Three indexes that refer to the initial two listings follow. The first of these (4.3) is arranged by *Akkadian word* and the second (4.4) by *English gloss*. The third index (4.5), which refers only to the Composite Logogram list, is organized by *sign number*. The numbers in bold always refer to the list of Composite Logograms.

The user may thus look up logograms in three different ways. The first two are self-explanatory. The third index allows the user to find a word that consists of logograms by *any* of the signs involved (an index is not necessary for individual logograms, which are already organized by sign number). For example, while working with a text, sign 328 is identified. To determine if this sign is part of a logogram string that constitutes one word, rather than representing a syllable or single logogram, refer to the third index in this section (4.5). Sign 328 occurs twice in the index. By consulting signs 133 and 208 in the Composite Logogram list (4.2), the user can determine if the combination of signs in the text indicates either *Bābilim* or *sīsû*.

There is one final way that the two logogram lists may be consulted. To search the lists by *sign designation*, e.g., DUG_4, consult the Value Index in *Part Five* (5.3) where the sign numbers are given. After discovering that DUG_4 is sign number 15, one can check below to see if DUG_4 occurs in either list. In this case, it does occur, in the Individual Logogram list (4.1), and indicates *qabû*, *'to say'*. This way of searching is especially helpful when working with texts in transliteration.

4.1 Individual Logograms

AŠ	1	*išten*, one
AŠ	1	*ina*, into
AŠ	1	*nadānu*, to give
ZU	6	*idû*, to know
ZU	6	*lamādu*, to learn
ABZU	6a	*apsû*, subt. water
KUŠ	7	*mašku*, hide
SU	7	*râbu*, to compensate
SILA	12	*sūqu*, street
AN	13	*Anu* (god)
AN	13	*šamû*, sky
DINGIR	13	*ilu*, god
DINGIR	13	*ana*, to
DUG$_4$	15	*qabû*, to say
GU$_3$	15	*šasû*, to cry
INIM	15	*awātu*, word
KA	15	*pû*, mouth
ZU$_2$	15	*šinnu*, tooth
KU$_2$	36	*akālu*, to eat
URU	38	*ālu*, city
UKKIN	40	*puḫur*, assembly
IR$_3$	50	*wardu*, slave
ITU	52	(*w*)*arḫu*, month
ŠAḪ	53	*šaḫû*, pig
KU$_4$	58	*erēbu*, to enter
PAP	60	*aḫu*, brother
MU	61	*zikru*, name
MU	61	*šumu*, name
MU	61	*nīšu*, life
MU	61	*zakāru*, speak
SILA$_3$	62	*qû*, liter measure
ŠUB	68	*maqātu*, to throw
ŠUB	68	*nadû*, to throw
BAD	69	*petû*, to open
IDIM	69	*Ea* (god)
IDIM	69	*kabtu*, heavy
SUMUN	69	*labīru*, old
SUN	69	*labīru*, old
TIL	69	*labāru*, get old
TIL	69	*qatû*, be ended
NUMUN	72	*zēru*, seed
MAŠ	74	*Ninurta* (god)
NU	75	*ul*, not
NU	75	*lā*, not
MUŠEN	78	*iṣṣūru*, bird
GAL$_2$	80	*bašû*, to be
ZI	84	*napištu*, life
GI	85	*qanû*, reed
GI	85	*târu*, to return
GI	85	*ḫurāṣu*, gold
NUN	87	*rubû*, prince
EN	99	*bēlu*, lord
GU$_2$	106	*kišadu*, neck
GUN	108*	*biltu*, tribute
SI	112	*qarnu*, horn
SAG	115	*rēšu*, head
TAG	126	*lapātu*, touch
MUL	129a	*kakkabu*, star
KA$_2$	133	*bābu*, gate
TA	139	*ištu*, from
TA	139	*ultu*, from
I	142	*nâdu*, to praise
DUMU	144	*māru*, son
TUR	144	*ṣeḫru*, small
AD	145	*abu*, father
LUGAL	151	*šarru*, king
KEŠDA	152	*rakāšu*, to bind
BAD$_3$	152[8]	*dūru*, city wall
SUM	164	*nadānu*, to give
KASKAL	166	*girru*, way
GABA	167	*irtu*, breast
EDIN	168	*ṣēru*, field
AM	170	*rīmu*, wild bull
IZI	172	*išātu*, fire
KUM	191	*ḫašālu*, to crush
UR$_2$	203	*sūnu*, lap
UR$_2$	203	*pēnu*, thigh
GIN	206	*alāku*, to go
GUB	206	*izuzzu*, to stand
TUM$_2$	206	*wabālu*, bring
ANŠE	208	*imēru*, ass
ANŠE	208	*imēru*, homer

EGIR	209	*warki*, after
GEŠTIN	210	*karānu*, wine
NITA	211	*zikaru*, male
SAḪAR	212	*epru*, dust
KAŠ	214	*šikaru*, beer
NA$_4$	229	*abnu*, stone
I$_3$	231	*šamnu*, oil
AMA	237	*ummu*, mother
DAGAL	237	*rapšu*, wide
UGULA	295	*waklu*, overseer
GIDRI	295	*ḫaṭṭu*, scepter
PA	295	*ar*(*t*)*u*, foliage
GARZA	295b	*parṣu*, relig. duty
SIPA	295m	*rēʾû*, shepherd
GIŠ	296	*iṣu*, tree, wood
GUD	297	*alpu*, ox
DUG	309	*karpatu*, pot
KALAM	312	*mātu*, land
UKU$_3$	312	*nišū*, people
UN	312	*nišū*, people
MEZ	314	*Marduk*
KUŠ$_3$	318	*ammatu*, cubit
U$_2$	318	*šammu*, plant
GA	319	*šizbu*, milk
SUKKAL	321	*sukkallu*, vizier
KALAG	322	*danānu*, be strong
GURUŠ	322	*eṭlu*, young man
E$_2$	324	*bītu*, house
GI$_4$	326	*târu*, to return
LU$_2$	330	*awīlu*, man
ŠEŠ	331	*aḫu*, brother
SAR	331e	*šaṭaru*, write
A$_2$	334	*idu*, arm, side
MURUB$_4$	337	*qablu*, middle
GAL	343	*rabû*, great
BARA$_2$	344	*parakku*, throne
AGA	347	*agû*, crown
ŠA	353	*manû*, mina
ŠU	354	*qātu*, hand
KUR	366	*kašādu*, to conquer
KUR	366	*mātu*, land
KUR	366	*šadû*, mountain
ŠE	367	*šēʾu*, barley
KAR	376*	*kāru*, quay
BABBAR	381	*peṣû*, white
U$_4$	381	*ūmu*, day
UTU	381	*šamšu*, sun
GEŠTU	383	*uznu*, ear
ŠA$_3$	384	*libbu*, heart
ERIN$_2$	393	*ṣābu*, soldier
ERIN$_2$	393	*ummānu*, army
DUG$_3$	396	*birku*, knee
DUG$_3$	396	*ṭābu*, good
ŠAR$_2$	396	*šāru*, 3600
TU$_{15}$	399	*šāru*, wind
IM	399	*šāru*, wind
IM	399	*ṭiṭṭu*, clay
IM	399	*ṭuppu*, tablet
ḪAR	401	*šemiru*, ring
U	411	*ešru*, ten
UGU	412	*eli*, upon
GE$_6$	427	*mūšu*, night
GE$_6$	427	*ṣalmu*, black
AMAR	437	*būru*, calf
GIM	440	*kīma*, like
GIR$_3$	444	*šēpu*, foot
GIG	446	*murṣu*, disease
IGI	449	*īnu*, eye
IGI	449	*pānu*, front
LIM	449	*līmu*, thousand
SIG$_5$	454	*damqu*, good
SA$_2$	457	*šanānu*, to equal
SILIM	457	*šulmu*, health
KI	461	*ašru*, place
KI	461	*erṣetu*, earth
KU$_3$	468	*ellu*, pure
NIŠ	471	*ešra*, twenty
UŠU$_3$	472	*šalāšā*, thirty
NIMIN	473	*erbâ*, forty
LIMMU$_3$	473	*erbe*, four
NINNU	475	*ḫanšā*, fifty
GIŠ$_2$	480	*šuššu*, sixty
DIŠ	480	*išten*, one
DIŠ	480	*šumma*, if
LA$_2$	481	*kamû*, prisoner
LA$_2$	481	*kamû*, to imprison

ENGUR	484	*Nammu* (goddess)	ID$_2$	579d	*nāru*, river
ME	532	*meʾat*, hundred	KU$_6$	589	*nūnu*, fish
DUR$_2$	536	*wašābu*, to sit	EŠ$_5$	593	*šalāšu*, three
TUKUL	536	*tukultu*, trust	GIN$_2$	595	*šiqlu*, shekel
DAB	537	*ṣabātu*, seize	LIMMU	597	*erbe*, four
DIB	537	*etēqu*, to pass	NINDA	597	*akalu*, food
UDU	537	*immeru*, sheep	GEŠIA	598a	5 *šušši* = 300
SIG$_2$	539	*šipātu*, wool	IA$_2$	598a	*ḫamiš*, five
MUNUS	554	*sinništu*, woman	AŠ$_3$	598b	*šeššu*, six
MI$_2$	554	*sinništu*, woman	GEŠAŠ	598b	6 *šušši* = 360
NIN	556	*bēltu*, lady	GEŠUMUN	598c	7 šušši = 420
DAM	557	*aššatu*, wife	IMIN	598c	*sebe*, seven
GEME$_2$	558	*amtu*, fem. servant	UMUN$_7$	598c	*sebe*, seven
SIKIL	564	*ellu*, pure	GEŠUSSU	598d	8 *šušši* = 480
MIN	570	*šinā*, two	USSU	598d	*šamānû*, eight
UR	575	*kalbu*, dog	GEŠILIMMU	598e	9 *šušši* = 540
A	579	*aplu*, heir	ILLIMU	598e	*tišu*, nine

4.2 Composite Logograms

^{d}AŠ	(13)**1**	*Aššur* (the god)
^{uru}ḪAL-*ṣu*	(38)**2**+555	*ḫalṣu*, fortification
AN.BAR	**13**+74	*parzillu*, iron
AN.DUL$_3$	**13**+329	*andullu*, sunshade
^{zá}AN.GUG.ME	(229)**13**+591+532	*sāndu*, red sandstone
^{kur}AŠŠUR^{ki}	(366)**14**(461)	*Aššur*, Assyria
ZU$_2$.LUM.MA	**15**+565+342	*suluppu*, date
U$_{18}$.LU	**49***+537	*šūtu*, south
^{giš}APIN	(296)**56**	*epinnu*, a plow
^{zá}TU	(229)**58**	*yaraḫḫu*, ruby
^{lú}KUR$_2$	(330)**60**	*nakru*, enemy
^{zá}NA.RU$_2$.A	(229)**70**+230+579	*narû*, stela
ŠIR.BUR.LA	**71**+349+55	*Lagaš* (city)
TI.LA	**73**+55	*balāṭu*, to live
KUNGA$_2$	**74**+13	*parû*, mule
^{anše}KUNGA$_2$	(208)**74**+13	*parû*, mule
MAŠ.DA$_3$	**74**+230	*ṣabītu*, gazelle
MAŠ.EN.KAK	**74**+99+230	*muškēnu*, common citizen
^{kur}NU.GI$_4$(.A)	(366)**75**+326(+579)	*erṣet lātâri*, netherworld
^{giš}IG	(296)**80**	*daltu*, door
^{mí}ḪUB$_2$	(554)**88**	*atānu*, jenny

EN.LIL$_2$^{ki}	**99**+313(461)	*Nippur* (city)
^{d}EN	(13)**99**	*Bēl*, *Marduk* (gods)
^{d}EN.ZU	(13)**99**+6	*Sîn* (god)
^{d}EN.LIL$_2$(.LA$_2$)	(13)**99**+313(+481)	*Enlil*, *Illil* (great god)
$^{m,\,d}$EN.ZU.ŠEŠ.MEŠ-*eri-ba*	(480,13)**99**+6+331 +533+38+5	*Sîn-aḫḫē-erība*, Sennacherib
^{lú}EN.NAM	(330)**99**+79	*bēl pīḫāti*, commissioner
^{d}INANNA	(13)**103**	*Ištar* (goddess)
SA.TU	**104**+58	*šadû*, mountain
GU$_2$.DU$_8$.A^{ki}	**106**+167+579(461)	*Kutû*, Kutha
SI.SA$_2$	**112**+457	*ešēru*, prosper
SI.SA$_2$	**112**+457	*ištānu*, north
^{giš}SAG.KUL	(296)**115**+72	*sikkūru*, lock
SAG.DU	**115**+206	*qaqqadu*, head
^{giš}MA$_2$	(296)**122**	*elippu*, boat
TAB.TAB	**124**+124	*ṣurrupu*, refined
LIMMU$_2$(.BA)	**124b**(+5)	*erbe*, four
KA$_2$.GAL	**133**+343	*abullu*, city gate
KA$_2$^{d}RA^{ki}	**133**+13+328(461)	*Bābilim*, Babylon
^{zá}I.DIB	(229)**142**+537	*askuppatu*, threshold
ḪE$_2$.GAL	**143**+343	*ḫegallu*, abundance
DUMU.MI$_2$	**144**+554	*mārtu*, daughter
^{lú}TUR	(330)**144**	*šerru*, child
AM.SI	**170**+112	*pīru*, elephant
UNU^{ki}	**195**(461)	*Uruk* (country)
NINA^{ki}	**200**(461)	*Ninua*, Nineveh
ANŠE.KUR.RA	**208**+366+328	*sīsû*, horse
^{lú}US$_2$	(537)**211**	*rēdû*, soldier
^{lú}NI.DU$_8$	(330)**231**+167	*ātû*, gatekeeper
^{d}IR.KAL	(13)**232**+322	*Irkallu*, netherworld
^{giš}PA	(296)**295**	*ḫuṭāru*, branch, staff
^{zá}PA	(229)**295**	*ayyartu*, a type of stone
^{m,d}MUATI.EN.MU.MEŠ	(480,13)**295**+99 +61+533	*Nabû-bēl-šumāti*, Nabubelshumati
GISSU	**296**+427	*ṣillu*, shade
KIRI$_6$	**296**+331e	*kirû*, orchard
^{d}GIŠ.NU$_{11}$.GAL	(13)**296**+71+343	*Šamaš* (god)
GIŠ.BAR	**296**+74	*girru*, fire
^{d}GIŠ.BAR	(13)**296**+74	*Girru* (god)
^{kur}MAR.TU^{ki}	(366)**307**+58(461)	*Amurru*, Westland
$^{tu_{15}}$MAR.TU	(399)**307**+58	*amurru*, west
^{mí}UN.E$_2$.GAL	(554)**312**+324+343	*sekertu*, woman of the palace

^{m,d}MEZ.A.SUM-*na*	(480,13)**314**+579 +164+70	*Marduk-apal-iddin*, Merodachbaladan
^{giš}ESI	(296)**322**	*ušu*, ebony
E_2.ABZU	**324**+6a	*Eabzu* (temple)
E_2.GAL	**324**+343	*ekallu*, palace
E_2.ZI.DA	**324**+84+335	*Ezida* (temple)
E_2.SAG.IL_2	**324**+115+205a	*Esagil*(*a*) (temple)
MA.NA	**342**+70	*manû*, mina
^{lú}TIRUM	(330)**343**+376	*tīru*, courtier
AGA.US_2	**347**+211	*rēdû*, soldier
ŠU.ḪA	**354**+589	*bāʾiru*, soldier
^{lú}NAR	(330)**355**	*nāru*, singer (m)
^{mí}NAR	(554)**355**	*nartu*, singer (f)
^{anše}GAM.MAL	(208)**362**+233	*gammalu*, camel
KUR-*ú*	**366**+318	*šadû*, east
GID_2(.DA)	**371**(+335)	*arku*, long
UD.KIB.NUN^{ki}	**381**+228+87(461)	*Sipparu*, Sippar
^{d}UTU	(13)**381**	*Šamaš* (god)
^{íd}UD.KIB.NUN	(579d)**381**+228+87	^{íd}*Purattu*, Euphrates
$^{mí}ŠA_3.E_2$.GAL	(554)**384**+324+343	*sekertu*, woman of the palace
$ERIN_2.ḪA_2$	**393**+404	*ummanāte*, army
$^{lú}ERIN_2$	(330)**393**	*ṣābu*, soldier
^{zá}NUNUZ	(229)**394**	*erimmatu*, egg-shaped bead
$MURU_9$	**399**+445	*imbaru*, mist
IM.$SUḪ_3$	**399**+569	*imsuḫḫu*, wind
^{d}IŠKUR	(13)**399**	*Adad* (god)
$KIŠ^{ki}$	**425**(461)	*Kiš*, Kish (country)
$^{giš}NA_2$	(296)**431**	*eršu*, bed
NIM.GIR_2	**433**+10	*birqu*, lightning
^{kur}ELAM.MA^{ki}	(366)**433**+342(461)	*Elamtu*, Elam
^{d}AMAR.UTU	(13)**437**+381	*Marduk* (god)
^{giš}BAN	(296)**439**	*qaštu*, bow
$^{lú}GIR_3.NITA_2$	(330)**444**+50	*šakkanakku*, official
$^{d}NE_3.IRI_{11}$.GAL	(13)**444**+195+343	*Nergal* (netherworld god)
$BAD_5.BAD_5$	**449**+449	*dabdû*, defeat
IGI.SA_2	**449**+457	*igisû*, gift
U_3.TU	**455**+58	*walādu*, birth
DI.KUD	**457**+12	*dayyānu*, judge
$SA_2.SA_2$	**457**+457	*kašādu*, reach
^{mí}KI.SIKIL	(554)**461**+564	*wardatu*, young woman
KARAŠ	**461**+323	*karāšu*, camp

KU$_3$.GI	**468**+85	*ḫurāṣu*, gold
GUŠKIN	**468**+85	*ḫurāṣu*, gold
KU$_3$.BABBAR	**468**+381	*kaspu*, silver
^{d}30	(13)**472**	*Sîn* (god)
^{giš}GIGIR	(296)**486**	*narkabtu*, chariot
^{giš}TUKUL	(296)**536**	*kakku*, weapon
^{giš}TAŠKARIN	(296)**536**	*taškarinnu*, box-wood
^{lú}ḪUN.GA$_2$	(330)**536**+233	*agru*, hired-person
UDU.NITA$_2$	**537**+50	*immeru*, sheep
EME$_3$	**554**+208	*atānu*, jenny
DAM.GAR$_3$	**557**+333	*tamkāru*, merchant
^{giš}GU.ZA	(296)**559**+586	*kussû*, seat
UR.MAḪ	**575**+57	*nēšu*, lion
A.RA$_2$	**579**+206	*adi*, up to
A.RA$_2$	**579**+206	*arû*, product
A.AB.BA	**579**+128+5	*tâmtu*, sea
A.ŠA$_3$	**579**+384	*eqlu*, field
A.MEŠ	**579**+533	*mû*, water
^{d}ID$_2$	(13)**579d**	*Id*, river(-god)
^{giš}ASAL$_2$	(296)**579**+58+167+377	*ṣarbatu*, poplar
NI$_3$.GA	**597**+319	*makkumru*, property
NI$_3$.ŠU	**597**+354	*bušû*, goods

4.3 Index of Akkadian Words

abnu	229	*amurru*	**307**
abu	145	*Amurru*	**307**
abullu	**133**	*ana*	13
Adad	**399**	*andullu*	**13**
adi	**579**	*Anu*	13
agru	**536**	*aplu*	579
agû	347	*apsû*	6a
aḫu	60	*arḫu*	52
aḫu	331	*arku*	**371**
ayyartu	**295**	*artu*	295
akalu	597	*aru*	295
akālu	36	*arû*	**579**
alāku	206	*askuppatu*	**142**
alpu	297	*ašru*	461
ālu	38	*aššatu*	557
ammatu	318	*Aššur*	**1**
amtu	558	*Aššur*	**14**

atānu	**88**
atānu	**554**
ātû	**231**
awīlu	330
awātu	15
Bābilim	**133**
bābu	133
bāʾiru	**354**
balāṭu	**73**
bašû	80
biltu	108*
birku	396
birqu	**433**
bītu	324
bušû	**597**
Bēl	**99**
bēl pīḫāti	**99**
bēltu	556
bēlu	99
būru	437
dabdû	**449**
daltu	**80**
dayyānu	**457**
damqu	454
danānu	322
dūru	152[8]
Ea	69
Eabzu	**324**
ekallu	**324**
Elamtu	**433**
eli	412
elippu	**122**
ellu	468
ellu	564
Enlil	**99**
epinnu	**56**
epru	212
eqlu	**579**
erbâ	473
erbe	**124**
erbe	473
erbe	597
erēbu	58
erimmatu	**394**
erṣet lātâri	**366**
erṣet lātâri	**75**
erṣetu	461
eršu	**431**
Esagil(a)	**324**
ešēru	**112**
ešra	471
ešru	411
etēqu	537
eṭlu	322
Ezida	**324**
gammalu	**362**
Girru	**296**
girru	**296**
girru	166
ḫalṣu	**2**
ḫamiš	598a
ḫanšā	475
ḫašālu	191
ḫaṭṭu	295
ḫegallu	**143**
ḫurāṣu	85
ḫurāṣu	**468**
ḫuṭāru	**295**
Id	**579d**
idu	334
idû	6
igisû	**449**
illilu	**99**
ilu	13
imbaru	**399**
immeru	537
immeru	**537**
imsuḫḫu	**399**
imēru	208
ina	1
īnu	449
Irkallu	**232**
irtu	167
iṣṣūru	78
iṣu	296
išātu	172

ištānu	**112**
Ištar	**103**
išten	1
išten	480
ištu	139
izuzzu	206
yaraḫḫu	**58**
kabtu	69
kakkabu	129a
kakku	**536**
kalbu	575
kamû	481
karānu	210
karāšu	**461**
karpatu	309
kāru	376*
kaspu	**468**
kašādu	**457**
kašādu	366
kīma	440
kirû	**296**
kussû	**559**
Kiš	**425**
kišadu	106
Kutû	**106**
lā	75
labāru	69
labīru	69
Lagaš	**71**
lamādu	6
lapātu	126
libbu	384
līmu	449
makkumru	**597**
manû	353
manû	**342**
maqātu	68
Marduk	**99**
Marduk	314
Marduk	**437**
Marduk-apal-iddin	**314**
mārtu	**144**
māru	144
mašku	7
mātu	312
mātu	366
*me*ᵓ*at*	532
mû	**579**
murṣu	446
muškēnu	**74**
mūšu	427
Nabû-bēl-šumāti	**295**
nadānu	1
nadānu	164
nadû	68
nâdu	142
nakru	**60**
Nammu	484
napištu	84
narkabtu	**486**
nartu	**355**
nāru	579d
nāru	**355**
narû	**70**
Nergal	**444**
Ninua	**200**
Ninurta	74
Nippur	**99**
nišū	312
nīšu	61
nūnu	589
nēšu	**575**
pānu	449
parakku	344
parṣu	295b
parû	**74**
parzillu	**13**
pēnu	203
petû	69
peṣû	381
pīru	**170**
pû	15
puḫur	40
Purattu	**381**
qablu	337
qabû	15

tīru	**343**
tišu	598e
tukultu	536
ṭābu	396
ṭiṭṭu	399
ṭuppu	399
ul	75
ultu	139
ummanāte	**393**
ummānu	393
ummu	237
ūmu	381
Uruk	**195**
ušu	**322**
uznu	383
wabālu	206
waklu	295
walādu	**455**
wardatu	**461**
wardu	50
warḫu	52
warki	209
wašābu	536
zakāru	61
zēru	72
zikaru	211
zikru	61

4.4 Index of English Glosses

abundance	**143**
Adad	**399**
after	209
Anu	13
arm	334
army	**393**
army	393
ass	208
assembly	40
Aššur	**1**
Assyria	**14**
Babylon	**133**
barley	367
be	80
bed	**431**
beer	214
Bēl	**99**
bind	152
bird	78
birth	**455**
black	427
boat	**122**
bow	**439**
box-wood	**536**
branch	**295**
breast	167
bring	206
brother	331
brother	60
bull	170
calf	437
camel	**362**
camp	**461**
chariot	**486**
child	**144**
city	38
city gate	**133**
city wall	152[8]
clay	399
commissioner	**99**
common citizen	**74**
compensate	7
conquer	366
courtier	**343**
crown	347
crush	191
cry	15
cubit	318
date	**15**
daughter	**144**
day	381
defeat	**449**

land	366
lap	203
learn	6
life	61
life	84
lightning	**433**
like	440
lion	**575**
live	**73**
lock	**115**
long	**371**
lord	99
male	211
man	330
Marduk	**99**
Marduk	314
Marduk	**437**
merchant	**557**
Merodachbaladan	**314**
middle	337
milk	319
mina	**342**
mina	353
mist	**399**
month	52
mother	237
mountain	**104**
mountain	366
mouth	15
mule	**74**
Nabubelshumati	**295**
name	61
Nammu	484
neck	106
Nergal	**444**
netherworld	**232**
netherworld	**75**
night	427
nine	598e
Nineveh	**200**
Ninurta	74
Nippur	**99**
north	**112**
not	75
official	**444**
oil	231
old	69
one	480
one	1
open	69
orchard	**296**
overseer	295
ox	297
palace	**324**
pass	537
people	312
pig	53
place	461
plant	318
plow	**56**
poplar	**579**
pot	309
praise	142
prince	87
prisoner	481
product	**579**
property	**597**
prosper	**112**
pure	468
pure	564
quay	376*
reach	**457**
red sandstone	**13**
reed	85
refined	124
relig. duty	295b
return	326
return	85
ring	401
river	579d
river(-god)	**579d**
ruby	**58**
say	15
scepter	295
sea	**579**
seat	**559**
seed	72
seize	537

4.5 Index of Composite Logograms by Constituent Sign Number

1	*Aššur*, **1**
2	*ḫalṣu*, **2**
5	*erbe*, **124b**
5	*Sîn-aḫḫē-erība*, **99**
5	*tâmtu*, **579**
6	*Sîn*, **99**
6	*Sîn-aḫḫē-erība*, **99**
6a	*Eabzu*, **324**
10	*birqu*, **433**
12	*dayyānu*, **457**
13	*Adad*, **399**
13	*andullu*, **13**
13	*Aššur* **1**
13	*Bābilim*, **133**
13	*Bēl*, **99**
13	*Enlil, Illil*, **99**
13	*Girru*, **296**
13	*Id*, **579d**
13	*Irkallu*, **232**
13	*Ištar*, **103**
13	*Marduk*, **437**
13	*Marduk-apla-iddina*, **314**
13	*Nabû-bēl-šumāti*, **295**
13	*Nergal*, **444**
13	*parû*, **74**
13	*parû*, **74**
13	*parzillu*, **13**
13	*sāndu*, **13**
13	*Sîn*, **99**
13	*Sîn*, **472**
13	*Sîn-aḫḫē-erība*, **99**
13	*Šamaš*, **296**
13	*Šamaš*, **381**
14	*Aššur*, **14**
15	*suluppu*, **15**
38	*ḫalṣu*, **2**
38	*Sîn-aḫḫē-erība*, **99**
49*	*šūtu*, **49***
50	*šakkanakku*, **444**
50	*immeru*, **537**
55	*balāṭu*, **73**
55	*Lagaš*, **71**
56	*epinnu*, **56**
57	*nēšu*, **575**
58	*šadû*, **104**
58	*Amurru*, **307**
58	*amurru*, **307**
58	*ṣarbatu*, **579**
58	*walādu*, **455**
58	*yaraḫḫu*, **58**
60	*nakru*, **60**
61	*Nabû-bēl-šumāti*, **295**
70	*manû*, **342**
70	*Marduk-apla-iddina*, **314**
70	*narû*, **70**
71	*Šamaš*, **296**
71	*Lagaš*, **71**
72	*sikkūru*, **115**
73	*balāṭu*, **73**
74	*girru*, **296**
74	*Girru*, **296**
74	*muškēnu*, **74**
74	*parû*, **74**
74	*parû*, **74**
74	*parzillu*, **13**
74	*ṣabītu*, **74**
75	*erṣet lātâri*, **75**
79	*bēl pīḫāti*, **99**
80	*daltu*, **80**
84	*Ezida*, **324**
85	*ḫurāṣu*, **468**
85	*ḫurāṣu*, **468**
87	^{id}*Purattu*, **381**
87	*Sipparu*, **381**
88	*atānu*, **88**
99	*bēl pīḫāti*, **99**
99	*Bēl*, **99**
99	*Enlil, Illil*, **99**

319 *makkumru*, **597**
322 *Irkallu*, **232**
322 *ušu*, **322**
323 *karāšu*, **461**
324 *Eabzu*, **324**
324 *ekallu*, **324**
324 *Esagil(a)*, **324**
324 *Ezida*, **324**
324 *sekertu*, **312**
324 *sekertu*, **384**
326 *erṣet lātâri*, **75**
328 *Bābilim*, **133**
328 *sīsû*, **208**
329 *andullu*, **13**
330 *agru*, **536**
330 *šakkanakku*, **444**
330 *bēl pīḫāti*, **99**
330 *ṣābu*, **393**
330 *šerru*, **144**
330 *nakru*, **60**
330 *nāru*, **355**
330 *ātû*, **231**
330 *tīru*, **343**
331 *Sîn-aḫḫē-erība*, **99**
331e *kirû*, **296**
333 *tamkāru*, **557**
335 *arku*, **371**
335 *Ezida*, **324**
342 *Elamtu*, **433**
342 *manû*, **342**
342 *suluppu*, **15**
343 *abullu*, **133**
343 *Šamaš*, **296**
343 *ḫegallu*, **143**
343 *ekallu*, **324**
343 *Nergal*, **444**
343 *sekertu*, **312**
343 *sekertu*, **384**
343 *tīru*, **343**
347 *rēdû*, **347**
349 *Lagaš*, **71**
354 *bāʾiru*, **354**
354 *bušû*, **597**
355 *nartu*, **355**
355 *nāru*, **355**
362 *gammalu*, **362**
366 *šadû*, **366**
366 *Amurru*, **307**
366 *Aššur*, **14**
366 *Elamtu*, **433**
366 *erṣet lātâri*, **75**
366 *sīsû*, **208**
371 *arku*, **371**
376 *tīru*, **343**
377 *ṣarbatu*, **579**
381 *Šamaš*, **381**
381 ^{íd}*Purattu*, **381**
381 *kaspu*, **468**
381 *Marduk*, **437**
381 *Sipparu*, **381**
384 *eqlu*, **579**
384 *sekertu*, **384**
393 *ṣābu*, **393**
393 *ummanāte*, **393**
394 *erimmatu*, **394**
399 *Adad*, **399**
399 *amurru*, **307**
399 *imbaru*, **399**
399 *imsuḫḫu*, **399**
404 *ummanāte*, **393**
425 *Kiš*, **425**
427 *ṣillu*, **296**
431 *eršu*, **431**
433 *birqu*, **433**
433 *Elamtu*, **433**
437 *Marduk*, **437**
439 *qaštu*, **439**
444 *šakkanakku*, **444**
444 *Nergal*, **444**
445 *imbaru*, **399**
449 *dabdû*, **449**
449 *dabdû*, **449**
449 *igisû*, **449**
455 *walādu*, **455**
457 *dayyānu*, **457**
457 *ešēru*, **112**

457 *igisû*, **449**
457 *ištānu*, **112**
457 *kašādu*, **457**
457 *kašādu*, **457**
461 *Amurru*, **307**
461 *Aššur*, **14**
461 *Bābilim*, **133**
461 *Elamtu*, **433**
461 *karāšu*, **461**
461 *Kiš*, **425**
461 *Kutû*, **106**
461 *Ninua*, **200**
461 *Nippur*, **99**
461 *Sipparu*, **381**
461 *Uruk*, **195**
461 *wardatu*, **461**
468 *kaspu*, **468**
468 *ḫurāṣu*, **468**
468 *ḫurāṣu*, **468**
472 *Sîn*, **472**
480 *Marduk-apla-iddina*, **314**
480 *Nabû-bēl-šumāti*, **295**
480 *Sîn-aḫḫē-erība*, **99**
481 *Enlil, Illil*, **99**
486 *narkabtu*, **486**
532 *sāndu*, **13**
533 *mû*, **579**
533 *Nabû-bēl-šumāti*, **295**
533 *Sîn-aḫḫē-erība*, **99**
536 *agru*, **536**
536 *kakku*, **536**
536 *taškarinnu*, **536**
537 *askuppatu*, **142**
537 *immeru*, **537**
537 *rēdû*, **211**
537 *šūtu*, **49***
554 *atānu*, **88**
554 *atānu*, **554**
554 *mārtu*, **144**
554 *nartu*, **355**
554 *sekertu*, **312**
554 *sekertu*, **384**
554 *wardatu*, **461**
555 *ḫalṣu*, **2**
557 *tamkāru*, **557**
559 *kussû*, **559**
564 *wardatu*, **461**
565 *suluppu*, **15**
569 *imsuḫḫu*, **399**
575 *nēšu*, **575**
579 *adi*, **579**
579 *arû*, **579**
579 *eqlu*, **579**
579 *erṣet lātâri*, **75**
579 *Kutû*, **106**
579 *mû*, **579**
579 *Marduk-apla-iddina*, **314**
579 *narû*, **70**
579 *ṣarbatu*, **579**
579 *tâmtu*, **579**
579d [íd]*Purattu*, **381**
579d *Id*, **579d**
586 *kussû*, **559**
589 *bāʾiru*, **354**
591 *sāndu*, **13**
597 *bušû*, **597**
597 *makkumru*, **597**

Part Five: Sign List

Introduction

This concise sign list places within a short space some of the most important information regarding Akkadian signs. Its primary sources are the sign lists of René Labat, *Manuel d'épigraphie akkadienne* (6th ed., 1988), and Rykle Borger, *Assyrisch-babylonische Zeichenliste* (2nd ed., 1981). For others, see the Bibliography. The present work is especially valuable in two ways. First, both the syllabic and logographic values of a given sign, distinguished by upper and lower case type, may be found very quickly. Second, when working with texts in transliteration, it allows the user easily to determine which sign is being indicated by the scholar providing the transliteration. Since various inconsistencies occur both between and within the lists of Labat and Borger, this section also serves to bring these to the user's attention (see the Summary of Differences, section 5.6).

Because the beginning student is usually introduced to signs of the Neo-Assyrian period, graphic representations of these signs are given in section 5.1. As do Labat and Borger, this list employs the numbering system of P. A. Deimel's *Šumerisches Lexikon*, modified occasionally as expedient (see the Chart of Correspondences, section 5.5). The signs are organized according to shape; note that the following signs are listed out of numerical order:

29	follows 381b	406	follows 398a
200	follows 133	515a	follows 529
204b	follows 185	554a	follows 562
382	follows 210	590	follows 379[2]
405	follows 396a		

Two indexes of sign values (5.2 and 5.3) follow the graphic sign chart. The most common syllabic and logographic values, as reflected in the lists of Labat and Borger, have been given here. Only values that are extremely rare, or (in the case of logograms) that occur only in

Sumerian, have been intentionally excluded. In addition, the list has been checked against the volumes of *CAD* published to date to assure that all logograms found in the summary section of each entry word are included. The vast majority of logograms found in *AHw* are also found here.

The Number Index (5.2) lists values according to sign number. Logographic values are listed in upper case letters, syllabic values in lower case. For composite logograms that have their own title (e.g., UKUR$_2$ consists of signs 343 and 53), the numbers of all signs involved are shown. The "#" symbol represents the present entry sign; for example, at 13 is found AZAG(468+#), which means that AZAG is composed of sign 468 + sign 13. The Number Index lists AZAG both in entry 13 and in entry 468. This allows the user to locate such values by looking up any of the signs involved (sometimes a string of four or more). Be aware that a few values indicated by either Labat's or Borger's lists as composite have their own separate entry and sign number in the present concise sign list. Also, the summary provided in the Number Index does *not* provide data on which values occur during the various dialect periods of the language. For this and other important information about the signs, consult the lists of Borger and Labat.

The Value Index (5.3) organizes the same information by sign value. In cases where a logographic designation involves several signs, the signs are listed in sequence, and the designation is followed by "#." For example, AZAG (composed of sign 468 + sign 13) is shown as AZAG# to the right of 468 on the first line, *and* to the right of 13 on the following line.

Following the Value Index comes two listings of determinatives (5.4). The first is organized alphabetically by sign value, the second in sequence by sign number.

A complication that arises from using the sign lists of Labat and Borger is the inconsistencies between (and occasionally within) them. Notations (B for Borger, L for Labat) are included in 5.2 and 5.3 to indicate these differences (see examples below). To further assist, a listing of sign number correspondences (5.5) and a summary of value differences (5.6) have been provided.

Abbreviations and Examples

The user is encouraged to become familiar with the following abbreviations and to pay attention only to those that are of interest or are helpful. While the basic design of the indexes is obvious, to make full use of them the examples below should be studied.

B	Borger
BI	Borger Index
d	difference; the values given agree, but the graphic representation of the sign differs.
e	entry; in some cases Labat lists sign "variants" under a given sign number, but with distinct values of their own; except in a few cases, Borger gives these same signs their own unique number.
foll	follows; following the entry for the number indicated, this sign has its own entry but no number is given (Labat's Main section only).
L	Labat
LI	Labat's Index (incl Addendum; pp. 249–281)
LL	Labat's Liste (pp. 29–32)
LM	Labat's Main entry (pp. 41–247)
mispr	misprint; this refers to a simple inconsistency, most often in LI, where a number is given that does not correspond to the sign list's number tag for the sign elsewhere. NOTE: Labat in many cases in the Liste, and even more so in the Index, gives a number for a sign without indicating its sub-listing; for example, "446" when sign "446a" is shown; these omissions have *not* been noted here.
v	variant; this indicates that two signs, while different, share some or all values; the word "also" is used in cases where the signs are not simply alternates; for example, sign 2a has the values "3" and "eš$_6$," and may also represent the values indicated for sign 472, but sign 472 does not have the values 3 and eš$_6$.
(?)	L and/or B have less than complete certainty on this value
=	indicates that the sign itself, its graphic image with all its values, is being addressed, not simply one of the values.
#	the number of the present entry sign; in the Value Index it indicates that the value attached to it is part of a composite logogram
+	two signs occur in sequence
x	one sign is written within the other

NOTE: When no comment is made regarding Borger or Labat, it indicates that either (1) the sign list agrees with *AAH*, or (2) that sign list omits the sign.

When no special letter (d, e, v) is given in connection with a reference to B or L, it means that the designated sign list has a different number tag for this sign. For example, 211b KAŠ$_3$ (= L 211a) means that Labat calls this particular combination of wedges 211a; *AAH* has used Borger's tag, 211b.

Further examples:

345 *kuk*(B:468) *kúk*(L:468) means that Labat has *kuk* as the value for sign 345 while Borger has *kuk* as the value for sign 468, and that Borger has *kúk* as the value for sign 345 while Labat has *kúk* as the value for 468.

34 ŠAKIR_3(LM) ŠAKIR_4(?) means that Labat's Main section shows the value to be ŠAKIR_3; the LM suggests either that Labat's Index disagrees with the Main section, or that this value is listed only in Labat's Main section. Borger shows this sign to have the value ŠAKIR_4, though this valuation is uncertain (hence the ?).

172a (= LM e172,B 172,51ff) means that Labat's Main section lists this sign in the entry for number 172 but with the distinctive values shown. Borger labels this sign 172,51ff.

443 UTU_2 (= LL 443*, LM foll 441) means that Labat's Liste shows 443* as the designation for this sign, while in Labat's Main section it follows number 441 but has no number.

29* (v98) means sign 29* is listed as a variant of sign 98, so that it has the values found for 98.

43a ru_{11} (= LM ev43) means that according to Labat's Main section (where it is displayed along with sign 43), in addition to the value of ru_{11}, this sign has the values of sign 43.

485 BARA_8(LI mispr 490) means that under BARA_8, LI displays sign 485 but erroneously calls it 490. The present work does *not* comment when LI simply omits the a, b, c, etc., following a number, for example, when 141 is written but sign 141a is shown.

Sign list begins on next page.

1	
2	
2a	
2b	
2c	
3	
4	
5	
6	
6a	
7	
8	
9	
10	
11	
12	
13	
14	
15	
16	
17	
17a	
18	
18*	
19	
20	
22*	
23	
24	
24′	
26	
27	
28	
28′	
29	*see after* 381b
29*	
30	
30*	
31	
32	
33	
34	
35	
36	
38	
38a	
39	
40	
41	
41′	
42	
43	
43a	
44	
46	
49	
49a	
49*	
50	
51	
52	
52a	
53	
54	
55	
56	
57	
58	
59	
60	
60a	
60b	
60c	
60d	
60e	
60*	
61	
62	
63a	
63b	
63c	
63d	
63e	
65	
66	
67	
68	
69	
69*	
70	
71	
72	
73	
74	
74a	
74*	

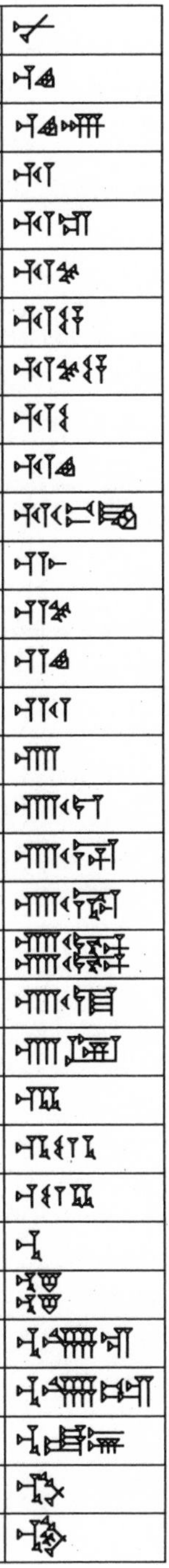

75	
76	
77	
78	
78a	
79	
79a	
79b	
80	
81	
82	
83	
84	
85	
86	
87	
87a	
87aa	
87b	
87c	
87d	
87m	
88	
89	
89a	
90	
91	
92a	
92b	
93	
94	
95	

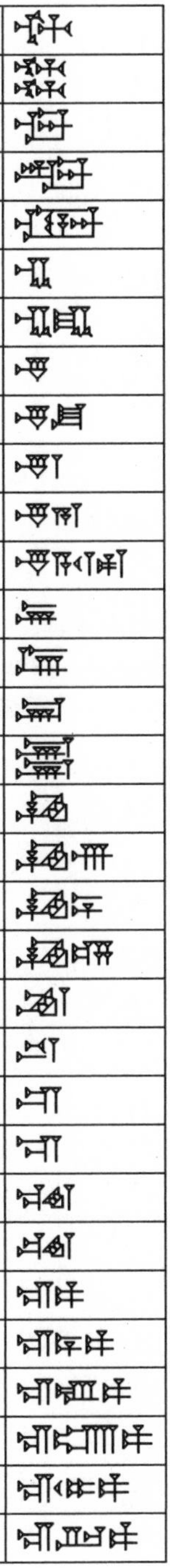

96	
96a	
97	
97a	
98	
99	
100	
101	
102	
103	
103a	
103b	
104	
104a	
105	
105a	
106	
107	
108	
108*	
109	
110	
111	
112	
113	
114	
115	
116	
117	
118	
119	
121	

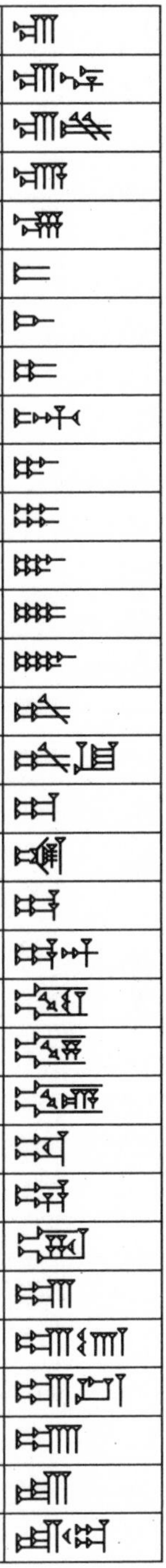

122	
122a	
122b	
123	
123a	
124	
124a	
124b	
125	
125b	
125c	
125d	
125e	
125f	
126	
126f	
128	
128a	
129	
129a	
130	
131	
131a	
132	
133	
200	
134	
135	
136	
138	
139	
140	

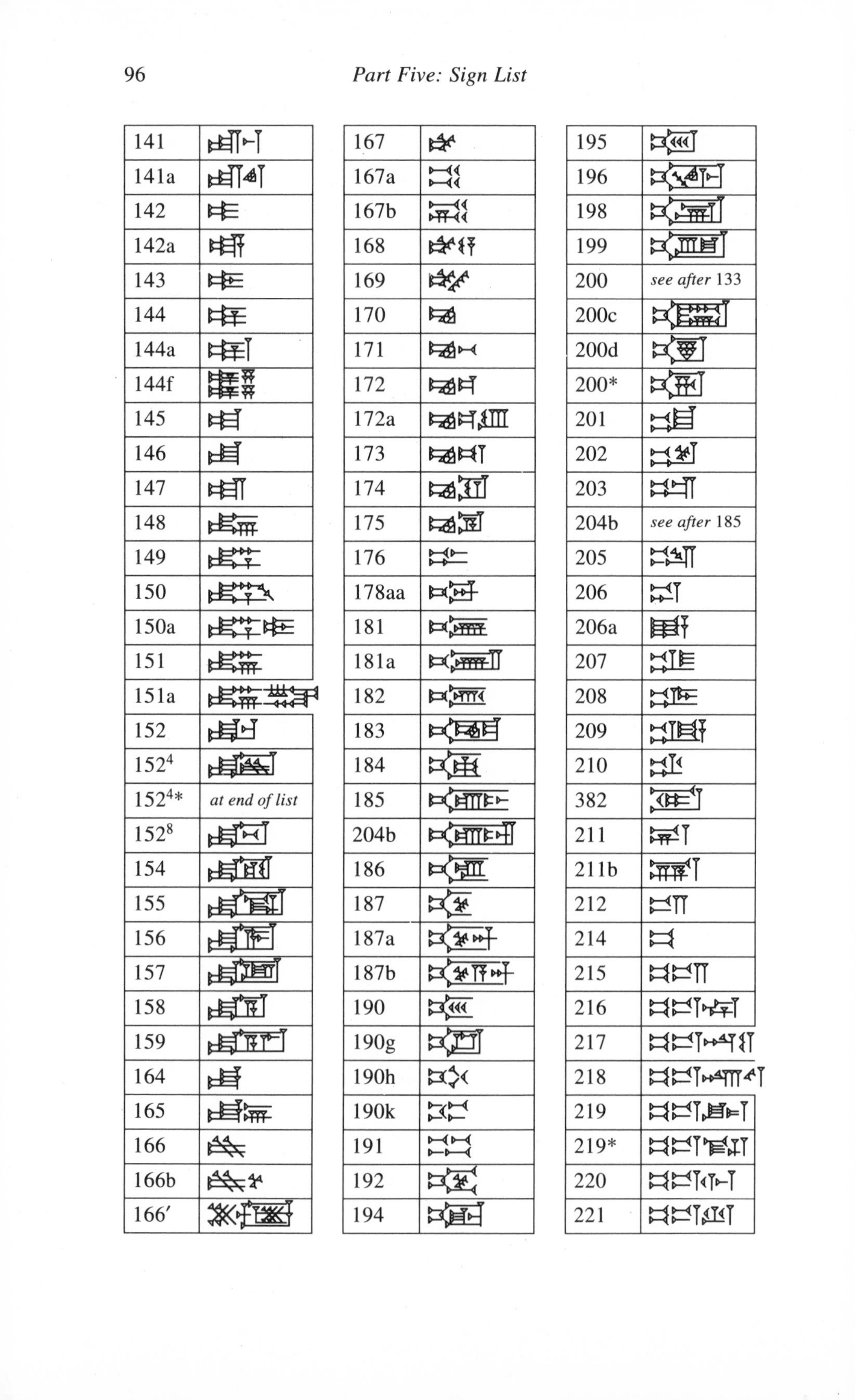

141	
141a	
142	
142a	
143	
144	
144a	
144f	
145	
146	
147	
148	
149	
150	
150a	
151	
151a	
152	
152^{4}	
152^{4}*	*at end of list*
152^{8}	
154	
155	
156	
157	
158	
159	
164	
165	
166	
166b	
166′	

167	
167a	
167b	
168	
169	
170	
171	
172	
172a	
173	
174	
175	
176	
178aa	
181	
181a	
182	
183	
184	
185	
204b	
186	
187	
187a	
187b	
190	
190g	
190h	
190k	
191	
192	
194	

195	
196	
198	
199	
200	*see after* 133
200c	
200d	
200*	
201	
202	
203	
204b	*see after* 185
205	
206	
206a	
207	
208	
209	
210	
382	
211	
211b	
212	
214	
215	
216	
217	
218	
219	
219*	
220	
221	

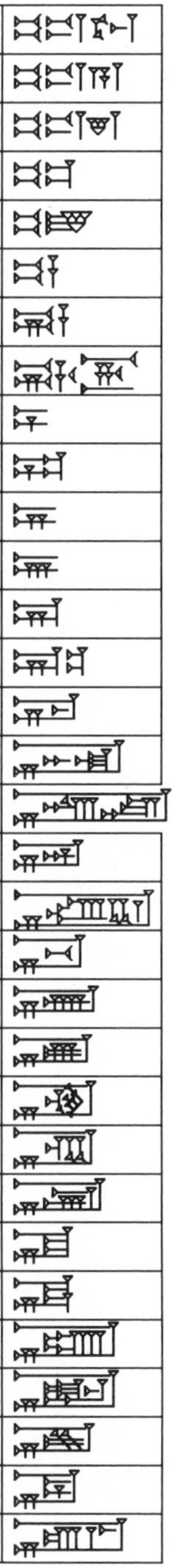

222	
224	
225	
226	
227	
228	
229	
229a	
230	
230*	
231	
232	
233	
233a	
234	
235	
236	
237	
239	
242	
244	
244a	
246	
247	
248	
249	
249b	
250	
250b	
250d	
251	
251a	

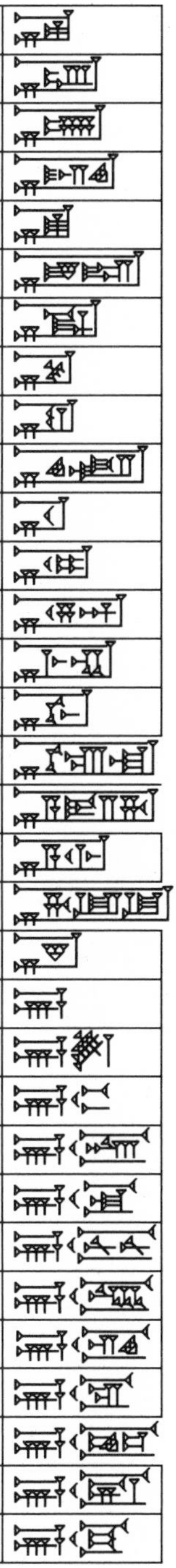

252	
252b	
255	
256	
257	
259	
260	
261	
262	
263	
264	
265	
269	
270	
271	
272	
273	
274	
277	
278	
280	
280a	
281	
281a	
282	
282a	
283	
284	
285	
286	
287	
288	

289	
290	
291	
292	
293	
294b	
294c	
295	
295a	
295b	
295bb	
295c	
295cc	
295d	
295e	
295ee	
295f	
295k	
295l	
295m	
296	
296a	
296b	
297	
298	
300	
301	
302	
305	
306	
307	
308	

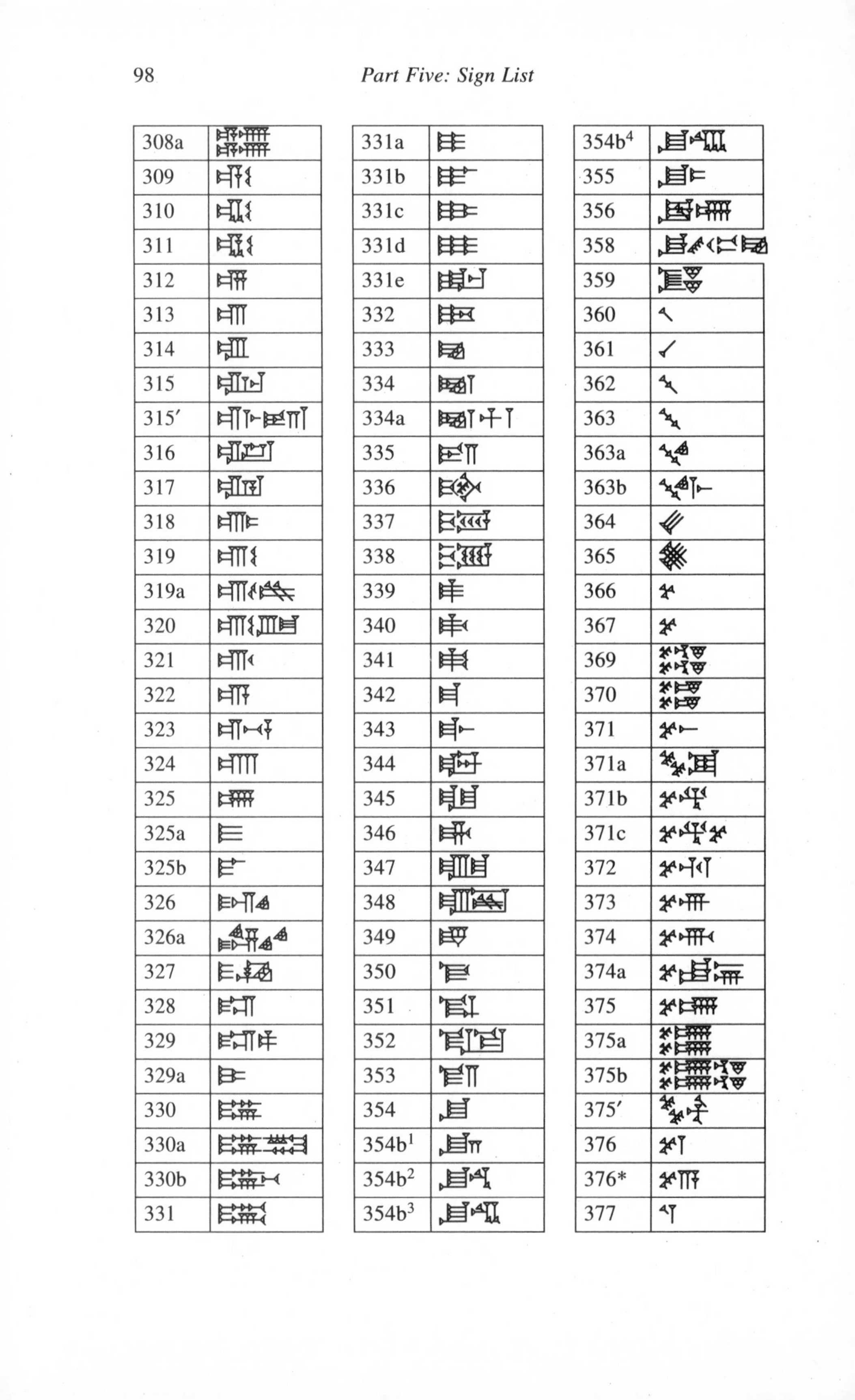

308a	
309	
310	
311	
312	
313	
314	
315	
315′	
316	
317	
318	
319	
319a	
320	
321	
322	
323	
324	
325	
325a	
325b	
326	
326a	
327	
328	
329	
329a	
330	
330a	
330b	
331	

331a	
331b	
331c	
331d	
331e	
332	
333	
334	
334a	
335	
336	
337	
338	
339	
340	
341	
342	
343	
344	
345	
346	
347	
348	
349	
350	
351	
352	
353	
354	
354b^1	
354b^2	
354b^3	

354b^4	
355	
356	
358	
359	
360	
361	
362	
363	
363a	
363b	
364	
365	
366	
367	
369	
370	
371	
371a	
371b	
371c	
372	
373	
374	
374a	
375	
375a	
375b	
375′	
376	
376*	
377	

378	
378a	
379[2]	
590	
380	
381	
381a	
381b	
382	*see after* 210
29	
383	
384	
385	
388	
389	
390	
391	
392	
393	
394	
394b	
394c	
394d	
395	
395a	
395*	
396	
396a	
405	
397	
398	
398a	

406	
399	
399a	
400	
401	
402	
403	
403*	
403**	
404	
404*	
405	*see after* 396a
405a	
405b	
406	*see after* 398a
406a	
409	
409a	
410	
411	
412	
413	
415	
416	
417	
418	
419	
420	
421	
422	
423	
424	

425	
426	
427	
428	
429	
430	
431	
433	
434	
434a	
435	
436	
437	
438	
439	
440	
440a	
441	
441a	
442	
443	
444	
445	
446	
446a	
447	
447a	
448	
449	
450	
451	
452	

452a	
454	
455	
456	
457	
458	
459	
459a	
459b	
460	
461	
462	
463	
464	
465	
466	
467	
468	
469	
470	
471	
472	
473	
475	
480	
481	
481a	
481b	
481c	
482	
482a	
482b	
482c	
483	
484	
485	
486	
487	
488a	
488b	
489a	
491	
492	
493	
494	
495	
496	
497	
498	
499	
500	
501	
502	
503	
506	
507	
508	
509	
510	
511	
512	
513	
514	
515	
515a	*see after* 529
516	
517	
518	
519	
520	
521	
522	
523	
524	
525	
526	
527	
528	
529	
515a	
532	
533	
533a	
534	
535	
536	
537	
537a	
537b	
537c	
538	
539	
540	
541	
542	
543	
543a	
544	
545	

546	
546a	
547	
548	
549	
550	
551	
552	
553	
554	
554a	*see after* 562
555	
556	
557	
558	
559	
560	
561	
562	
554a	
563	
564	
565	
566	
566b	

567	
568	
569	
570	
571	
572	
573	
574	
575	
575a	
576	
577	
578a	
579	
579a	
579b	
579c	
579d	
579e	
579f	
580	
581	
582	
583	

584	
585	
585a	
585b	
585c	
586	
589	
590	*see after* 379^2
591	
592	
593	
593a	
593b	
594	
595	
596	
597	
598a	
598b	
598c	
598d	
598d*	
598e	
598e*	

152^4

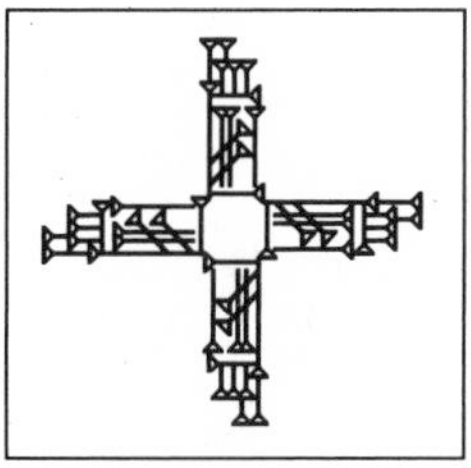

5.2 Number Index

1	1 àna às àṣ aš àz dàl dil dili eš$_{20}$ in$_6$ ina inna rám rim$_5$ rù rum šùp(B:295k) tàl til$_4$ ṭil AŠ DIL DILI ḪIL$_2$ INA RUM UBU
2	(det) ḫal ḫala BULUḪ BURU$_8$ DIDLI (LI mispr 1) ḪAL
2a	3 eš$_6$ (also v472)
2b	(v472; see B p180)
2c	(v472; see B p180)
3	buk mug muk muq puk šúk wuk MUG MUK
4	mùg mùk mùq ZADIM
5	ba pá BA
6	sú ṣú zu ZU ZUEN(99+#)
6a	ABZU
7	(det) $\frac{1}{36}$ guš kus kuš kuz su sùm śu šu$_{11}$ KUŠ SU ŠURUPPAK (#+366+68)
8	rig$_4$ rik$_4$ riq$_4$ rug ruk ruq sán sun$_6$ šin šun DUR$_6$ ŠEN
9	bal bala bùl pal pala pùl BAL BALA
10	ád át áṭ gír gíri ul$_4$ AD$_5$(318+#;L:330b) GIR$_2$ KIŠI$_{16}$(318+#) TAB$_2$ UL$_4$
11	bál búl púl BU$_{13}$(?, LI; B:30) BULUG$_2$ BUR$_2$ BURU$_2$ DU$_9$ UŠU(LI mispr 10) UŠUM UŠUMGAL(343+#)
12	dim$_5$(B:352) gùg ḫas ḫaṣ ḫaš ḫaz ḫús kud kut kuṭ qud qut qutu sil ṣìl(B:13+329) šar$_7$ šil tar ṭar(LM) tara tím(B:207) tír ṭar ṭur$_6$ ṭír ḪAŠ KU$_5$ KUD SIL SILA TAR
13	(det) an ána d(det) èl ìl ila ili(B) ìli(L) ilu(B) ìlu(L) iti$_4$(#+579d) itu$_4$(#+579d) le$_4$ li$_4$ nán(#+331+461) sa$_8$ ṣìl(#+329;L:12) šubul AN ANZU(#+399+445) AZAG(468+#) DINGIR KUNGA$_2$(74+#;L:547) MITTA(536+#) NAGGA(#+70) NANNA$_4$(#+331+461; LM:NANNA) NANNAR(#+331+461) ULUŠIN(214+339+579+#) ULUŠIN$_2$(214+339+#+70)
14	Aš-šur (=L 1+101)
15	du$_{11}$ e$_7$ en$_4$ ga$_{14}$ gù iš$_5$ ka pe$_4$ pi$_4$ qà su$_{11}$ zib$_4$ zú BAḪAR$_2$(309+#+349) DU$_{11}$ DUG$_4$ GU$_3$ GUG$_6$(#+230) GUGU INIM KA KIR$_4$ PIḪU$_3$(#+230) ZU$_2$ ZUḪ
16	MU$_7$ TU$_6$
17	UG$_8$(B:330^8) UḪ$_4$ US$_{11}$ UŠ$_{11}$(L:372) UŠ$_{12}$(L) (= LM foll 16)
17a	(see B p64)
18	NUNDUN
18*	SU$_6$ SUL$_3$ SUN$_4$(LI SUN$_8$)
19	ba$_{11}$ bù(LI mispr 26) bu$_6$(LI) pù(LI:26) pu$_4$(LI) BUZUR$_5$ PUZUR$_5$
20	NIGRU
22*	MURGU$_2$
23	IBIRA(LI mispr 22) TIBIRA$_2$
24	šiq$_4$
24′	UŠ$_{13}$

B = Borger BI = Borger Index d = difference e = entry foll = following L = Labat
LI = Labat's Index LL = Labat's Liste LM = Labat's Main entry mispr = misprint v = variant

26 ba$_{12}$ bum pum BU$_3$ PU$_3$ PUZUR$_4$(#+353) SUD$_4$(B:371) ŠU$_{12}$ ŠUD$_3$ (B:also v19)

27 TUKUR$_2$

28 IMMIN ZU$_5$

28′ UŠ$_{14}$

29 (det) ZABAR(L) ZABAR$_2$(B) (=LM e381,B 381,111ff+29)

29* (v98)

30 ba$_5$ BU$_{13}$(LI:11) BUN$_2$

30* pû (=LL 30a; see L p55)

31 KAN$_4$(B:133)

32 em$_4$ im$_4$(B:206) EME

33 ma$_5$ MA$_5$ MU$_3$

34 ŠAKIR$_3$(LM) ŠAKIR$_4$(?)

35 nag nak naq nik$_5$ NAG NAK

36 GU$_7$ KU$_2$

38 (det) ala ali alu er$_4$ eri(B) eri$_4$(L) ir$_4$ iri(B) iri$_4$(L) ré rí ru$_9$ ERI(B) ERI$_4$(L) RI$_2$ U$_{19}$ URU

38a ála (=LM e38)

39 (v15)

40 UKKIN UNKIN (=LM foll 38)

41 BANŠUR

41′ kapru (=LL 42; see L p57)

42 ŠAKIR$_3$

43 ru$_4$ URU$_2$

43a ru$_{11}$ (=LM ev43)

44 ASAR SILIG ŠILIG

46 kur$_{12}$ GUR$_5$ GURUŠ$_3$ ŠAKIR

49 ERIM$_3$ ERIN$_3$

49a (v49*;=L 49*)

49* gàl qàl sùk GIŠGAL LU$_7$ QAL$_3$ U$_{17}$(B:383) U$_{18}$(B) ULU$_3$ (=LL foll 49*,LM v49*)

50 èr ìr ir$_{11}$(LM:50x367; B,LI:51) wàr ARAD DUR$_3$(#+208) IR$_3$ IR$_{11}$(LM:50x367;B,LI:51) IRDA NITA$_2$ ŠAGAN$_2$(444+#) ŠAGAN$_3$(208+#)

51 ir$_{11}$(LM:50x367) AMME(?) ARAD$_2$ IR$_{11}$(LM:50x367) (=LI 50,51)

52 (det) ITI ITU

52a ARAḪ$_2$

53 sáḫ siḫ ṣáḫ ṣeḫ šaḫ šiḫ šúḫ SUBAR SUBUR ŠAḪ ŠUBUR ŠUBURA UKUR$_2$(343+#)

54 BAR$_8$(B) BAR$_{12}$(L) BURU$_{15}$ EBUR SULLIM ŠIBIR$_2$

55 ḫir$_4$ la LA LAGAS(71+349+#) ŠIKA

56 bin pin APIN ENGAR URU$_4$

57 maḫ meḫ miḫ MAḪ

58 dú ku$_4$ pi$_{10}$ tu ṭú ASAL$_2$(579+#+167+377) GUR$_8$ KU$_4$ TU TUD URU$_5$ UNU$_7$(L:337)

59 gúb gúp le li EN$_3$ ENSI(99+532+#) GUB$_2$ LE LI

60 aḫ$_4$(B:397) ba$_{14}$ bab bap gur$_{12}$ kúr pa$_4$ pap qur$_4$ ENKUM(99+#+363b+87+532+152^4) KUR$_2$ PAB PAP ŠUŠŠUB(#+#+69*)

60a púš PUŠ$_2$ (=L e60, B 60,24ff)

60b PA$_6$ (=L e60)

60c PA$_5$ (=L e60)

60d bur$_{13}$ pur$_{13}$ BULUG$_3$ DIM$_4$ GEŠPU$_2$(354+#) MUNU$_6$ (=L e60,B 60,33ff)

(?) = L and/or B uncertain on value = graphic image of sign itself # = number of the current sign
+ = two signs occur in sequence x = one sign is written within the other

60e BULUG$_4$(B:560) MUNU$_4$ (=L e60)

60* GAM$_3$ ZUBI

61 i$_{14}$ ia$_5$ mu šád šát šu$_{10}$ šùm šúmu wu$_4$ MU MUḪALDIM

62 ga$_5$ ka$_4$ qa šál LILLU(309+#+349) QA SIL$_3$ SILA$_3$ ŠITA$_6$

63a gát kád kát qad$_6$ qat$_6$ šíd KAD$_2$ (=L e63)

63b SASIRRA (see L p267)

63c gàt kàd kàt KAD$_3$ (=L e63)

63d dad dat gid$_6$ kít šìd šít(LI) šìt šíṭ(LI) šìṭ tad tak$_5$ tat taṭ ṭad ṭat KID$_2$ TAG$_4$ TAK$_4$ (=L e63)

63e EGA$_2$(B:87c)

65 ŠEŠLAM

66 GUG$_4$ LAMAḪUŠ NUMUN$_2$ ZUKUM (=L d66,B 66C)

67 gil kíl qíl GE$_{16}$ GIB GIL GILIM ḪIL

68 ru šub šup ARATTA(435+366+#+461) ARATTA$_2$(436+#+461) ILLAR(296+#) RU ŠUB ŠURUPPAK(7+366+#)

69 bad bat baṭ be bi$_4$ bít bíṭ gam$_5$ mát me$_4$ med mid mit miṭ mút pát páṭ pè pì pít qìd qìt sun ṣiṣ šum$_4$ ti$_5$ til ṭíl úš zaz zis ziz ADAMA(#+427) ARALI(324+366+#) BAD BARA$_2$(B,LM:344) BAT BE EŠE$_3$ IDIM LUGUD(#+381) MED MID MUD$_2$ SUMUN SUN TIL UG$_7$ ULAL UŠ$_2$ ZIZ

69* BURU$_7$(LM) GURUN(LM) ŠUŠŠUB(60+60+#)

70 na NA NAGGA(13+#) ULUŠIN$_2$(214+339+13+#)

71 nu$_{11}$ šer šir BURU$_4$(#+349) LAGAS(#+349+55) NU$_{11}$ SIR$_4$ ŠIR ŠUR$_3$

72 gúl kul qul zar$_4$ zer zir KUL NUMUN

73 de$_9$ dì te$_9$ ti ṭe$_6$ ṭì ESA(366+#) TI

74 $\frac{1}{2}$ ba$_7$ bar baš ma$_7$ mas maṣ maš pár para(B:381) pára(L:344) sutu(296+#) war waš BAN$_2$ BAR KUNGA$_2$(#+13;L:547) MAŠ PAR$_2$ SA$_9$ SUTU(296+#)

74a GIDIM$_2$ (=B 74,335)

74* DALLA IDIGNA (=B 74,238f)

75 là nu úl NU

76 kun$_8$ máš MAŠ$_2$

77 ku$_{14}$ kun kunu qun KUN

78 (det) ʾu$_5$ baḫ bak baq ḫu mus$_8$ pag pak paq púq u$_{11}$ ARAB(381+87+#) BIBE(372+144+#) ḪU MUŠEN

78a u$_5$ U$_5$ (=L 78*)

79 bir$_5$ na$_7$ nam pir$_6$ sim śím šam$_4$ ším NAM PALA(#+151) SIM SIN$_2$

79a bur$_5$ BUR$_5$ BURU$_5$ (=L v79*)

79b (v79a;=L v79*)

80 eg ek eq gál ig ik iq GAL$_2$ IG IK

81 màt mu$_{12}$ mud mut muṭ MUD

82 sa$_4$ ša$_{22}$ še$_{18}$(L) še$_{21}$(B) SA$_4$

83 ra$_4$ rad rat raṭ rít rud ruṭ RAD SUD$_2$ ŠITA$_3$

84 sé sí ṣé ṣí ze zi SE$_2$ SI$_2$ ZI ZID

B = Borger BI = Borger Index d = difference e = entry foll = following L = Labat
LI = Labat's Index LL = Labat's Liste LM = Labat's Main entry mispr = misprint v = variant

85 (det) ge gi ké kí qán qè qì DUSU(#+320) GE GI GUŠKIN(468+#)
86 dal re ri sar$_5$ tal tala ṭal ARU(335+#) DAL DI$_5$ RE RI TAL
87 nu$_6$ nun síl ṣil zil ABRIG$_2$(420+#+532+206) ADAB(381+#) ARAB(381+#+78) BURANUN(579d+381+228+#+461) BURUNUN(579d+381+228+#+461) ENKUM(99+60+363b+#+532+152^4) NUN ZIMBIR(381+228+#+461)
87a tùr TUR$_3$
87aa ARḪUŠ$_3$ IMMAL
87b ARḪUŠ$_2$ ŠALLAM(?;L:87m) ŠILAM
87c AKAR EGA$_2$(L:63e)
87d KURUDA
87m ŠALLAM(?;B:87b)
88 gáb gáp ḫúb ḫúp kab kap kùb kùp qáb qáp qùb qùp EME$_5$(554+#) GUB$_3$ ḪUB$_2$ KAB
89 ḫub ḫup kúb kúp qúb qúp ḪUB TU$_{10}$ TUN
89a (v89)
90 (det) gad gada gat kad kat kaṭ kit$_9$ kút qàd qàt qid$_4$ GAD GADA KAD
91 KINDA
92a AKKIL (=L 92)
92b UMBIN
93 ŠINIG
94 di$_{11}$ dim tàm tì tim tum$_8$ ṭim ṭúm DIM
95 mun MUN MUNU
96 BULUG
96a MENBULUG$_2$
97 a$_5$ ag ak aka aq aqa AG AK KID$_3$ NA$_3$ ŠA$_5$
97a ^{d}NA$_3$ (=L e97,B 97)
98 ME$_3$
99 en in$_4$ EN ENKUM(#+60+363b+87+532+152^4) ENSI(#+532+59) NIBRU(#+313) ZUEN(#+6)
100 dàr tàr tàra ṭàr DARA$_3$
101 sur śur šur ṭìr SUR ŠUR
102 múš siḫ$_4$ suḫ šuḫ AḪULAB AŠKUD(334+#) ḪALBA$_2$(586+#) MUŠ$_2$ SUḪ ŠUBA(586+#) TIŠPAK
103 mùš INANNA INNANA INNIN MUŠ$_3$ NIDBA(469+#)
103a ŠE$_{12}$
103b AŠUGI SED ŠE$_4$ ŠED$_7$
104 (det) sa śa ša$_{10}$ SA
104a AŠGAB (=B 104,6)
105 gà gán gar$_{19}$ garak kán kár kára GAN$_2$ GANA$_2$ GURU$_6$ IKU KAN$_2$ KAR$_2$
105a ALʾAL$_2$
106 gú qu$_6$ tik tiq GU$_2$ GUN$_2$
107 USAN
108 dur túr ṭur DUR
108* bilti biltu GUN
109 làl ALAMMUŠ(LI:141a) LAL$_3$
110 GURUŠDA KU$_7$ KUŠ$_6$
111 gur guru kùr qur tari taru GUR KUR$_3$
112 se si ṣì śe śi šé ší ENSI$_2$(295+376+#) SI
113 si$_4$(LI mispr 114) su$_4$ śí śú ši$_5$ šu$_7$ GUN$_3$ SI$_4$ SU$_4$ (confusion w/114)
114 dar d̠ar(LM) dír dàš(B:339) tár tìr ṭár ṭir$_4$ DAR TAR$_2$ (confusion w/ 113; =B v114)

(?) = L and/or B uncertain on value = graphic image of sign itself # = number of the current sign
+ = two signs occur in sequence x = one sign is written within the other

115 res reš ris riš sag sak saq ša$_{24}$ šag šak šaq AZUKNA(401+#) BALLA(536+597+#+320+152+211) BALLA$_2$(536+597+#+320+152+554) DUL$_7$ SAG

116 MUḪ$_2$ (=LL d116)

117 (v118)

118 DILIB$_3$ (=B d118)

119 KAN$_3$

121 GUD$_2$ GUDU$_2$

122 (det) má MA$_2$ SANGA$_2$(320+#+352+352)

122a DELLU DIMGUL

122b UD$_5$ UZ$_3$

123 dir mál sa$_5$ su$_{12}$(B:164) ter$_4$ ṭir ADDIR(579+295+226+469+#) DIR DIRI DIRIG MAL$_2$ SA$_5$

123a nìg nìk nìq

124 2 dáb dáp dapa$_2$ tab taba tap tapa ṭab ṭap TAB

124a 3 eš$_{21}$

124b 4 LAMMU$_2$ LIM$_2$ LIMMU$_2$ (=LM e124,B 124,42)

125 MEGIDA

125b 5 IA$_7$

125c 6 AŠ$_4$

125d 7 IMIN$_2$

125e 8 USSU$_2$ (LI shows 598d)

125f 9 ILIMMU$_2$

126 báḫ paḫ$_2$ sum$_6$ tà tag tak taka taq tuk$_5$ śum šu$_{14}$ šum TAG TIBIR ŠUM

126f UTTU (=L e126)

128 ab ap ès èṣ èš ìs ìṣ iš$_7$ ìz AB ABA EŠ$_3$ IZ$_3$

128a šību (=L e128)

129 nab nap

129a (det) mul náp MUL

130 ug uk uq UG PIRIG$_3$

131 as asa aṣ az uṣ$_4$ uz$_4$ AZ

131a NIB(B) NIB$_2$(L)

132 (det) da$_5$ gi$_{27}$ gin$_6$ kin$_6$(?) TABIRA(#+560) TIBIRA(#+560) URUDU

133 bàb bába(B) bàba(L) ká pápa(B) pàpa(L) KA$_2$ KAN$_4$(L:31)

134 díḫ u$_{16}$ um UM UMMEDA(#+532;L:315) UMU

135 SAMAG$_2$(L:138) SUMUG(B:138)

135a SAMAG$_3$(L:314) (=134x411)

136 SAMAG(B:138)

138 dub dup tub tup ṭub ṭup DIḪ DUB MES$_2$ MEZ$_2$ SAMAG(L:136) SAMAG$_2$(B:135) SUMUG(L:135) SUMUG$_2$(L) TUP

139 (det w/579b) dá ta ṭá TA

140 GANMUŠ GANSIS

141 GANMUŠ$_2$

141a ALAMMUŠ(LI;B:109) LAL$_4$(B:v140)

142 i nád nát náṭ I KUN$_4$(#+537)

142a i-a ia ie iu yí (=LM foll 142)

143 (det) gan ḫé ḫí kám kan kana li$_6$ qan qàm DIM$_9$(151+#) ERIŠ$_7$ GAN GANA ḪE$_2$ KAM$_2$ KAN UDUL$_7$ UTUL$_7$

144 du$_{13}$ mar$_5$ mara$_5$ maru(LM) maru$_5$ tu$_{19}$(L:230) tur tura turu ṭùr BAN$_3$ BANDA$_3$ BIBE(372+#+78) DI$_4$ DUMU IBILA(#+211) KUN$_5$(#+536) TUKUMBI(354+597+#+481+214) TUR

B = Borger BI = Borger Index d = difference e = entry foll = following L = Labat LI = Labat's Index LL = Labat's Liste LM = Labat's Main entry mispr = misprint v = variant

144a	GENA GENNA GINA GINNA (=LM e144)
144f	ZIZNA
145	àb àba ad at aṭ àp AD
146	ḪAŠḪUR
147	se$_{20}$ si$_{20}$ ṣe ṣi zé zí ZE$_2$
148	en$_6$ in ini IN
149	rab rap RAB
150	DIM$_3$
150a	DIM$_8$ (=L e150)
151	šàr šarri šarru DIM$_9$(#+143) LILAN LILLAN LUGAL PALA(79+#)
151a	ADAMEN$_2$ DADRUM
152	ḫir sìr šìr u$_9$ BALLA(536+597+115+320+#+211) BALLA$_2$(536+597+115+320+#+554) EZEN GIR$_{11}$ KEŠ$_2$ KEŠDA SAḪAR$_2$(LM;B:331e;LI:309+#) SIR$_3$ ŠAKAR(LM;B,LI:331e) ŠER$_3$ ŠIR$_3$ (also v331e)
152^4	ENKUM(99+60+363b+87+532+#) UBARA
152^{4*}	GUGU$_2$
152^8	bàd bàt dur$_8$ ug$_5$ uq$_5$ BAD$_3$ UG$_5$
154	(see B p101)
155	(see B p101)
156	ASILA ASILAL
157	LUBUN
158	ASILAL$_3$ SIL$_6$
159	SIL$_7$
164	sè sì sím su$_{12}$(L:123) sum śúm še$_{19}$(B) še$_{21}$(B:82) šúm SE$_3$ SI$_3$ SUM
165	nák EREŠ$_2$ NAGA TE$_3$ TU$_5$(354+#) UGA(318+#+319)
166	buš íš kas kasa ras raš BU$_2$ DANNA(#+371) KAS KASKAL KAŠ$_2$ RAŠ
166b	BALIḪA ILLAT (=L e166)
166′	tāḫāzu (see L p109)
167	dáḫ du$_8$ duḫ gab gaba gap káp qab qap táḫ tuḫ tuḫu ṭáḫ ṭuḫ ASAL$_2$(579+58+#+377) DU$_8$ DUḪ GAB GABA
167a	(partial v167;=L e167)
167b	(v167;=L e167)
168	ru$_6$ ṣeri ṣeru BIR$_4$ EDIN ERU$_4$(579+#) MURU$_5$(554+381+#) RU$_6$
169	daḫ taḫ taḫa túḫ ṭaḫ DAḪ TAḪ
170	am AM ILDAG$_2$(579+#)
171	(det) šir$_4$ šira širi UZU
172	be$_8$ bí bil dè kun$_9$ kúm li$_9$ ne ni$_5$ pi$_5$ pil pil$_4$(296+#) qúm saḫ$_5$ suḫ$_8$ ṣaḫ ṣéḫ te$_4$ ṭè ṭi$_5$ BI$_2$ BIL DE$_3$ DU$_{14}$(330+#) GENE(461+#) GUNNI(461+#) IZI IZI$_2$(461+#) IZU KUM$_2$ LAM$_2$ NE NIMUR(461+#) ŠE$_6$ ŠEG$_6$ ṬE$_3$ ZAḪ
172a	rìm rúm ERIM$_2$ (=LM e172,B 172,51ff.)
173	be$_7$ bi$_5$ bíl bìl(296+#) ne$_8$ píl pìl(296+#) BIL$_2$ GIBIL
174	EŠ$_{12}$
175	EŠ$_{13}$
176	NINDA$_2$
178aa	sàn šàm šan(LI:180) ŠAM$_3$ (=L 176′)
181	AZU UZU$_2$ (=LL d181)
181a	UŠBAR(L) UŠBAR$_2$(B) (=LM e181)
182	AZU$_2$ SUBAR$_2$ SUMAŠ
183	ág ám ram rama AG$_2$ AGA$_2$ EM$_3$
184	(see B p106)
185	MURU$_{11}$ MURUM UBUDILI UGUDILI UŠBAR$_3$(B:204b)

(?) = L and/or B uncertain on value = graphic image of sign itself # = number of the current sign
+ = two signs occur in sequence x = one sign is written within the other

186 URU$_{11}$

187 šám SA$_{10}$ SAM$_2$ ŠAM$_2$

187a (partial v187) (=L e187)

187b (partial v187) (=L e187,B 187)

190 ḫáš ḫíš ṣíb ṣíp zaq$_4$ zek zíb zik ziq ḪAŠ$_2$ ZIB$_2$

190g NIGIN$_6$

190h (v190k)

190k GALAM SUKUD

191 gu$_8$ gum ku$_{13}$ kum kùn qu qum ri$_{12}$(B:230) GUM KUM

192 gas gaṣ gaz kàs kaṣ(L) kàṣ(B) GAZ NAGA$_2$(L) NAGA$_3$(B)

194 EŠGAL URUGAL

195 ab$_4$ aba$_4$ ABA$_4$ ERI$_{11}$ GUN$_4$ GUNU$_4$ IRI$_{11}$ LARSA(381+#) LARSAM(381+#) UNU UNU$_2$(376+#) UNUG URI$_2$(331+#+461) URIM$_2$(331+#+461)

196 UNUGI

198 AGARIN$_2$

199 AGARIN

200 NANŠE NINA SIRARA

200c ZI$_4$

200d EŠEMIN$_4$

200* (v200;=L 200)

201 kas$_5$ GIGRI(#+#) GIR$_6$ GIRI$_6$ SUḪ$_6$ SUḪUŠ

202 e$_{12}$(459a+#) ed$_4$(459a+#) ím kas$_4$ GIGRI$_2$(#+#) GIR$_5$ IM$_2$ KAŠ$_4$

203 úr UR$_2$

204b MURU$_2$(LM;B:337) MURU$_4$(B,LI) URU$_7$ UŠBAR$_3$(L:185) (=L e185)

205 él il IL

206 du e$_{11}$(459a+#) gub gup im$_4$(L:32) kin$_7$ kub kup qub qup rá ša$_4$ tù ṭù ABRIG$_2$(420+87+532+#) DU E$_{11}$(459a+#) GEN GIN GUB MEN$_3$ RA$_2$ TUM$_2$ UKU$_2$(482+#)

206a laḫ$_4$ súp LAḪ$_4$

207 dàm du$_4$ dum éb ép íb íp tam$_4$ tím(L:12) tìm(L) tu$_4$ tum ṭu$_4$ ṭum DUM EGIR$_3$(B:554a) EGIR$_4$(B) IB$_2$ TUM

208 (det) ANŠE DUR$_3$(#+50) EME$_3$(554+#) ŠAGAN$_3$(#+50)

209 EGIR

210 wi$_5$ GEŠTIN

211 60 iš$_{10}$ nid nit niṭ ús úṣ uš úz AŠLUG(324+#+371+335) BALLA(536+597+115+320+152+#) GALA(#+536) GIŠ$_3$ IBILA(144+#) NIDLAM(554+#+435) NIDLAM$_2$(554+#) NITA US$_2$ UŠ

211b KAŠ$_3$ (=L 211a)

212 es$_5$ eš$_{15}$ eš$_{16}$(LI;B:325a) ís íṣ iš iši íz mil mili IŠ KUŠ$_7$ SAḪAR SAḪARDUB SAḪARPEŠ UKUM

214 bi bé gaš kás kaš pé pí sa$_{18}$ su$_{15}$ ša$_{21}$ šu$_{13}$ BE$_2$ BI KAŠ KAŠBIR(#+579+373) TUKUMBI(354+597+144+481+#) ULUŠIN(#+339+579+13) ULUŠIN(#+339+579+13) ULUŠIN$_2$(#+339+13+70)

B = Borger BI = Borger Index d = difference e = entry foll = following L = Labat
LI = Labat's Index LL = Labat's Liste LM = Labat's Main entry mispr = misprint v = variant

215 (det) rig rik riq ši$_6$ šim AGARIN$_5$(237+#) BAPPIR$_2$ LUMGI(L:255) NUNGI SIRIS(LM:224) ŠEM ŠIM
216 BULUG$_6$ NUG ŠEMBULUG$_2$ ŠIMBULUG$_2$
217 NUG$_4$
218 BULUG$_7$ ŠEMMUG ŠIMMUG
219 ŠAQA$_2$
219* ŠEMBI ŠEMKAŠ ŠIMKAŠ
220 BULUG$_8$(?)
221 NUG$_2$
222 ŠEMEŠAL
224 DUMGAL LUMGI$_2$ LUNGA(L) LUNGA$_2$(B) NUNGI$_2$ SIRIS(LM; B,LI:215) SIRIS$_2$(B)
225 AGARIN$_4$(237+#) BAPPIR LUMGI(B:215) LUMGI$_3$(B) NUNGI$_3$
226 ADDIR(579+295+#+469+123) GISAL
227 BANŠUR$_2$ KIŠI$_{11}$
228 gíb gíp kep kib kip qib qip tur$_4$ ṭur$_4$ ùl BURANUN(579d+381+#+87+461) BURUNUN(579d+381+#+87+461) KIB UL$_3$ ULLU$_2$(LI mispr 229) ŠENNUR ZIMBIR(381+#+87+461)
229 (det) dàg dàk dàq ia$_4$ tàg tàk tàq NA$_4$ ZA$_2$
229a ḪUNIN(see B p292,L p257)
230 ban$_4$ dà dù gag ka$_{15}$ kak ki$_7$ kàl qaq qi$_6$ re$_{13}$ ri$_{12}$(L:191) ri$_{13}$(L) rú tu$_{19}$(B:144) DA$_3$ DALA(449+#;L) DALA$_2$(449+#;B) DU$_3$ GAG GUG$_6$(15+#) ḪENBUR ḪENBUR$_2$(367+#) KAK SUR$_7$(461+#) PIḪU$_3$(15+#)
230* (v233a)
231 dig dik diq ì ià ia$_6$(#+579) lé lí né ni ṣá(?) ṣal šàl tiq(LM) tíq wá(?) za$_7$(?) zal zár DIG DILMUN(#+574) I$_3$ IA$_3$ MU$_5$ NI SANTANA(343+#) ZAL ZANGA
232 er ir ER IR
233 gá mà mal mala BA$_4$ MA$_3$ MAL DALḪAMUN(399+#) GA$_2$ PISAN ŠITA
233a ŠITA$_2$ (=B 233,40)
234 IKU$_2$
235 GAḪALLA
236 GAGIRSU
237 AGARIN$_3$(#+595) AGARIN$_4$(#+225) AGARIN$_5$(#+215) AMA DAGAL
239 ESIBIR
242 SABAD$_2$
244 GANUN UŠUŠ
244a (v244)
246 MUNU$_3$
247 GARAŠ
248 DAN$_4$
249 par$_4$ KISAL PAR$_4$
249b (see B pp118,119)
250 EMEDUB
250b GAZI$_3$ (=L e252)
250d ME$_7$
251 AM$_4$ AMA$_4$
251a GALILLA
252 GAZI(L:257) GAZI$_2$(L) IŠḪARA(LM) IŠḪARA$_4$ SILA$_4$
252b EMEDUB$_2$
255 ùr DAN$_3$(B:341) UR$_3$
256 GAGIA
257 GAZI(B:252)
259 GABURRA
260 BARA$_{10}$

(?) = L and/or B uncertain on value   = graphic image of sign itself   # = number of the current sign
+ = two signs occur in sequence   x = one sign is written within the other

261 ESAG$_2$

262 ERIM$_4$

263 GAḪILI

264 SABAD

265 ITIMA

269 GAZAG

270 MEN

271 ARḪUŠ UŠ$_3$

272 GASIKILLA

273 EDAKUA

274 PIRU

277 ḪALUBBA

278 GALGA

280 dag dak daq pàr pàra(B; LI:488b) para$_{10}$(B:344) tág ták táq ṭak BAR$_3$ BARA$_3$(LI:488b) DAG PAR$_3$ PARA$_3$(LI:485[488b])

280a IL$_8$ (=LM e205)

281 UTUA$_2$(B LI:293)

281a KEŠ$_8$ KISIM$_4$ KIŠI$_8$

282 LAḪTA LAḪTAN

282a RAPIL RAPIQU

283 ZIBIN

284 KIŠI$_7$

285 KISIM$_2$

286 ŠURUN$_4$

287 UDUL$_6$ UTUA UTUL$_6$

288 ḪARA$_4$

289 UTUL$_5$

290 ḪARUB KEŠ$_9$ KIŠI$_9$ ŠARIN ŠURIN$_5$ ZIBIN$_2$

291 AGAN$_2$ UBUR

292 ŠARAN

293 AMAŠ UDUL$_3$ UTUA$_2$(LM:281) UTUL$_3$

294b MAGANZA

294c KU$_{12}$

295 ari$_5$(#+533) aru bá ḫad ḫás ḫáṣ ḫat ḫaṭ pa sàk šàg šàk šàq wí(?) zág zák záq ADDIR(579+#+226+469+123) BANMIN EN$_5$(#+376) ENSI$_2$(#+376+112) GIDRI GIDRU KUNGA(B:547) MUATI NINGIDAR(597+#) PA SAG$_3$ SIG$_3$ UGULA

295a GARSU

295b BILLUDA GARZA

295bb ZILULU (=LL,LM foll 295b)

295c RIG$_7$

295cc GARZA$_2$ GIRZA (=LM foll 295c)

295d MAŠKIM$_2$

295e MAŠKIM

295ee MAŠKIM$_3$

295f ŠABRA

295k sab sap šab šap šip(B) šip$_4$(L) šùb(L:547) šùp(L:1) SAB ŠAB ŠABA

295l ENŠADA

295m sàp síp šab$_5$ šáp(L) šap$_5$(B) SIB$_2$ SIPA

296 (det) bìl(#+173) es eṣ eš$_{19}$ ez gis giṣ giš is iṣ iš$_6$ iz kák(#+536) nís níš pìl(#+173) pil$_4$(#+172) sutu(#+74) túkul(#+536) GEŠ GEŠTU$_2$(#+536+383) GEŠTU$_3$(#+383+536) GISSU(#+427) GIŠ ILLAR(#+68) IŠ$_6$ IZ KIRI$_6$(#+331e) LUḪUMMU(#+427) SUTU(#+74) ṬIL$_2$(#+427)

296a GUR$_{17}$ GURU$_{17}$

296b GIŠḪAR(B) GIŠḪAR$_2$(L)

297 (det) gu$_4$ ku$_{15}$ BAḪAR EŠTUB(#+381+589) GU$_4$ GUD

298 al AL

300 ḪIBIS$_2$ ḪIBIZ$_2$

301 GIŠBAR

302 LIDIM(?)

B = Borger BI = Borger Index d = difference e = entry foll = following L = Labat
LI = Labat's Index LL = Labat's Liste LM = Labat's Main entry mispr = misprint v = variant

305 ḪIBIRA

306 ár ub up AR$_2$ ARA$_2$ UB UP

307 mar wár MAR

308 e i$_{15}$ yì E EG$_2$

308a ḪILIBU

309 (det) dug duk duq lud lut luṭ líṭ tùg tùk tùq BAḪAR$_2$(#+15+349) DUG LUD LILLU(#+62+349) LUM$_3$ SAḪAR$_2$(LI:#+152; B:331e;LM:152) ŠAKAR(LI:#+331e;B:331e; LM:152) URRUB URSUB ZURZUB

310 (v69*)

311 BURU$_7$ GURIN GURUN (also v69*)

312 ùku un KALAM UKU$_3$ UN

313 gid git giṭ ki$_4$(L:326) kid kit kiṭ líl qi$_5$ qid qit qiṭ saḫ síḫ suḫ$_4$ šíḫ GE$_2$ GID KID LIL$_2$ NIBRU(99+#)

314 lag lak laka laq lík líq mèš mis miṣ miš rid rit riṭ síd sít sìn šid šit šiṭ KIŠIB LAG LIG$_2$ MES MEZ PISAN$_2$ SAMAG$_3$(?;B:135a) SANGA SANGU SIL$_x$(LM) SIL$_{11}$ SILA$_{11}$ SILAG ŠID ŠITA$_5$ UMBISAG

315 EME$_2$ UMMEDA(?;B:134+532)

315′ UMMEDA$_2$(B:137 =134x532+335)

316 SAMAG$_4$

317 PISAN$_3$ UMBISAG$_2$

318 (det) $\frac{1}{10}$ (411+#) ba$_6$ bu$_8$(L) bu$_{11}$(B) pu$_8$(L) pu$_{11}$(B) sam ša$_{17}$(B:455) šam ú AD$_5$(#+10;L:330b) BA$_6$ KIŠI$_{16}$(#+10) KUŠ$_3$ ŠIMBIRIDA(#+366+328) U$_2$ UGA(#+165+319)

319 ga kà qá GA GAR$_2$(LM) GAR$_9$ UGA(318+165+#)

319a (see L p145,B p131)

320 gìl íl íli BALLA(536+597+115+#+152+211) BALLA$_2$(536+597+115+#+152+554) DUSU(85+#) GUR$_3$ IL$_2$(LI mispr 205) SANGA$_2$(#+122+352+352)

321 làḫ lìḫ luḫ luḫu naḫ raḫ riḫ ruḫ LAḪ$_3$ LUḪ RAḪ SUKAL SUKKAL

322 dan dín gal$_9$ kal kala lab lap líb líp qal$_4$ rab$_4$ rib rip rub tan tana ṭan ALAD$_2$ BAD$_4$(461+#) ESI ESIG GURUŠ ILLU(579+#) KAL KALA KALAG KALAGA KANKAL(461+#) LAMA$_2$(L) LAMA$_3$(B) LAMAR LAMMA LAMMAR LIRUM(354+#) SIG$_{15}$ SI$_{21}$

323 ALAD(B) ALAD$_3$(L) KARAŠ(461+#)

324 (det) ʾà ʾè àʾ é èʾ bid bit biti biṭ mét míd pi$_{11}$ pid pit ARALI(#+366+69) AŠLUG(#+211+371+335) E$_2$ INGAR(#+567) U$_6$(449+#)

325 nàr nir NIR

325a 3 EŠ$_{16}$(LI:212)

325b 4 LIMMU$_4$

326 ge$_4$ gi$_4$ ki$_4$(B:313) qe$_4$ qi$_4$ GI$_4$

326a gigi

327 USAN$_2$ (also v107)

328 ra RA ŠIMBIRIDA(318+366+#)

329 dùl súr śúr ṣìl(13+#; L:12) šúr ANDUL DUL$_3$ KUŠ$_2$ SUR$_2$ ŠUR$_2$

329a 5 ia$_9$

(?) = L and/or B uncertain on value = graphic image of sign itself # = number of the current sign
+ = two signs occur in sequence x = one sign is written within the other

330 (det) lú na$_6$ qál DU$_{14}$(#+172) LU$_2$ NIGA$_2$(#+367)

330a ADAMEN

330b ad$_5$(L) ad$_6$(B) at$_5$(L) at$_6$(B) AD$_5$(B:318+10) AD$_6$(B) (=L e330, B 330^6; LI mispr 69)

331 áḫ áḫa aḫi(LI:334) nan nán(13+#+461) nanna$_4$(13+#+461) sis siš šas(LI:also 366) šaṣ šaš(LI:also 366) šes šis šiṣ šiš šiz ùri MUŠ$_5$ NANNA(#+461) NANNA$_4$(13+#+461; LM:NANNA) NANNAR(13+#+461) SIS SIŠ ŠEŠ URI$_2$(#+195+461) URI$_3$ URIM$_2$(#+195+461) URU$_3$

331a 6 AŠ$_9$

331b 7 IMIN$_3$

331c 8 USSU$_3$

331d 9 ILIMMU$_3$

331e (det) sar śar šar šer$_9$ šir$_9$ šur$_4$(482+#) KIRI$_6$(296+#) MA$_4$ MU$_2$ NISSA SAR SAḪAR$_2$(LM:152;LI:309+152) ŠAKAR(LM:152) USAR(482+#) USUR(482+#) UŠAR(482+#) UŠUR(482+#) (=L e152)

332 bute buti butu en$_7$ puta puti putu sak$_6$ ṣak zà zag zak zaq ZA$_3$ ZAG

333 gàr kàr qar qer$_5$ GAR$_3$ KAR$_3$ QAR ZEḪ(556+#) ZEḪ$_x$(554+#)

334 á aḫi(?;B:331) ed et eṭ id ídi it iṭ A$_2$ AḪ$_5$(#+579d) AŠKUD(#+102) ID IDI$_2$

334a ti$_8$ TE$_8$ (=LM e334)

335 da ìdi tá ṭa ARU(#+86) AŠLUG(324+211+371+#) DA

336 lil LIL

337 múr muri múru MUR$_2$ MURU$_2$(LM:185[204b]) MURUB$_4$ NISAG UNU$_7$(B:58)

338 ṭe$_5$ DE$_2$ SIMUG UMUM UMUN$_2$

339 ás áṣ áš áša(LI:579) áz dàš(L:114) es$_4$ is$_4$ tàš AŠ$_2$ BANEŠ IMGAGA(#+579b; see L p155) ULUŠIN(214+#+579+13) ULUŠIN$_2$(214+#+13+70) ZIZ$_2$

340 four sūtu

341 five sūtu DAN$_3$(L:255)

342 ma wa$_6$ MA PEŠ$_3$

343 gal gala kál qal ráb ráp GAL SANTANA(#+231) SUR$_6$(461+#) TIRU(#+376) TIRUM(#+376) UKUR$_2$(#+53) UŠUMGAL(#+11)

344 bár bára par$_6$ pára(B:74) ša$_{23}$ BAR$_2$ BARA$_2$(LI:69) PARA$_{10}$(L:280) TITAB

345 kuk(B:468) kúk(L:468) lù GUG$_2$ LU$_3$

346 bís biš gir giri kar$_4$ kir kiri peš pis piš piša pùš qer qir qiri GIR ḪA$_6$ PEŠ

347 aga mere mir miri AGA MER MIR NIGIR NIMGIR UKU

348 DUN$_4$ NIGIR$_2$ NIMGIR$_2$

349 bur buru pur puru BAḪAR$_2$(309+15+#) BUR BURU$_4$(71+#) LAGAS(71+#+55) LILLU(309+62+#)

350 BUR-U GAŠAN

351 10,000 sig$_7$ ši$_7$ SIG$_7$ ŠI$_7$(LM:24) UKTIN(#+358)

B = Borger BI = Borger Index d = difference e = entry foll = following L = Labat
LI = Labat's Index LL = Labat's Liste LM = Labat's Main entry mispr = misprint v = variant

352 búm dim$_5$(L:12) dúb dúp túb túp ṭúb ṭúp BALAG DUB$_2$ SANGA$_2$(320+122+#+#) TIGI(#+355)

353 en$_8$ na$_5$ ša zur$_8$ ARA NA$_5$ PUZUR$_4$(26+#) ŠA

354 kat$_6$(L) kat$_7$(B) qad qat qata šu GEŠPU$_2$(#+60d) LIRUM(#+322) SAḪAB(#+480) SAḪAB$_2$(#+457+472) ŠU TU$_5$(#+165) TUKUMBI(#+597+144+481+214) (=LM e354b)

354b^1 qa$_4$ qád qát (=L e354b)

354b^2 kad$_4$ kat$_4$ kaṭ$_4$ qat$_5$ KAD$_4$ KARA$_4$ PEŠ$_5$ (=L e354b,B 354b(205))

354b^3 KAD$_7$

354b^4 kad$_5$ kat$_5$ kaṭ$_5$ qat$_8$ KAD$_5$ KAM$_3$ PEŠ$_6$ (=L v354b,B 354b(206))

355 (det) bàḫ buḫ láb lib lip lu$_5$ lub lul lulu lup nar paḫ piḫ puḫ KA$_5$ LUL NAR NARI PAḪ TIGI(352+#) ŠATAM

356 sa$_6$ ša$_6$ GIŠIMMAR SA$_6$ SIG$_6$ ŠA$_6$ ŠANGA

358 ALAM ALAN UKTIN(351+#)

359 TILLA URI (=B v359)

360 eš$_{18}$ iš$_8$ EŠ$_{18}$ GE$_{23}$(B) GE$_{22}$(L) (=LM 362′; cf. 411)

361 GE$_{22}$(B) GE$_{23}$(L)

362 ar$_5$ gam gar$_{17}$ gum$_4$ gúr gúru qam qìr GAM GUR$_2$

363 9 sìp(L:395) ILIMMU$_4$ (sign of hyphen, line break, repetition)

363a (v350)

363b ENKUM(99+60+#+87+532+152^4) (v351)

364 ŠUŠUR

365 KAD$_8$ ŠUŠUR$_2$

366 (det) gur$_{16}$ gìn kur kìn lad lat laṭ mad mat maṭ nad nat naṭ qìn(?) qúr sad sat saṭ šad šada šadi šas(LI;see 331) šaš(LI; see 331) šat šaṯ(L) šaṭ ARALI(324+#+69) ARATTA(435+#+68+461) ESA(#+73) GIN$_3$ GUDIBIR$_2$(#+#) KUR MAD SAT ŠIMBIRIDA(318+#+328) ŠURUPPAK(7+#+68)

367 (det) ir$_{11}$(LM:50x367; B,LI:51) še AŠNAN(#+375) DABIN(536+#) EZIN$_2$(#+375) EZINA$_2$(#+375) EZINU$_2$(#+375) ḪENBUR$_2$(#+230) IR$_{11}$(LM:50x367;B,LI:51) NIGA NIGA$_2$(330+#) ŠE

369 KARADIN$_2$

370 KARADIN$_3$

371 bu gíd gít gíṭ pu qíd qít ra$_5$ sír šír šúd AŠLUG(324+211+#+335) BU DANNA(166+#) GID$_2$ KIM$_3$ SIR$_2$

371a SIRSIR

371b MUNU$_5$ (=L e371,LL 371a)

371c MUNU$_7$ (=L e371b)

372 us uṣ uš$_{10}$(B) uš$_{11}$(L) uz BIBE(#+144+78) UŠ$_{10}$(B) UŠ$_{11}$(B:17) UZ

373 sar$_4$ sir sù śù šir$_8$ šud šut šuṭ šuz BIR$_8$(579+#) KAŠBIR(214+579+#) SIR SU$_3$ SUD

374 muš ṣir ṣiri ṣúr šir10 wuš zìr MUŠ

374a NIDABA NISABA (=LL 165,LM foll 374)

(?) = L and/or B uncertain on value = graphic image of sign itself # = number of the current sign
+ = two signs occur in sequence x = one sign is written within the other

375 dir$_4$ ter tir ṭir$_5$ AŠNAN(367+#) EŠA(579+#) EZIN$_2$(367+#) EZINA$_2$(367+#) EZINU$_2$(367+#) GAMUN(465+#+427) TIR

375a KARADIN$_6$ NINNI$_5$ (=L e375,B 375,45)

375b KARADIN

375′ MUNU$_8$

376 (det) de$_4$ di$_{12}$ te ti$_7$ ṭe$_4$ ṭi$_4$ EN$_5$(295+#) ENSI$_2$(295+#+112) GAL$_5$ MUL$_2$ TE TEMEN TIRU(343+#) TIRUM(343+#) UNU$_2$(#+195)

376* gar$_{14}$ kar kara kir$_8$ qár KAR

377 liḫ$_4$ lis liš liz mal$_4$ ASAL$_2$(579+58+167+#) DILIM$_2$ LIŠ

378 (sign of separation)

378a $\frac{1}{4}$

379[2] AD$_4$(LI no#)

380 (v406)

381 a$_{12}$ bír dám ḫàš ḫiš ḫúd ḫút ḫúṭ laḫ liḫ par para(L:74) para$_{11}$(L) per pir sa$_{15}$(?;B:597) sa$_{16}$(L:597) ta$_5$ tam tú ṭám u$_4$ ud úm ut uṭ ADAB(#+87) AMNA ARAB(#+87+78) AZALAG(536+#) AZLAG(536+#) BABBAR BAR$_6$ BURANUN(579d+#+228+87+461) BURUNUN(579d+#+228+87+461) DADAG(#+#) EŠTUB(297+#+589) ḪA$_5$ ḪAD$_2$ KISLAḪ(461+#) LARSA(#+195) LARSAM(#+195) LUGUD(69+#) MURU$_5$(554+#+168) PAR PIRIG$_2$ TAM TU$_2$ U$_4$ UD UTU ZIMBIR(#+228+87+461)

381a è i$_{10}$ ARA$_4$ E$_3$ ED$_2$ (=L e381)

381b ḫùb (=LL 382,LM e381; v89? see L p175[2])

382 ITIMA$_2$ (LI mispr 26)

383 à aw be$_6$ bì i$_{16}$ ia$_8$ íu iw ya ye yi yu ma$_9$ me$_8$ mi$_5$ pa$_{12}$ pe pi tál tála u$_{17}$ U$_{17}$(L:49*) wa we wi wu GEŠTU GEŠTU$_2$(296+536+#) GEŠTU$_3$(296+#+536) PI TAL$_2$

384 lìb lìp šà PEŠ$_{12}$ ŠA$_3$

385 NANAM

388 BIR$_6$

389 GUDU$_5$

390 IŠKILA IŠKILLA PEŠ$_4$

391 algamešu (see B p158)

392 uʾ$_4$ úḫ úḫu AKŠAK UḪ$_2$ UPE

393 bìr ḫìš láḫ líḫ nura nuri nuru par$_5$ pír sáp ṣab ṣap tam$_5$ zab zap EREN$_2$ ERIM ERIN$_2$ RIN$_2$ ZALAG$_2$

394 NUNUZ

394b LAḪTAN (=LL 394a,LM e394)

394c USAN$_3$

394d MUD$_3$

395 sìp(B:363) ṣib ṣibi ṣip šìp zib zip zúb ZIB

395a $\frac{1}{6}$

395* (v395)

396 (det w/579) 3,600 ʾì da$_{10}$ de$_8$ dí du$_{10}$ ḫe ḫi i$_{11}$ sár šár ta$_8$ té tí ṭà ṭé ṭí DU$_{10}$ DUG$_3$ ḪI ŠAR$_2$

396a tàp (=LM foll 396)

B = Borger BI = Borger Index d = difference e = entry foll = following L = Labat
LI = Labat's Index LL = Labat's Liste LM = Labat's Main entry mispr = misprint v = variant

397 ʾa ʾe ʾi ʾu aʾ aḫ$_4$(L:60) eʾ éḫ iʾ íḫ uʾ uḫ$_5$

398 ʾá ʾé ʾí ʾú(B) ʾù(B:494) áʾ aḫ éʾ eḫ íʾ iḫ u$_{13}$ úʾ(B) ùʾ(B:494) uḫ AḪ UḪ UḪU

398a GUDU$_4$ (=L e398)

399 (det) 3600 em im ní tum$_9$(L:557) tum$_{10}$(B:557) tumu šar$_5$(LM:also 86) ANZU(13+#+445) DALḪAMUN(#+233) IM IŠKUR MURU$_9$(#+445) NI$_2$ ŠAR$_5$ TU$_{15}$

399a DUNGU

400 bir pìr BIR DUBUR ELLAG$_2$ GIRIŠ

401 ḫar ḫara ḫaru ḫír ḫur ḫuru kín mur muru ur$_5$ AR$_3$ ARA$_3$ AZUKNA(#+115) GADIBDIM ḪAR ḪUR KIN$_2$ MUR SAGGAR$_2$ UR$_5$

402 ḫiš$_4$ ḫuš ruš ḪUŠ RUŠ

403 sìḫ súḫ SUḪUR

403* (v403)

403** (v403)

404 (det) ḫá ḪA$_2$

404* KISIM$_5$ (also v396)

405 ḫir$_5$ KAZAZA MUL$_3$ SUR$_3$ (=L v405)

405a (v405;see L p189)

405b (v405;see L p189)

406 (det) gám ka$_{13}$ kam kama qám KAM TU$_7$ UDUL$_2$(LI missing) UTUL$_2$

406a (v406;=LL 406,LM foll 405)

409 36,000 DUBUR$_2$

409a (v409)

410 GUKIN$_2$ TIKKIN

411 $\frac{1}{10}$(#+318) $\frac{1}{6}$ 10 600(480+#) a$_6$ bu$_{12}$ guru$_{12}$ iš$_8$ šu$_4$ u BUR$_3$ BUZUR GIGURU ŠU$_4$ ŠUŠ U UNUN (also v360)

412 eli muḫ màḫ UGU

413 SIBIR ŠIBIR UŠBAR$_5$ (cf. 54)

415 UDUN

416 GAKKUL

417 U-GUR

418 UGUN

419 SAGŠU

420 áb áp le$_8$ li$_8$ lid lit liti liṭ liṭi réme rím rími AB$_2$ ABRIG$_2$(#+87+532+206) LId UDUL(#+536/537) UNU$_3$(#+536/537) UTUL(#+536/537)

421 ALIM

422 LILIS LILIZ

423 kir$_6$(cf LM,LI) qir$_6$ ŠEM$_5$ (=L e424;see LI)

424 kír qír KIR$_2$ ŠEM$_3$ UB$_3$

425 kis kiš qis qiš KIŠ

426 MEZE ŠEM$_4$

427 gi$_6$ mé mi ṣíl wi$_4$ ADAMA(69+#) DUGUD$_2$(?) GAMUN(465+375+#) GE$_6$ GI$_6$ GIG$_2$ GISSU(296+#) KU$_{10}$ LUḪUMMU(296+#) MI ṬIL$_2$(296+#)

428 ŠAGAN ŠAKAN ŠAMAN$_2$

429 gul gulu kúl qúl sún šùn GUL SUN$_2$

430 GIR$_4$ qìr(?;LI)

431 ná nú NA$_2$ NU$_2$

433 nàm nam$_4$(LI) ni$_6$ nim nù num tu$_8$ tum$_4$ DIḪ$_3$ ELAM NIM NUM

434 tùm TUM$_3$ (also v424; see B pp168f,L pp193,195)

434a kir$_7$ tum$_{11}$ KIR$_7$

(?) = L and/or B uncertain on value = graphic image of sign itself # = number of the current sign
+ = two signs occur in sequence x = one sign is written within the other

435 la$_{11}$(L) la$_{12}$(B) lam lama ARATTA(#+366+68+461) GANBA(461+#) LAM NIDLAM(554+211+#)
436 iš$_{11}$ lam$_{7}$ ARATTA$_{2}$(#+68+461)
437 ṣár ṣur ṣuru zur AMAR MAR$_{2}$
438 SISKUR SISKUR$_{2}$(#+#; LI SIZKUR)
439 ban pan BAN PAN
440 dím gim gimi ki$_{5}$ kim qim qín(?) tam$_{6}$ ṭém ṭím DIM$_{2}$ GIM GIN$_{7}$ MUŠDA ŠIDIM
440a GIR$_{9}$
441 (det) du$_{7}$ ru$_{5}$ ul DU$_{7}$ UL
441a nakkāpû (see B p171)
442 ŠITA$_{4}$
443 UTU$_{2}$ (=LL 443*,LM foll 441)
444 gèr gìr kir$_{10}$ qir$_{7}$ úg wir GIR$_{3}$ NE$_{3}$ PIRIG SAKKAN SUMUKAN SUMUQAN ŠAGAN$_{2}$(#+50) UG$_{2}$
445 ANZU(13+399+#) DUGUD MURU$_{9}$(399+#)
446 gig qiq GIG
446a BUZUR$_{3}$ PUZUR$_{3}$
447 NIGIN$_{4}$
447a NIGIN$_{3}$
448 KIŠI$_{10}$ KUŠ$_{5}$ KUŠU KUZU
449 1,000 bad$_{5}$ bat$_{5}$ gi$_{8}$ igi ín ína íni ini$_{4}$(#+570) ínu làm$_{5}$ lem lì lim limi lúm pàn si$_{17}$ še20 ši zi$_{5}$ BAD$_{5}$ DALA(#+230;L) DALA$_{2}$(#+230;B) GE$_{8}$ IGI LIM ŠI U$_{6}$(#+324)
450 pà PAD$_{3}$
451 ar AR
452 AGRIG GISKIM GIŠKIM
452a (v452)
454 KUR$_{7}$ KURU$_{7}$ KURUM$_{7}$ SIG$_{5}$
455 ša$_{17}$(B) ša$_{19}$(L) ù LIBIR SI$_{5}$ U$_{3}$
456 ḫul ḪUL
457 de di sá śá ša$_{18}$ šùb(B:295k) ti$_{4}$ ṭe ṭi DI SA$_{2}$ SAḪAB$_{2}$(354+#+472) SI$_{8}$ SILIM
458 EMEŠ(554+#) LAGAR MURUB$_{2}$(554+#)
459 dul tul DUL
459a dul$_{6}$ e$_{11}$(#+206) e$_{12}$(#+202) ed$_{4}$(#+202) tul$_{5}$ tu$_{21}$ tíl ṭùl DU$_{6}$ E$_{11}$(#+206) TILLU (=L e459)
459b ŠUMUNDA(B mispr 459a)
460 SU$_{7}$
461 (det) ge$_{5}$ gi$_{5}$ ke ki nán(13+331+#) qé qí ARATTA(435+366+68+#) ARATTA$_{2}$(436+68+#) BAD$_{4}$(#+322) BURANUN(579d+381+228+87+#) BURUNUN(579d+381+228+87+#) GANBA(#+435) GENE(#+172) GUNNI(#+172) IZI$_{2}$(#+172) KANKAL(#+322) KARAŠ(#+323) KI KISLAḪ(#+381) NANNA(331+#) NANNA$_{4}$(13+331+#; LM:NANNA) NANNAR(13+331+#) NIMUR(#+172) SUR$_{6}$(#+343) SUR$_{7}$(#+230) URI$_{2}$(331+195+#) URIM$_{2}$(331+195+#) ZIMBIR(381+228+87+#)
462 ḪABRUD
463 KISLAḪ$_{2}$
464 (sign of repetition) u$_{7}$ KIMIN (=B 461,280+464)

B = Borger BI = Borger Index d = difference e = entry foll = following L = Labat
LI = Labat's Index LL = Labat's Liste LM = Labat's Main entry mispr = misprint v = variant

465 dan$_5$ din dini dún tin tén ṭin DIN GAMUN(#+375+427) KURUN$_2$ TIN
466 keš$_4$ kiš$_4$ kiši$_4$
467 dun sul šáḫ šul tun$_4$ DUN ŠAḪ$_2$ ŠUL
468 kù kuk(L:345) kúk(B:345) qu$_5$ AZAG(#+13) GUŠKIN(#+85) KU$_3$
469 bád bát báṭ pad pat paṭ šug šuk šuq ADDIR(579+295+226+#+123) KUR$_6$ KURUM$_6$ NIDBA(#+103) PAD ŠUG
470 15 UIA
471 20 21(#+480) mam man mìm mìn naš nis niš šar$_4$ šárru wan BUZUR$_2$ MAN MIN$_3$ NIŠ PUZUR$_2$ ŠUŠANA$_2$
472 30 bà és eš is$_5$ ìš sin BA$_3$ EŠ SAḪAB$_2$(354+457+#) SIN UŠU$_3$
473 4 40 LIMMU(LM) LIMMU$_3$ NIMIN NIN$_5$ ŠANABI$_2$
475 50 KINGUSILI$_2$ KINGUSILLA$_2$ NINNU
480 (det; indic sentences and paragraphs) 1 21(471+#) 60 600(#+411) ana dáš diš dúš eš$_4$ gè gì il$_4$ ili$_6$ iš$_4$ li$_5$ táš tis tiš tiz ṭiš DIŠ EŠ$_4$ EŠ$_{18}$(LM) GI$_3$ GIŠ$_2$ I(det) MAKKAŠ SAḪAB(354+#) SANTAK$_4$ TAL$_4$
481 lá lal sur$_5$(#+483) šur$_5$(#+483) LA$_2$ LAL TUKUMBI(354+597+144+#+214)
481a ribbātu (=LL 481*,LM e481)
481b ribbātu (=LL 481*,LM e481)
481c DUG$_5$(?) (=B 481,73)
482 lál šur$_4$(#+331e[LM:152]) LAL$_2$ UKU$_2$(#+206) USAR(#+331e) USUR(#+331e) UŠAR(#+331e) UŠUR(#+331e) (see L p105)
482a ribbātu (=LL 482*,LM e482)
482b ribbātu (=LL 482*,LM e482,B 482,20)
482c GAR$_2$ (=B 319,9;see B p395)
483 gíl gili$_4$ gir$_8$ ḫab ḫaba ḫap kele kil kìr qil qìr(LI:430) rè reme rì rim rimi rin sur$_5$(481+#) šur$_5$(481+#) ELLAG GIRAG GIRIM GIRIN GUD$_8$ GUR$_4$ ḪAB KIL KUR$_4$ LAGAB LUGUD$_2$ NIGIN$_2$ RIM RIN
484 ENGUR ZIKUM
485 BARA$_8$(LI mispr 490) PARA$_8$
486 GIGIR (=LL 485)
487 ESIR$_2$
488a (see B p183)
488b BARA$_3$(LI) BARA$_5$ PARA$_5$(LI mispr 485, also PARA$_3$)
489a SIDUG
491 sar$_6$ ṣar ṣara zar ZAR
492 ŠERIMSUR ŠERINŠUR$_2$
493 GANA$_5$ GANAM$_5$
494 ʾù(L:398) u$_8$ ùʾ(L:398) LAḪAR ŠURUN U$_8$ US$_5$ (=B 494+493)
495 UDUB
496 KUNIN$_3$(?)
497 ME$_9$
498 GALA$_4$
499 UGRA
500 AGAR$_2$

(?) = L and/or B uncertain on value = graphic image of sign itself # = number of the current sign
+ = two signs occur in sequence x = one sign is written within the other

501 AGAR$_4$
502 BARA$_9$ PARA$_9$
503 GIGIR$_3$
506 GAḪURIN
507 MUŠŠAGANA
508 ŠEDUR
509 UMUN$_6$
510 BUN DILIM$_3$ ELAMKUŠ NINDA$_3$
511 bu$_4$ ḫáb ḫáp pú túl ṭul GIGIR$_2$ ḪAB$_2$ PU$_2$ TUL$_2$
512 DAGRIN UMAḪ UMUN$_5$
513 GARIN
514 GALA$_5$
515 bu$_5$ bul pul BUL NINNA$_2$ NUSSU TUKU$_4$
515a NENNI NINNA NINNI (=L v515,B 515,9)
516 BUGIN$_3$ BUNIN$_3$
517 BARA$_6$ MEN$_4$
518 ELAMKUŠ$_2$
519 GUKIN
520 ŠU$_5$
521 ŠU$_6$
522 as$_4$ sug suk suq zuk zuq AMBAR AS$_4$ BUGIN BUNIN SUG
523 INDA$_2$
524 EDAKUA$_2$
525 ABLAL
526 AGAR$_3$
527 ELAMKUŠ$_3$ (=LM 526)
528 BUGIN$_2$ BUNIN$_2$ NINDU
529 NIGIN
532 (det) 100 me méš mì qad$_4$ qat$_4$ sib sip šep šib šip ABRIG$_2$(420+87+#+206) ENKUM(99+60+363b+87+#+152[4]) ENSI(99+#+59) IŠIB LUKUR(554+#) ME MEŠ$_2$ UMMEDA(134+#;L:315)
533 (det) ari$_5$(295+#) eš$_{17}$ mès meš míš wiš MEŠ (=B v533)
533a (v533;=B 533)
534 (v348;=L 377*)
535 eb ep ib ip urta DAR$_2$ DARA$_2$ IB URAŠURTA
536 (det) $\frac{1}{6}$ 60 dúr duš ge$_7$ gi$_7$ gu$_5$ ḫun iš$_9$ kák(296+#) ku náḫ qú ši$_4$ túk tukul túkul(296+#) túq tur$_7$ tus tuš túš ṭúr ṭuš úb úp uš$_4$ záp AZALAG(#+381) AZLAG(#+381) AZLAG$_2$ BALLA(#+597+115+320+152+211) BALLA$_2$(#+597+115+320+152+554) DAB$_5$ DABIN(#+367) DUL$_5$ DUR$_2$ DURU$_2$ DURUN EŠ$_2$ GALA(211+#) GEŠTU$_2$(296+#+383) GEŠTU$_3$(296+383+#) GI$_7$ ḪUN KU KUN$_5$(144+#) MITTA(#+13) MU$_4$ NAM$_2$ SUḪ$_5$ ŠE$_3$ TASKARIN TAŠKARIN TU$_9$ TUG$_2$ TUK$_2$ TUKUL TUŠ UB$_2$ UDUL(420+#/537) UMUŠ UNU$_3$(420+#/537) UTUL(420+#/537) ZI$_3$ ZID$_2$
537 (det) dab dap dib dip lu tib tip ṭàb ṭib ṭip DAB DIB GUKKAL(#+550) KUN$_4$(142+#) LU UDU UDUL(420+536/#) UNU$_3$(420+536/#) UTUL(420+536/#)
537a (v537c;see L p249)
537b (v537c;see B p189)
537c AD$_3$ (=B 537,65+537*)
538 kin kun$_{10}$ qe qi qin GUR$_{10}$ KIN
539 (det) šík šíq SIG$_2$ SIK$_2$ SIKI

B = Borger BI = Borger Index d = difference e = entry foll = following L = Labat
LI = Labat's Index LL = Labat's Liste LM = Labat's Main entry mispr = misprint v = variant

540 DAR$_4$ DARA$_4$ GANA$_6$ INNA NINA$_2$ U$_{10}$

541 EREN ERIN ŠEŠ$_4$

542 GUR$_7$

543 MUNSUB MUNŠUB

543a AŠ$_5$ MUNSUB$_2$ MUNŠUB$_2$ (L e543,B e543; cf. BI,LI)

544 ŠEŠ$_2$

545 $\frac{1}{6}$ šú ŠU$_2$ ŠUŠ$_2$

546 EN$_2$

546a KEŠ$_3$ (=LM e546,B 546,6)

547 KUNGA$_2$(B:74+13) KUNGA(L:295) ŠUḪUB

548 GIBIL$_2$ KIBIR(L) KIBIR$_2$(B)

549 ŠUDUN

550 ḫúl BIBRA BIBRI GUKKAL(537+#) ḪUL$_2$ UKUŠ$_2$

551 KIŠI$_6$ ŠEG$_9$

552 LIL$_5$

553 LIL$_3$

554 (det) mám mán mim mín rag rak raq sal sala ša$_{12}$ šal šel$_4$ BALLA$_2$(536+597+115+320+152+#) EME$_3$(#+208) EME$_5$(#+88) EMEŠ(#+458;LI:562) GAL$_4$ LUKUR(#+532) MI$_2$ MUNUS MURU$_5$(#+381+168) MURUB$_2$(#+458) NIDLAM(#+211+435) NIDLAM$_2$(#+211) RAG RAK SAL ŠAL ZEḪ$_x$(#+333)

554a EGI$_2$ EGIR$_3$(L:207) (=B 554,84+556,8)

555 ríg rík ríq sim$_6$ súm ṣim ṣu ṣum zum zù RIG$_2$ SUM$_2$ ZUM

556 e$_5$ eriš in$_5$ min$_4$ ním nin EREŠ NIN ZEḪ(#+333)

557 da$_4$ dam dùm ta$_4$ tám tum$_9$(B:399) tum$_{10}$(L:399) ṭa$_4$ ṭam DAM

558 amat amtu GEME$_2$ GIM$_3$

559 gu ku$_8$ qù GU

560 alla ALLA BULUG$_4$(L:60e) NAGAR NAGARA TABIRA(132+#) TIBIRA(132+#)

561 TUGUL TUḪUL (=B d561)

562 ùḫ KUŠU$_2$

563 nig nik niq NIG

564 el il$_5$ ili$_5$ SIKIL

565 gúm ḫum ḫus kús kúṣ kúz lu$_4$ lum lumu nim$_4$ nu$_4$ núm qùm GUZ ḪUM LUM MUR$_8$ NUM$_2$

566 GUḪŠU(B:568) GUḪŠU$_2$(L:568) (=LM e565)

566b LUGUD$_3$

567 GAR$_8$ INGAR(324+#) KULLA MUR$_7$ MURGU SIG$_4$

568 GUḪŠU(L:566) GUḪŠU$_2$(B:566) (=LM e567,LI 566)

569 saḫ$_4$ SUḪ$_3$ (=B v569)

570 (det; sign of repetition) $\frac{2}{60}$ 2 120 ini$_4$(449+#) šina II(det) MIN

571 $\frac{1}{3}$ ŠUŠANA

572 $\frac{2}{3}$ ŠANABI

573 $\frac{5}{6}$ KINGUSILA KINGUSILI KINGUSILLA

574 dúg dúk dúq ráš tug tuk tuq DILMUN(231+#) DU$_{12}$ TUG TUK TUKU

575 das daš lig lik liq tàn tas taṣ taš taša taz téš tís tíš tíz ur TEŠ$_2$ UR

575a neša (=L e575)

576 GIDIM

577 GIDIM$_4$ UDUG UTUG

578a 2+30 2+$\frac{1}{2}$ 150 (=LL 577′,LM 578)

(?) = L and/or B uncertain on value = graphic image of sign itself # = number of the current sign
+ = two signs occur in sequence x = one sign is written within the other

579 (det w/396) ʾe$_{4}$ ʾi$_{4}$ ʾu$_{4}$ a ia$_{6}$(231+#) me$_{5}$ ṭur$_{5}$ A ADDIR(#+295+226+469+123) ASAL$_{2}$(#+58+167+377) BIR$_{8}$(#+373) DURU$_{5}$ E$_{4}$ ERU$_{4}$(#+168) EŠA(#+375) ILDAG$_{2}$(#+170) ILLU(#+322) KAŠBIR(214+#+373) ULUŠIN(214+339+#+13) ZAḪ$_{2}$(589+#)

579a aʾa a-a ai aia aiia aiiu aiye aiyi aya aye ayi ayya ayye ayyi ayyu ayu A-A (=L e579)

579b (det; also det w/139) a$_{4}$ àm AM$_{3}$ IMGAGA(339+#; see L p155) ŠEG$_{3}$ (=L e579)

579c ér ESEŠ IR$_{2}$ ISIŠ$_{2}$ ŠEŠ$_{5}$ (=L e579)

579d (det) íd ít iti$_{4}$(13+#) itu$_{4}$(13+#) AḪ$_{5}$(334+#) BURANUN(#+381+228+87+461) BURUNUN(#+381+228+87+461) I$_{7}$ ID$_{2}$ IT$_{2}$ (=L e579)

579e ESIR (=L e579)

579f ŠEG$_{4}$

580 AGAM

581 IR$_{6}$

582 ŠEDU$_{3}$

583 EDURU

584 ZAḪ$_{3}$

585 ESAG

585a NIMIN$_{3}$ (=2PI, 383)

585b (see B p202;=LL 482)

585c NIEŠ (=3PI, 383)

586 4 sà ṣa za ḪALBA$_{2}$(#+102) LIMMU$_{5}$ NINI$_{2}$(#+595) NIR$_{2}$(#+595) ŠUBA(#+102) ZA

589 ʾa$_{4}$ a$_{7}$ gir$_{14}$ ḫa kir$_{9}$ ku$_{6}$ EŠTUB(297+381+#) ḪA KU$_{6}$ ZAḪ$_{2}$(#+579)

590 ZUBUD$_{2}$ ZUGUD

591 gug guq GUG

592 bik pik piq se$_{11}$ si$_{11}$ sig sik siq śé ŝì šak$_{6}$ še$_{19}$ ŝì šik šiq zík zíq SIG

593 3 EŠ$_{5}$ (=L e593)

593a 3+20 3+$\frac{1}{3}$ 200 EŠŠABA EŠŠANA IŠŠEBU (=L e593, B 593, 8–9)

593b (sign of repetition) (=L e593)

594 ur$_{4}$ UR$_{4}$

595 puš$_{4}$ ṭu ṭun AGA$_{3}$ AGARIN$_{3}$(237+#) DUN$_{3}$ GIN$_{2}$ NINI$_{2}$(586+#) NIR$_{2}$(586+#) TUN$_{3}$

596 KILIM KISI$_{5}$ KIŠ$_{5}$ KIŠIB$_{2}$ PEŠ$_{2}$ PIŠ$_{2}$

597 4 ga$_{4}$ gar gara garak$_{5}$ kar$_{5}$ nì níg ník níq qàr sa$_{15}$(L:381) sa$_{16}$(?;B:381) šá BALLA(536+#+115+320+152+211) BALLA$_{2}$(536+#+115+320+152+554) ER$_{2}$ GAR LAMMU LIMMU NI$_{3}$ NIG$_{2}$ NINDA NINGIDAR(#+295) TUKUMBI(354+#+144+481+214)

598a 5 300 í iá yá GEŠIA I$_{2}$ IA$_{2}$

598b $\frac{1}{6}$ 6 360 àš AŠ$_{3}$ GEŠAŠ

598c 7 420 GEŠUMUN IMIN UMUN(LM) UMUN$_{7}$

598d 8 480 GEŠUSSU USSU (=B v598d)

598d* (v598d;=B 598d)

598e 9 540 GEŠILIMMU ILIMMU

598e* (v598e)

B = Borger BI = Borger Index d = difference e = entry foll = following L = Labat
LI = Labat's Index LL = Labat's Liste LM = Labat's Main entry mispr = misprint v = variant

5.3 Value Index

397	ᵓa
398	ᵓá
324	ᵓà
589	ᵓa_4
397	ᵓe
398	ᵓé
324	ᵓè
579	ᵓe_4
397	ᵓi
398	ᵓí
396	ᵓì
579	ᵓi_4
397	ᵓu
398	ᵓú(B)
398	ᵓù(L)
494	ᵓù(B)
579	ᵓu_4
78	ᵓu_5
579	a
579	A
334	á
334	A_2
383	à
579b	a_4
97	a_5
411	a_6
589	a_7
381	a_{12}
397	aᵓ
398	áᵓ
324	àᵓ
579a	aᵓa
579a	a-a
579a	A-A
128	ab
128	AB
420	áb
420	AB_2
145	àb
195	ab_4
128	ABA
145	àba
195	aba_4
195	ABA_4
525	ABLAL
420	$ABRIG_2$#
87	$ABRIG_2$#
532	$ABRIG_2$#
206	$ABRIG_2$#
6a	ABZU
145	ad
145	AD
10	ád
537c	AD_3
379^{2}	AD_4
330b	ad_5(L)
330b	AD_5(L)
318	AD_5#(B)
10	AD_5#(B)
330b	ad_6(B)
330b	AD_6(B)
381	ADAB#
87	ADAB#
69	ADAMA#
427	ADAMA#
330a	ADAMEN
151a	$ADAMEN_2$
579	ADDIR#
295	ADDIR#
226	ADDIR#
469	ADDIR#
123	ADDIR#
97	ag
97	AG
183	ág
183	AG_2
347	aga
347	AGA
183	AGA_2
595	AGA_3
580	AGAM
291	$AGAN_2$
500	$AGAR_2$
526	$AGAR_3$
501	$AGAR_4$
199	AGARIN
198	$AGARIN_2$
237	$AGARIN_3$#
595	$AGARIN_3$#
237	$AGARIN_4$#
225	$AGARIN_4$#
237	$AGARIN_5$#
215	$AGARIN_5$#
452	AGRIG
398	aḫ
398	AḪ
331	áḫ
60	$aḫ_4$(L)
397	$aḫ_4$(B)
334	$AḪ_5$#
579d	$AḪ_5$#
331	áḫa
331	aḫi(B)
334	aḫi(?;LI)
102	AḪULAB
579a	ai
579a	aia
579a	aiia
579a	aiiu
579a	aiye
579a	aiyi
579a	aya
579a	aye
579a	ayi
579a	ayya
579a	ayye
579a	ayyi
579a	ayyu
579a	ayu
97	ak
97	AK
97	aka
87c	AKAR

92a	AKKIL
392	AKŠAK
298	al
298	AL
105a	ALʾAL$_2$
38	ala
38a	ála
323	ALAD(B)
322	ALAD$_2$
323	ALAD$_3$(L)
358	ALAM
109	ALAMMUŠ
141a	ALAMMUŠ(LI)
358	ALAN
38	ali
421	ALIM
560	alla
560	ALLA
38	alu
170	am
170	AM
183	ám
579b	àm
579b	AM$_3$
251	AM$_4$
237	AMA
251	AMA$_4$
437	AMAR
293	AMAŠ
558	amat
522	AMBAR
51	AMME(?)
381	AMNA
558	amtu
13	an
13	AN
480	ana
13	ána
1	àna
329	ANDUL
208	ANŠE
13	ANZU#
399	ANZU#
445	ANZU#
128	ap
420	áp
145	àp
56	APIN
97	aq
97	aqa
451	ar
451	AR
306	ár
306	AR$_2$
401	AR$_3$
362	ar$_5$
353	ARA
306	ARA$_2$
401	ARA$_3$
381a	ARA$_4$
381	ARAB#
87	ARAB#
78	ARAB#
50	ARAD
51	ARAD$_2$
52a	ARAḪ$_2$
324	ARALI#
366	ARALI#
69	ARALI#
435	ARATTA#
366	ARATTA#
68	ARATTA#
461	ARATTA#
436	ARATTA$_2$#
68	ARATTA$_2$#
461	ARATTA$_2$#
271	ARḪUŠ
87b	ARḪUŠ$_2$
87aa	ARḪUŠ$_3$
295	ari$_5$#
533	ari$_5$#
295	aru
335	ARU#
86	ARU#
131	as
339	ás
1	às
522	as$_4$
522	AS$_4$
131	asa
579	ASAL$_2$#
58	ASAL$_2$#
167	ASAL$_2$#
377	ASAL$_2$#
44	ASAR
156	ASILA
156	ASILAL
158	ASILAL$_3$
131	aṣ
339	áṣ
1	àṣ
1	aš
1	AŠ
339	áš
339	AŠ$_2$
598b	àš
598b	AŠ$_3$
125c	AŠ$_4$
543a	AŠ$_5$
331a	AŠ$_9$
339	áša
579	áša(LI)
104a	AŠGAB
334	AŠKUD#
102	AŠKUD#
324	AŠLUG#
211	AŠLUG#
371	AŠLUG#
335	AŠLUG#
367	AŠNAN#
375	AŠNAN#
14	Aš-šur
103b	AŠUGI
145	at
10	át
330b	at$_5$(L)
330b	at$_6$(B)
145	aṭ
10	áṭ

383 aw
131 az
131 AZ
339 áz
1 àz
468 AZAG#
13 AZAG#
536 AZALAG#
381 AZALAG#
536 AZLAG#
381 AZLAG#
536 AZLAG$_2$
181 AZU
182 AZU$_2$
401 AZUKNA#
115 AZUKNA#
5 ba
5 BA
295 bá
472 bà
472 BA$_3$
233 BA$_4$
30 ba$_5$
318 ba$_6$
318 BA$_6$
74 ba$_7$
19 ba$_{11}$
26 ba$_{12}$
60 ba$_{14}$
60 bab
133 bàb
133 bába(B)
133 bàba(L)
381 BABBAR
69 bad
69 BAD
469 bád
152[8] bàd
152[8] BAD$_3$
461 BAD$_4$#
322 BAD$_4$#
449 bad$_5$
449 BAD$_5$
78 baḫ
126 báḫ
355 bàḫ
297 BAḪAR
309 BAḪAR$_2$#
15 BAḪAR$_2$#
349 BAḪAR$_2$#
78 bak
9 bal
9 BAL
11 bál
9 bala
9 BALA
352 BALAG
166b BALIḪA
536 BALLA#
597 BALLA#
115 BALLA#
320 BALLA#
152 BALLA#
211 BALLA#
536 BALLA$_2$#
597 BALLA$_2$#
115 BALLA$_2$#
320 BALLA$_2$#
152 BALLA$_2$#
554 BALLA$_2$#
439 ban
439 BAN
74 BAN$_2$
144 BAN$_3$
230 ban$_4$
144 BANDA$_3$
339 BANEŠ
295 BANMIN
41 BANŠUR
227 BANŠUR$_2$
60 bap
225 BAPPIR
215 BAPPIR$_2$
78 baq
74 bar
74 BAR
344 bár
344 BAR$_2$
280 BAR$_3$
381 BAR$_6$
54 BAR$_8$(B)
54 BAR$_{12}$(L)
344 bára
344 BARA$_2$
69 BARA$_2$(LI)
280 BARA$_3$
488b BARA$_3$(LI)
488b BARA$_5$
517 BARA$_6$
485 BARA$_8$
502 BARA$_9$
260 BARA$_{10}$
74 baš
69 bat
69 BAT
469 bát
152[8] bàt
449 bat$_5$
69 baṭ
469 báṭ
69 be
69 BE
214 bé
214 BE$_2$
383 be$_6$
173 be$_7$
172 be$_8$
214 bi
214 BI
172 bí
172 BI$_2$
383 bì
69 bi$_4$
173 bi$_5$
372 BIBE#
144 BIBE#
78 BIBE#
550 BIBRA
550 BIBRI

324	bid
592	bik
172	bil
172	BIL
173	bíl
173	BIL$_2$
296	bìl#
173	bìl#
295b	BILLUDA
108*	bilti
108*	biltu
56	bin
400	bir
400	BIR
381	bír
393	bìr
168	BIR$_4$
79	bir$_5$
388	BIR$_6$
579	BIR$_8$#
373	BIR$_8$#
346	bís
346	biš
324	bit
69	bít
324	biti
324	biṭ
69	bíṭ
371	bu
371	BU
166	BU$_2$
19	bù
26	BU$_3$
511	bu$_4$
515	bu$_5$
19	bu$_6$(LI)
318	bu$_8$(L)
318	bu$_{11}$(B)
411	bu$_{12}$
30	BU$_{13}$(B)
11	BU$_{13}$(?;LI)
522	BUGIN
528	BUGIN$_2$
516	BUGIN$_3$
355	buḫ
3	buk
515	bul
515	BUL
11	búl
9	bùl
96	BULUG
11	BULUG$_2$
60d	BULUG$_3$
60e	BULUG$_4$(L)
560	BULUG$_4$(B)
216	BULUG$_6$
218	BULUG$_7$
220	BULUG$_8$(?)
2	BULUḪ
26	bum
352	búm
510	BUN
30	BUN$_2$
522	BUNIN
528	BUNIN$_2$
516	BUNIN$_3$
349	bur
349	BUR
11	BUR$_2$
411	BUR$_3$
79a	bur$_5$
79a	BUR$_5$
60d	bur$_{13}$
579d	BURANUN#
381	BURANUN#
228	BURANUN#
87	BURANUN#
461	BURANUN#
349	buru
350	BUR-U
11	BURU$_2$
71	BURU$_4$#
349	BURU$_4$#
79a	BURU$_5$
69*	BURU$_7$(LM)
311	BURU$_7$
2	BURU$_8$
54	BURU$_{15}$
579d	BURUNUN#
381	BURUNUN#
228	BURUNUN#
87	BURUNUN#
461	BURUNUN#
166	buš
332	bute
332	buti
332	butu
411	BUZUR
471	BUZUR$_2$
446a	BUZUR$_3$
19	BUZUR$_5$
13	d(det)
335	da
335	DA
139	dá
230	dà
230	DA$_3$
557	da$_4$
132	da$_5$
396	da$_{10}$
537	dab
537	DAB
124	dáb
536	DAB$_5$
536	DABIN#
367	DABIN#
63d	dad
381	DADAG#+#
151a	DADRUM
280	dag
280	DAG
229	dàg
237	DAGAL
512	DAGRIN
169	daḫ
169	DAḪ
167	dáḫ
280	dak
229	dàk

309	DUG
574	dúg
396	DUG$_3$
15	DUG$_4$
481c	DUG$_5$(?)
445	DUGUD
427	DUGUD$_2$(?)
167	duḫ
167	DUḪ
309	duk
574	dúk
459	dul
459	DUL
329	dùl
329	DUL$_3$
536	DUL$_5$
115	DUL$_7$
459a	dul$_6$
207	dum
207	DUM
557	dùm
224	DUMGAL
144	DUMU
467	dun
467	DUN
465	dún
348	DUN$_4$
595	DUN$_3$
399a	DUNGU
138	dup
352	dúp
309	duq
574	dúq
108	dur
108	DUR
536	dúr
536	DUR$_2$
208	DUR$_3$#
50	DUR$_3$#
8	DUR$_6$
152[8]	dur$_8$
536	DURU$_2$
579	DURU$_5$
536	DURUN
85	DUSU#
320	DUSU#
536	duš
480	dúš
308	e
308	E
324	é
324	E$_2$
381a	è
381a	E$_3$
579	E$_4$
556	e$_5$
15	e$_7$
459a	e$_{11}$#
206	e$_{11}$#
459a	E$_{11}$#
206	E$_{11}$#
459a	e$_{12}$#
202	e$_{12}$#
397	eʾ
398	éʾ
324	èʾ
535	eb
207	éb
54	EBUR
334	ed
381a	ED$_2$
459a	ed$_4$#
202	ed$_4$#
273	EDAKUA
524	EDAKUA$_2$
168	EDIN
583	EDURU
80	eg
308	EG$_2$
63e	EGA$_2$(L)
87c	EGA$_2$(B)
554a	EGI$_2$
209	EGIR
207	EGIR$_3$(L)
554a	EGIR$_3$(B)
207	EGIR$_4$(B)
398	eḫ
397	éḫ
80	ek
564	el
205	él
13	èl
433	ELAM
510	ELAMKUŠ
518	ELAMKUŠ$_2$
527	ELAMKUŠ$_3$
412	eli
483	ELLAG
400	ELLAG$_2$
399	em
183	EM$_3$
32	em$_4$
32	EME
315	EME$_2$
554	EME$_3$#
208	EME$_3$#
554	EME$_5$#
88	EME$_5$#
250	EMEDUB
252b	EMEDUB$_2$
554	EMEŠ#
548	EMEŠ#
562	EMEŠ(LI)
99	en
99	EN
546	EN$_2$
59	EN$_3$
15	en$_4$
295	EN$_5$#
376	EN$_5$#
148	en$_6$
332	en$_7$
353	en$_8$
56	ENGAR
484	ENGUR
99	ENKUM#
60	ENKUM#
363b	ENKUM#
87	ENKUM#

532	ENKUM#
152^4	ENKUM#
99	ENSI#
532	ENSI#
59	ENSI#
295	ENSI$_2$#
376	ENSI$_2$#
112	ENSI$_2$#
295l	ENŠADA
535	ep
207	ép
80	eq
232	er
232	ER
579c	ér
579c	ER$_2$
50	èr
38	er$_4$
541	EREN
393	EREN$_2$
556	EREŠ
165	EREŠ$_2$
38	eri(B)
38	ERI(B)
38	eri$_4$(L)
38	ERI$_4$(L)
195	ERI$_{11}$
393	ERIM
172a	ERIM$_2$
49	ERIM$_3$
262	ERIM$_4$
541	ERIN
393	ERIN$_2$
49	ERIN$_3$
556	eriš
143	ERIŠ$_7$
579	ERU$_4$#
168	ERU$_4$#
296	es
472	és
128	ès
339	es$_4$
212	es$_5$

366	ESA#
73	ESA#
585	ESAG
261	ESAG$_2$
579c	ESEŠ
322	ESI
239	ESIBIR
322	ESIG
579e	ESIR
487	ESIR$_2$
296	eṣ
128	èṣ
472	eš
472	EŠ
536	EŠ$_2$
128	èš
128	EŠ$_3$
480	eš$_4$
480	EŠ$_4$
593	EŠ$_5$
2a	eš$_6$
174	EŠ$_{12}$
175	EŠ$_{13}$
212	eš$_{15}$
212	eš$_{16}$(LI)
325a	EŠ$_{16}$(B)
533	eš$_{17}$
360	eš$_{18}$
480	EŠ$_{18}$(LM)
296	eš$_{19}$
1	eš$_{20}$
124a	eš$_{21}$
579	EŠA#
375	EŠA#
69	EŠE$_3$
200d	EŠEMIN$_4$
194	EŠGAL
593a	EŠŠABA
593a	EŠŠANA
297	EŠTUB#
381	EŠTUB#
589	EŠTUB#
334	et

334	eṭ
296	ez
152	EZEN
367	EZIN$_2$#
375	EZIN$_2$#
367	EZINA$_2$#
375	EZINA$_2$#
367	EZINU$_2$#
375	EZINU$_2$#
319	ga
319	GA
233	gá
233	GA$_2$
105	gà
597	ga$_4$
62	ga$_5$
15	ga$_{14}$
167	gab
167	GAB
88	gáb
167	gaba
167	GABA
259	GABURRA
90	gad
90	GAD
90	gada
90	GADA
401	GADIBDIM
230	gag
230	GAG
256	GAGIA
236	GAGIRSU
235	GAḪALLA
263	GAḪILI
506	GAḪURIN
416	GAKKUL
343	gal
343	GAL
80	gál
80	GAL$_2$
49*	gàl
554	GAL$_4$
376	GAL$_5$

322	gal$_{9}$
343	gala
211	GALA#
536	GALA#
498	GALA$_{4}$
514	GALA$_{5}$
190k	GALAM
278	GALGA
251a	GALILLA
362	gam
362	GAM
406	gám
60*	GAM$_{3}$
69	gam$_{5}$
465	GAMUN#
375	GAMUN#
427	GAMUN#
143	gan
143	GAN
105	gán
105	GAN$_{2}$
143	GANA
105	GANA$_{2}$
493	GANA$_{5}$
540	GANA$_{6}$
493	GANAM$_{5}$
461	GANBA#
435	GANBA#
140	GANMUŠ
141	GANMUŠ$_{2}$
140	GANSIS
244	GANUN
167	gap
88	gáp
597	gar
597	GAR
482c	GAR$_{2}$
319	GAR$_{2}$(LM)
333	gàr
333	GAR$_{3}$
567	GAR$_{8}$
319	GAR$_{9}$
376*	gar$_{14}$
362	gar$_{17}$
105	gar$_{19}$
597	gara
105	garak
597	garak$_{5}$
247	GARAŠ
513	GARIN
295a	GARSU
295b	GARZA
295cc	GARZA$_{2}$
272	GASIKILLA
192	gaṣ
214	gaš
350	GAŠAN
90	gat
63a	gát
63c	gàt
192	gaz
192	GAZ
269	GAZAG
257	GAZI(L)
252	GAZI(B)
252	GAZI$_{2}$(L)
250b	GAZI$_{3}$
85	ge
85	GE
313	GE$_{2}$
480	gè
326	ge$_{4}$
461	ge$_{5}$
427	GE$_{6}$
536	ge$_{7}$
449	GE$_{8}$
67	GE$_{16}$
361	GE$_{22}$(B)
360	GE$_{22}$(L)
360	GE$_{23}$(B)
361	GE$_{23}$(L)
558	GEME$_{2}$
206	GEN
144a	GENA
461	GENE#
172	GENE#
144a	GENNA
444	gèr
296	GEŠ
598b	GEŠAŠ
598a	GEŠIA
598e	GEŠILIMMU
354	GEŠPU$_{2}$#
60d	GEŠPU$_{2}$#
210	GEŠTIN
383	GEŠTU
296	GEŠTU$_{2}$#
536	GEŠTU$_{2}$#
383	GEŠTU$_{2}$#
296	GEŠTU$_{3}$#
383	GEŠTU$_{3}$#
536	GEŠTU$_{3}$#
598c	GEŠUMUN
598d	GEŠUSSU
85	gi
85	GI
480	gì
480	GI$_{3}$
326	gi$_{4}$
326	GI$_{4}$
461	gi$_{5}$
427	gi$_{6}$
427	GI$_{6}$
536	gi$_{7}$
536	GI$_{7}$
449	gi$_{8}$
132	gi$_{27}$
67	GIB
228	gíb
173	GIBIL
548	GIBIL$_{2}$
313	gid
313	GID
371	gíd
371	GID$_{2}$
63d	gid$_{6}$
576	GIDIM
74a	GIDIM$_{2}$
577	GIDIM$_{4}$

295	GIDRI
295	GIDRU
446	gig
446	GIG
427	GIG$_2$
326a	gigi
486	GIGIR
511	GIGIR$_2$
503	GIGIR$_3$
201	GIGRI#+#
202	GIGRI$_2$#+#
411	GIGURU
67	gil
67	GIL
483	gíl
320	gìl
483	gili$_4$
67	GILIM
440	gim
440	GIM
558	GIM$_3$
440	gimi
206	GIN
595	GIN$_2$
366	gìn
366	GIN$_3$
132	gin$_6$
440	GIN$_7$
144a	GINA
144a	GINNA
228	gíp
346	gir
346	GIR
10	gír
10	GIR$_2$
444	gìr
444	GIR$_3$
430	GIR$_4$
202	GIR$_5$
201	GIR$_6$
483	gir$_8$
440a	GIR$_9$
152	GIR$_{11}$
589	gir$_{14}$
483	GIRAG
346	giri
10	gíri
201	GIRI$_6$
483	GIRIM
483	GIRIN
400	GIRIŠ
295cc	GIRZA
296	gis
226	GISAL
452	GISKIM
296	GISSU#
427	GISSU#
296	giṣ
296	giš
296	GIŠ
480	GIŠ$_2$
211	GIŠ$_3$
301	GIŠBAR
49*	GIŠGAL
296b	GIŠḪAR (B)
296b	GIŠḪAR$_2$ (L)
356	GIŠIMMAR
452	GIŠKIM
313	git
371	gít
313	giṭ
371	gíṭ
559	gu
559	GU
106	gú
106	GU$_2$
15	gù
15	GU$_3$
297	gu$_4$
297	GU$_4$
536	gu$_5$
36	GU$_7$
191	gu$_8$
206	gub
206	GUB
59	gúb
59	GUB$_2$
88	GUB$_3$
297	GUD
121	GUD$_2$
483	GUD$_8$
366	GUDIBIR$_2$#+#
121	GUDU$_2$
398a	GUDU$_4$
389	GUDU$_5$
591	gug
591	GUG
345	GUG$_2$
12	gùg
66	GUG$_4$
15	GUG$_6$#
230	GUG$_6$#
15	GUGU
152^{4*}	GUGU$_2$
568	GUḪŠU (B)
566	GUḪŠU (L)
566	GUḪŠU$_2$ (B)
568	GUḪŠU$_2$ (L)
519	GUKIN
410	GUKIN$_2$
537	GUKKAL#
550	GUKKAL#
429	gul
429	GUL
72	gúl
429	gulu
191	gum
191	GUM
565	gúm
362	gum$_4$
108*	GUN
106	GUN$_2$
113	GUN$_3$
195	GUN$_4$
461	GUNNI#
172	GUNNI#
195	GUNU$_4$
206	gup
59	gúp

591	guq
111	gur
111	GUR
362	gúr
362	GUR$_2$
483	GUR$_4$
320	GUR$_3$
46	GUR$_5$
542	GUR$_7$
58	GUR$_8$
538	GUR$_{10}$
60	gur$_{12}$
366	gur$_{16}$
296a	GUR$_{17}$
311	GURIN
111	guru
362	gúru
105	GURU$_6$
411	guru$_{12}$
296a	GURU$_{17}$
69*	GURUN(LM)
311	GURUN
322	GURUŠ
46	GURUŠ$_3$
110	GURUŠDA
7	guš
468	GUŠKIN#
85	GUŠKIN#
565	GUZ
589	ḫa
589	ḪA
404	ḫá
404	ḪA$_2$
381	ḪA$_5$
346	ḪA$_6$
483	ḫab
483	ḪAB
511	ḫáb
511	ḪAB$_2$
483	ḫaba
462	ḪABRUD
295	ḫad
381	ḪAD$_2$
2	ḫal
2	ḪAL
2	ḫala
586	ḪALBA$_2$#
102	ḪALBA$_2$#
277	ḪALUBBA
483	ḫap
511	ḫáp
401	ḫar
401	ḪAR
401	ḫara
288	ḪARA$_4$
401	ḫaru
290	ḪARUB
12	ḫas
295	ḫás
12	ḫaṣ
295	ḫáṣ
12	ḫaš
12	ḪAŠ
190	ḫáš
190	ḪAŠ$_2$
381	ḫàš
146	ḪAŠḪUR
295	ḫat
295	ḫaṭ
12	ḫaz
396	ḫe
143	ḫé
143	ḪE$_2$
230	ḪENBUR
367	ḪENBUR$_2$#
230	ḪENBUR$_2$#
396	ḫi
396	ḪI
143	ḫí
305	ḪIBIRA
300	ḪIBIS$_2$
300	ḪIBIZ$_2$
67	ḪIL
1	ḪIL$_2$
308a	ḪILIBU
152	ḫir
401	ḫír
381	ḫiš
190	ḫíš
393	ḫìš
402	ḫiš$_4$
78	ḫu
78	ḪU
89	ḫub
89	ḪUB
88	ḫúb
88	ḪUB$_2$
381b	ḫùb
381	ḫúd
456	ḫul
456	ḪUL
550	ḫúl
550	ḪUL$_2$
565	ḫum
565	ḪUM
536	ḫun
536	ḪUN
229a	ḪUNIN
89	ḫup
88	ḫúp
401	ḫur
401	ḪUR
401	ḫuru
565	ḫus
12	ḫús
402	ḫuš
402	ḪUŠ
381	ḫút
381	ḫúṭ
142	i
142	I
480	I(det)
598a	í
598a	I$_2$
231	ì
231	I$_3$
579d	I$_7$
381a	i$_{10}$
396	i$_{11}$

61	i$_{14}$
308	i$_{15}$
383	i$_{16}$
397	iʾ
398	íʾ
142a	i-a
142a	ia
598a	iá
598a	IA$_{2}$
231	ià
231	IA$_{3}$
229	ia$_{4}$
61	ia$_{5}$
231	ia$_{6}$#
579	ia$_{6}$#
125b	IA$_{7}$
383	ia$_{8}$
329a	ia$_{9}$
535	ib
535	IB
207	íb
207	IB$_{2}$
144	IBILA#
211	IBILA#
23	IBIRA
334	id
579d	íd
579d	ID$_{2}$
334	ídi
334	IDI$_{2}$
335	ìdi
74*	IDIGNA
69	IDIM
142a	ie
80	ig
80	IG
449	igi
449	IGI
398	iḫ
397	íḫ
570	II(det)
80	ik
80	IK
105	IKU
234	IKU$_{2}$
205	il
205	IL
320	íl
320	IL$_{2}$
13	ìl
480	il$_{4}$
564	il$_{5}$
205a	IL$_{8}$
13	ila
579	ILDAG$_{2}$#
170	ILDAG$_{2}$#
13	ili
320	íli
564	ili$_{5}$
480	ili$_{6}$
598e	ILIMMU
125f	ILIMMU$_{2}$
331d	ILIMMU$_{3}$
363	ILIMMU$_{4}$
296	ILLAR#
68	ILLAR#
166b	ILLAT
579	ILLU#
322	ILLU#
13	ilu
399	im
399	IM
202	ím
202	IM$_{2}$
32	im$_{4}$(L)
206	im$_{4}$(B)
32	IM$_{4}$(L)
206	IM$_{4}$(B)
339	IMGAGA#
579b	IMGAGA#
598c	IMIN
125d	IMIN$_{2}$
331b	IMIN$_{3}$
87aa	IMMAL
28	IMMIN
148	in
148	IN
449	ín
99	in$_{4}$
556	in$_{5}$
1	in$_{6}$
1	ina
1	INA
449	ína
103	INANNA
523	INDA$_{2}$
324	INGAR#
567	INGAR#
148	ini
449	íni
449	ini$_{4}$#
570	ini$_{4}$#
15	INIM
1	inna
540	INNA
103	INNANA
103	INNIN
449	ínu
535	ip
207	íp
80	iq
232	ir
232	IR
579c	IR$_{2}$
50	ìr
50	IR$_{3}$
38	ir$_{4}$
581	IR$_{6}$
51	ir$_{11}$(B, LI)
50	ir$_{11}$(LM:50x367)
367	ir$_{11}$(LM:50x367)
51	IR$_{11}$(B, LI)
50	IR$_{11}$(LM:50x367)
367	IR$_{11}$(LM:50x367)
50	IRDA
38	iri
195	IRI$_{11}$
296	is
212	ís

128	ìs
339	is$_4$
472	is$_5$
579c	ISIŠ$_2$
296	iṣ
212	íṣ
128	ìṣ
212	iš
212	IŠ
166	íš
472	ìš
480	iš$_4$
15	iš$_5$
296	iš$_6$
296	IŠ$_6$
128	iš$_7$
360	iš$_8$
411	iš$_8$
536	iš$_9$
211	iš$_{10}$
436	iš$_{11}$
252	IŠḪARA (LM)
252	IŠḪARA$_4$
212	iši
532	IŠIB
390	IŠKILA
390	IŠKILLA
399	IŠKUR
593a	IŠŠEBU
334	it
579d	ít
579d	IT$_2$
52	ITI
13	iti$_4$#
579d	iti$_4$#
265	ITIMA
382	ITIMA$_2$
52	ITU
13	itu$_4$#
579d	itu$_4$#
334	iṭ
142a	iu
383	íu
383	iw
296	iz
296	IZ
212	íz
128	ìz
128	IZ$_3$
172	IZI
461	IZI$_2$#
172	IZI$_2$#
172	IZU
383	ya
598a	yá
383	ye
383	yi
142a	yí
308	yì
383	yu
15	ka
15	KA
133	ká
133	KA$_2$
319	kà
62	ka$_4$
355	KA$_5$
406	ka$_{13}$
230	ka$_{15}$
88	kab
88	KAB
90	kad
90	KAD
63a	kád
63a	KAD$_2$
63c	kàd
63c	KAD$_3$
354b^2	kad$_4$
354b^2	KAD$_4$
354b^4	kad$_5$
354b^4	KAD$_5$
354b^3	KAD$_7$
365	KAD$_8$
230	kak
230	KAK
296	kák#
536	kák#
322	kal
322	KAL
343	kál
230	kàl
322	kala
322	KALA
322	KALAG
322	KALAGA
312	KALAM
406	kam
406	KAM
143	kám
143	KAM$_2$
354b^4	KAM$_3$
406	kama
143	kan
143	KAN
105	kán
105	KAN$_2$
119	KAN$_3$
31	KAN$_4$ (L)
133	KAN$_4$ (B)
143	kana
461	KANKAL#
322	KANKAL#
88	kap
167	káp
376*	kar
376*	KAR
105	kár
105	KAR$_2$
333	kàr
333	KAR$_3$
346	kar$_4$
597	kar$_5$
376*	kara
105	kára
354b^2	KARA$_4$
375b	KARADIN
369	KARADIN$_2$
370	KARADIN$_3$
375a	KARADIN$_6$

110	KU$_7$
559	ku$_8$
427	KU$_{10}$
294c	KU$_{12}$
191	ku$_{13}$
77	ku$_{14}$
297	ku$_{15}$
206	kub
89	kúb
88	kùb
12	kud
12	KUD
345	kuk(L)
468	kuk(B)
345	kúk(B)
468	kúk(L)
72	kul
72	KUL
429	kúl
567	KULLA
191	kum
191	KUM
172	kúm
172	KUM$_2$
77	kun
77	KUN
191	kùn
142	KUN$_4$#
537	KUN$_4$#
144	KUN$_5$#
536	KUN$_5$#
76	kun$_8$
172	kun$_9$
538	kun$_{10}$
295	KUNGA(L)
547	KUNGA(B)
547	KUNGA$_2$(L)
74	KUNGA$_2$#(B)
13	KUNGA$_2$#(B)
496	KUNIN$_3$(?)
77	kunu
206	kup
89	kúp
88	kùp
366	kur
366	KUR
60	kúr
60	KUR$_2$
111	kùr
111	KUR$_3$
483	KUR$_4$
469	KUR$_6$
454	KUR$_7$
46	kur$_{12}$
454	KURU$_7$
87d	KURUDA
469	KURUM$_6$
454	KURUM$_7$
465	KURUN$_2$
7	kus
565	kús
565	kúṣ
7	kuš
7	KUŠ
329	KUŠ$_2$
318	KUŠ$_3$
448	KUŠ$_5$
110	KUŠ$_6$
212	KUŠ$_7$
448	KUŠU
562	KUŠU$_2$
12	kut
90	kút
12	kuṭ
7	kuz
565	kúz
448	KUZU
55	la
v55	LA
481	lá
481	LA$_2$
75	là
435	la$_{11}$(L)
435	la$_{12}$(B)
322	lab
355	láb
366	lad
314	lag
314	LAG
483	LAGAB
458	LAGAR
71	LAGAS#
349	LAGAS#
55	LAGAS#
381	laḫ
393	láḫ
321	làḫ
321	LAḪ$_3$
206a	laḫ$_4$
206a	LAḪ$_4$
494	LAḪAR
282	LAḪTA
394b	LAḪTAN
314	lak
314	laka
481	lal
481	LAL
482	lál
482	LAL$_2$
109	làl
109	LAL$_3$
141a	LAL$_4$
435	lam
435	LAM
172	LAM$_2$
449	lam$_5$
436	lam$_7$
435	lama
322	LAMA$_2$(L)
322	LAMA$_3$(B)
66	LAMAḪUŠ
322	LAMAR
322	LAMMA
322	LAMMAR
597	LAMMU
124b	LAMMU$_2$
322	lap
314	laq
381	LARSA#

195	LARSA#
381	LARSAM#
195	LARSAM#
366	lat
366	laṭ
59	le
59	LE
231	lé
13	le$_4$
420	le$_8$
449	lem
59	li
59	LI
231	lí
449	lì
13	li$_4$
480	li$_5$
143	li$_6$
420	li$_8$
172	li$_9$
355	lib
322	líb
384	lìb
455	LIBIR
420	lid
420	LID
302	LIDIM(?)
575	lig
314	LIG$_2$
381	liḫ
393	líḫ
321	lìḫ
377	liḫ$_4$
575	lik
314	lík
336	lil
336	LIL
313	líl
313	LIL$_2$
553	LIL$_3$
552	LIL$_5$
151	LILAN
422	LILIS
422	LILIZ
151	LILLAN
309	LILLU#
62	LILLU#
349	LILLU#
449	lim
449	LIM
124b	LIM$_2$
449	limi
597	LIMMU
473	LIMMU(LM)
124b	LIMMU$_2$
473	LIMMU$_3$
325b	LIMMU$_4$
586	LIMMU$_5$
355	lip
322	líp
384	lìp
575	liq
314	líq
354	LIRUM#
322	LIRUM#
377	lis
377	liš
377	LIŠ
420	lit
420	liti
420	liṭ
309	líṭ
420	liṭi
377	liz
537	lu
537	LU
330	lú
330	LU$_2$
345	lù
345	LU$_3$
565	lu$_4$
355	lu$_5$
49*	LU$_7$
355	lub
157	LUBUN
309	lud
309	LUD
151	LUGAL
69	LUGUD#
381	LUGUD#
483	LUGUD$_2$
566b	LUGUD$_3$
321	luḫ
321	LUḪ
321	luḫu
296	LUḪUMMU#
427	LUḪUMMU#
554	LUKUR#
532	LUKUR#
355	lul
355	LUL
355	lulu
565	lum
565	LUM
449	lúm
309	LUM$_3$
215	LUMGI(B)
225	LUMGI(L)
224	LUMGI$_2$
225	LUMGI$_3$(B)
565	lumu
224	LUNGA(L)
224	LUNGA$_2$(B)
355	lup
309	lut
309	luṭ
342	ma
342	MA
122	má
122	MA$_2$
233	mà
233	MA$_3$
331e	MA$_4$
33	ma$_5$
33	MA$_5$
74	ma$_7$
383	ma$_9$
366	mad
366	MAD

294b	MAGANZA
57	maḫ
57	MAḪ
412	màḫ
480	MAKKAŠ
233	mal
233	MAL
123	mál
123	MAL$_2$
377	mal$_4$
233	mala
471	mam
554	mám
471	man
471	MAN
554	mán
307	mar
307	MAR
437	MAR$_2$
144	mar$_5$
144	mara$_5$
144	maru (LM)
144	maru$_5$
74	mas
74	maṣ
74	maš
74	MAŠ
76	máš
76	MAŠ$_2$
295e	MAŠKIM
295d	MAŠKIM$_2$
295ee	MAŠKIM$_3$
366	mat
69	mát
81	màt
366	maṭ
532	me
532	ME
427	mé
98	ME$_3$
69	me$_4$
579	me$_5$
250d	ME$_7$
383	me$_8$
497	ME$_9$
69	med
69	MED
125	MEGIDA
57	meḫ
270	MEN
206	MEN$_3$
517	MEN$_4$
96a	MENBULUG$_2$
347	MER
347	mere
314	MES
138	MES$_2$
533	mès
533	meš
533	MEŠ
532	méš
532	MEŠ$_2$
314	mèš
324	mét
314	MEZ
138	MEZ$_2$
426	MEZE
427	mi
427	MI
554	MI$_2$
532	mì
383	mi$_5$
69	mid
69	MID
324	míd
57	miḫ
212	mil
212	mili
554	mim
471	mìm
570	MIN
554	mín
471	mìn
471	MIN$_3$
556	min$_4$
347	mir
347	MIR
347	miri
314	mis
314	miṣ
314	miš
533	míš
69	mit
536	MITTA#
13	MITTA#
69	miṭ
61	mu
61	MU
331e	MU$_2$
33	MU$_3$
536	MU$_4$
231	MU$_5$
16	MU$_7$
81	mu$_{12}$
295	MUATI
81	mud
81	MUD
69	MUD$_2$
394d	MUD$_3$
3	mug
3	MUG
4	mùg
412	muḫ
116	MUḪ$_2$
61	MUḪALDIM
3	muk
3	MUK
4	mùk
129a	mul
129a	MUL
376	MUL$_2$
405	MUL$_3$
95	mun
95	MUN
543	MUNSUB
543a	MUNSUB$_2$
543	MUNŠUB
543a	MUNŠUB$_2$
95	MUNU

246	MUNU$_{3}$
60e	MUNU$_{4}$
371b	MUNU$_{5}$
60d	MUNU$_{6}$
371c	MUNU$_{7}$
375′	MUNU$_{8}$
554	MUNUS
3	muq
4	mùq
401	mur
401	MUR
337	múr
337	MUR$_{2}$
567	MUR$_{7}$
565	MUR$_{8}$
567	MURGU
22*	MURGU$_{2}$
337	muri
401	muru
337	múru
337	MURU$_{2}$(B, LI)
204b	MURU$_{2}$(LM)
204b	MURU$_{4}$(B, LI)
554	MURU$_{5}$#
381	MURU$_{5}$#
168	MURU$_{5}$#
399	MURU$_{9}$#
445	MURU$_{9}$#
185	MURU$_{11}$
554	MURUB$_{2}$#
458	MURUB$_{2}$#
337	MURUB$_{4}$
185	MURUM
78	mus$_{8}$
374	muš
374	MUŠ
102	múš
102	MUŠ$_{2}$
103	mùš
103	MUŠ$_{3}$
331	MUŠ$_{5}$
440	MUŠDA
78	MUŠEN
507	MUŠŠAGANA
81	mut
69	mút
81	muṭ
70	na
70	NA
431	ná
431	NA$_{2}$
97	NA$_{3}$
97a	NA$_{3}$
229	NA$_{4}$
353	na$_{5}$
353	NA$_{5}$
330	na$_{6}$
79	na$_{7}$
129	nab
366	nad
142	nád
35	nag
35	NAG
165	NAGA
192	NAGA$_{2}$(L)
192	NAGA$_{3}$(B)
560	NAGAR
560	NAGARA
13	NAGGA#
70	NAGGA#
321	naḫ
536	náḫ
35	nak
35	NAK
165	nák
79	nam
79	NAM
536	NAM$_{2}$
433	nàm
433	nam$_{4}$(LI)
331	nan
13	nán#
331	nán#
461	nán#
385	NANAM
331	NANNA#
461	NANNA#
13	nanna$_{4}$#
331	nanna$_{4}$#
461	nanna$_{4}$#
13	NANNA$_{4}$#
331	NANNA$_{4}$#
461	NANNA$_{4}$#
13	NANNAR#
331	NANNAR#
461	NANNAR#
200	NANŠE
129	nap
129a	náp
35	naq
355	nar
355	NAR
325	nàr
355	NARI
471	naš
366	nat
142	nát
366	naṭ
142	náṭ
172	ne
172	NE
231	né
444	NE$_{3}$
173	ne$_{8}$
515a	NENNI
575a	neša
231	ni
231	NI
399	ní
399	NI$_{2}$
597	nì
597	NI$_{3}$
172	ni$_{5}$
433	ni$_{6}$
131a	NIB (B)
131a	NIB$_{2}$(L)
99	NIBRU#
313	NIBRU#
211	nid

374a	NIDABA
469	NIDBA#
103	NIDBA#
554	NIDLAM#
211	NIDLAM#
435	NIDLAM#
554	NIDLAM$_2$#
211	NIDLAM$_2$#
585c	NIEŠ
563	nig
563	NIG
597	níg
597	NIG$_2$
123a	nìg
367	NIGA
330	NIGA$_2$#
367	NIGA$_2$#
529	NIGIN
483	NIGIN$_2$
447a	NIGIN$_3$
447	NIGIN$_4$
190g	NIGIN$_6$
347	NIGIR
348	NIGIR$_2$
20	NIGRU
563	nik
597	ník
123a	nìk
35	nik$_5$
433	nim
433	NIM
556	ním
565	nim$_4$
347	NIMGIR
348	NIMGIR$_2$
473	NIMIN
585a	NIMIN$_3$
461	NIMUR#
172	NIMUR#
556	nin
556	NIN
473	NIN$_5$
200	NINA
540	NINA$_2$
597	NINDA
176	NINDA$_2$
510	NINDA$_3$
528	NINDU
597	NINGIDAR#
295	NINGIDAR#
586	NINI$_2$#
595	NINI$_2$#
515a	NINNA
515	NINNA$_2$
375a	NINNI$_5$
475	NINNU
563	niq
597	níq
123a	nìq
325	nir
325	NIR
586	NIR$_2$#
595	NIR$_2$#
471	nis
296	nís
374a	NISABA
337	NISAG
331e	NISSA
471	niš
471	NIŠ
296	níš
211	nit
211	NITA
50	NITA$_2$
211	niṭ
75	nu
75	NU
431	nú
431	NU$_2$
433	nù
565	nu$_4$
87	nu$_6$
71	nu$_{11}$
71	NU$_{11}$
216	NUG
221	NUG$_2$
217	NUG$_4$
433	num
433	NUM
565	núm
565	NUM$_2$
72	NUMUN
66	NUMUN$_2$
87	nun
87	NUN
18	NUNDUN
215	NUNGI
224	NUNGI$_2$
225	NUNGI$_3$
394	NUNUZ
393	nura
393	nuri
393	nuru
515	NUSSU
295	pa
295	PA
5	pá
450	pà
60	pa$_4$
60c	PA$_5$
60b	PA$_6$
383	pa$_{12}$
60	PAB
469	pad
469	PAD
450	PAD$_3$
78	pag
355	paḫ
355	PAḪ
126	paḫ$_2$
78	pak
9	pal
9	pala
79	PALA#
151	PALA#
439	pan
439	PAN
449	pàn
60	pap

60	PAP
133	pápa(B)
133	pàpa(L)
78	paq
381	par
381	PAR
74	pár
74	PAR$_2$
280	pàr
280	PAR$_3$
249	par$_4$
249	PAR$_4$
393	par$_5$
344	par$_6$
381	para(B)
74	para(L)
74	pára(B)
344	pára(L)
280	pàra(B)
280	PARA$_3$(B)
488b	PARA$_3$(LI)
488b	PARA$_5$(B, LI)
485	PARA$_8$
502	PARA$_9$
280	para$_{10}$(L)
344	PARA$_{10}$(B)
381	para$_{11}$(L)
469	pat
69	pát
469	paṭ
69	páṭ
383	pe
214	pé
69	pè
15	pe$_4$
381	per
346	peš
346	PEŠ
596	PEŠ$_2$
342	PEŠ$_3$
390	PEŠ$_4$
354b^{2}	PEŠ$_5$
354b^{4}	PEŠ$_6$
384	PEŠ$_{12}$
383	pi
383	PI
214	pí
69	pì
15	pi$_4$
172	pi$_5$
58	pi$_{10}$
324	pi$_{11}$
324	pid
355	piḫ
15	PIḪU$_3$#
230	PIḪU$_3$#
592	pik
172	pil
173	píl
296	pìl#
173	pìl#
296	pil$_4$#
172	pil$_4$#
56	pin
592	piq
381	pir
393	pír
400	pìr
79	pir$_6$
444	PIRIG
381	PIRIG$_2$
130	PIRIG$_3$
274	PIRU
346	pis
233	PISAN
314	PISAN$_2$
317	PISAN$_3$
346	piš
596	PIŠ$_2$
346	piša
324	pit
69	pít
371	pu
511	pú
511	PU$_2$
19	pù
26	pù(LI)
19	PU$_3$
26	PU$_3$(LI)
19	pu$_4$(LI)
318	pu$_8$(L)
318	pu$_{11}$(B)
355	puḫ
3	puk
515	pul
11	púl
9	pùl
26	pum
78	púq
349	pur
60d	pur$_{13}$
349	puru
60a	púš
60a	PUŠ$_2$
346	pùš
595	puš$_4$
332	puta
332	puti
332	putu
471	PUZUR$_2$
446a	PUZUR$_3$
26	PUZUR$_4$#
353	PUZUR$_4$#
19	PUZUR$_5$
62	qa
62	QA
319	qá
15	qà
354b^{1}	qa$_4$
167	qab
88	qáb
354	qad
354b^{1}	qád
90	qàd
532	qad$_4$
63a	qad$_6$
343	qal
330	qál
49*	qàl

49*	QAL$_3$
322	qal$_4$
362	qam
406	qám
143	qàm
143	qan
85	qán
167	qap
88	qáp
230	qaq
333	qar
333	QAR
376*	qár
597	qàr
354	qat
354b^1	qát
90	qàt
532	qat$_4$
354b^2	qat$_5$
63a	qat$_6$
354b^4	qat$_8$
354	qata
538	qe
461	qé
85	qè
326	qe$_4$
346	qer
333	qer$_5$
538	qi
461	qí
85	qì
326	qi$_4$
313	qi$_5$
230	qi$_6$
228	qib
313	qid
371	qíd
69	qìd
90	qid$_4$
483	qil
67	qíl
440	qim
538	qin
440	qín(?)
366	qìn(?)
228	qip
446	qiq
346	qir
424	qír
430	qìr(?;LI)
483	qìr
423	qir$_6$
444	qir$_7$
346	qiri
425	qis
425	qiš
313	qit
371	qít
69	qìt
313	qiṭ
191	qu
536	qú
559	qù
468	qu$_5$
106	qu$_6$
206	qub
89	qúb
88	qùb
12	qud
72	qul
429	qúl
191	qum
172	qúm
565	qùm
77	qun
206	qup
89	qúp
88	qùp
111	qur
366	qúr
362	qùr
60	qur$_4$
12	qut
12	qutu
328	ra
328	RA
206	rá
206	RA$_2$
83	ra$_4$
371	ra$_5$
149	rab
149	RAB
343	ráb
322	rab$_4$
83	rad
83	RAD
554	rag
554	RAG
321	raḫ
321	RAḪ
554	rak
554	RAK
183	ram
1	rám
183	rama
149	rap
343	ráp
282a	RAPIL
282a	RAPIQU
554	raq
166	ras
166	raš
166	RAŠ
574	ráš
83	rat
83	raṭ
86	re
86	RE
38	ré
483	rè
230	re$_{13}$
483	reme
420	réme
115	res
115	reš
86	ri
86	RI
38	rí
38	RI$_2$

483 rì
191 ri$_{12}$(L)
230 ri$_{12}$(B)
230 ri$_{13}$(L)
322 rib
314 rid
215 rig
555 ríg
555 RIG$_{2}$
8 rig$_{4}$
295c RIG$_{7}$
321 riḫ
215 rik
555 rík
8 rik$_{4}$
483 rim
483 RIM
420 rím
172a rìm
1 rim$_{5}$
483 rimi
420 rími
483 rin
483 RIN
393 RIN$_{2}$
322 rip
215 riq
555 ríq
8 riq$_{4}$
115 ris
115 riš
314 rit
83 rít
314 riṭ
68 ru
68 RU
230 rú
230 RU$_{2}$
1 rù
43 ru$_{4}$
441 ru$_{5}$
168 ru$_{6}$
168 RU$_{6}$
38 ru$_{9}$
43a ru$_{11}$
322 rub
83 rud
8 rug
321 ruḫ
8 ruk
1 rum
1 RUM
172a rúm
8 ruq
402 ruš
402 RUŠ
83 ruṭ
104 sa
104 SA
457 sá
457 SA$_{2}$
586 sà
82 sa$_{4}$
82 SA$_{4}$
123 sa$_{5}$
123 SA$_{5}$
356 sa$_{6}$
356 SA$_{6}$
13 sa$_{8}$
74 SA$_{9}$
187 SA$_{10}$
597 sa$_{15}$(B)
381 sa$_{15}$(?;L)
597 sa$_{16}$(?;L)
381 sa$_{16}$(B)
214 sa$_{18}$
295k sab
295k SAB
264 SABAD
242 SABAD$_{2}$
366 sad
115 sag
115 SAG
295 SAG$_{3}$
401 SAGGAR$_{2}$
419 SAGŠU
313 saḫ
53 sáḫ
569 saḫ$_{4}$
172 saḫ$_{5}$
354 SAḪAB#
480 SAḪAB#
354 SAḪAB$_{2}$#
457 SAḪAB$_{2}$#
472 SAḪAB$_{2}$#
212 SAḪAR
152 SAḪAR$_{2}$(LM)
331e SAḪAR$_{2}$(B)
309 SAḪAR$_{2}$#(LI)
152 SAḪAR$_{2}$#(LI)
212 SAḪARDUB
212 SAḪARPEŠ
115 sak
295 sàk
332 sak$_{6}$
444 SAKKAN
554 sal
554 SAL
554 sala
318 sam
187 SAM$_{2}$
138 SAMAG(B)
136 SAMAG(L)
135 SAMAG$_{2}$(B)
138 SAMAG$_{2}$(L)
135a SAMAG$_{3}$(B)
314 SAMAG$_{3}$(?;L)
316 SAMAG$_{4}$
8 sán
178aa sàn
314 SANGA
320 SANGA$_{2}$#
122 SANGA$_{2}$#
352 SANGA$_{2}$#+#
314 SANGU
480 SANTAK$_{4}$
343 SANTANA#
231 SANTANA#
295k sap

393	sáp
295m	sàp
115	saq
331e	sar
331e	SAR
396	sár
373	sar$_{4}$
86	sar$_{5}$
491	sar$_{6}$
63b	SASIRRA
366	sat
366	SAT
366	saṭ
112	se
84	sé
84	SE$_{2}$
164	sè
164	SE$_{3}$
592	se$_{11}$
147	se$_{20}$
103b	SED
112	si
112	SI
84	sí
84	SI$_{2}$
164	sì
164	SI$_{3}$
113	si$_{4}$
113	SI$_{4}$
455	SI$_{5}$
457	SI$_{8}$
592	si$_{11}$
449	si$_{17}$
147	si$_{20}$
322	SI$_{21}$
532	sib
295m	SIB$_{2}$
413	SIBIR
314	síd
489a	SIDUG
592	sig
592	SIG
539	SIG$_{2}$
295	SIG$_{3}$
567	SIG$_{4}$
454	SIG$_{5}$
356	SIG$_{6}$
351	sig$_{7}$
351	SIG$_{7}$
322	SIG$_{15}$
53	siḫ
313	síḫ
403	sìḫ
102	siḫ$_{4}$
592	sik
539	SIK$_{2}$
539	SIKI
564	SIKIL
12	sil
12	SIL
87	síl
62	SIL$_{3}$
158	SIL$_{6}$
159	SIL$_{7}$
314	SIL$_{11}$
12	SILA
62	SILA$_{3}$
252	SILA$_{4}$
314	SILA$_{11}$
314	SILAG
44	SILIG
457	SILIM
79	sim
79	SIM
164	sím
555	sim$_{6}$
338	SIMUG
472	sin
472	SIN
314	sìn
79	SIN$_{3}$
532	sip
295m	síp
363	sìp(B)
395	sìp(L)
295m	SIPA
592	siq
373	sir
373	SIR
371	sír
371	SIR$_{2}$
152	sìr
152	SIR$_{3}$
71	SIR$_{4}$
200	SIRARA
215	SIRIS
224	SIRIS(LM)
224	SIRIS$_{2}$(B)
371a	SIRSIR
331	sis
331	SIS
438	SISKUR
438	SISKUR$_{2}$#+#
438	SIZKUR(LI)
331	siš
331	SIŠ
314	sít
7	su
7	SU
6	sú
373	sù
373	SU$_{3}$
113	su$_{4}$
113	SU$_{4}$
18*	SU$_{6}$
460	SU$_{7}$
15	su$_{11}$
164	su$_{12}$(B)
123	su$_{12}$(L)
214	su$_{15}$
53	SUBAR
182	SUBAR$_{2}$
53	SUBUR
373	SUD
83	SUD$_{2}$
26	SUD$_{4}$(L)
371	SUD$_{4}$(B)
522	sug
522	SUG

102	suḫ
102	SUḪ
403	súḫ
569	SUḪ$_3$
313	suḫ$_4$
536	SUḪ$_5$
201	SUḪ$_6$
172	suḫ$_8$
403	SUḪUR
201	SUḪUŠ
522	suk
49*	sùk
321	SUKAL
321	SUKKAL
190k	SUKUD
467	sul
18*	SUL$_3$
54	SULLIM
164	sum
164	SUM
555	súm
555	SUM$_2$
7	sùm
126	sum$_6$
182	SUMAŠ
135	SUMUG(L)
138	SUMUG(B)
138	SUMUG$_2$(L)
444	SUMUKAN
69	SUMUN
444	SUMUQAN
69	sun
69	SUN
429	sún
429	SUN$_2$
18*	SUN$_4$
8	sun$_6$
18*	SUN$_8$(LI)
206a	súp
522	suq
101	sur
101	SUR
329	súr
329	SUR$_2$
405	SUR$_3$
481	sur$_5$#
483	sur$_5$#
461	SUR$_6$#
343	SUR$_6$#
461	SUR$_7$#
230	SUR$_7$#
296	sutu#
74	sutu#
296	SUTU#
74	SUTU#
586	ṣa
231	ṣá(?)
393	ṣab
172	ṣaḫ
53	ṣáḫ
332	ṣak
231	ṣal
393	ṣap
491	ṣar
437	ṣár
491	ṣara
147	ṣe
84	ṣé
53	ṣeḫ
172	ṣéḫ
168	ṣeri
168	ṣeru
147	ṣi
84	ṣí
112	ṣì
395	ṣib
190	ṣíb
395	ṣibi
87	ṣil
427	ṣíl
296	SIL$_2$#
427	SIL$_2$#
12	ṣìl(L)
13	ṣìl#(B)
329	ṣìl#(B)
555	ṣim
395	ṣip
190	ṣíp
374	ṣir
374	ṣiri
69	ṣiṣ
555	ṣu
6	ṣú
555	ṣum
437	ṣur
374	ṣúr
437	ṣuru
104	śa
457	śá
331e	śar
112	śe
592	śé
112	śi
113	śí
592	śì
79	śím
7	śu
113	śú
373	śù
126	śum
164	śúm
101	śur
329	śúr
353	ša
353	ŠA
597	šá
384	šà
384	ŠA$_3$
206	ša$_4$
97	ŠA$_5$
356	ša$_6$
356	ŠA$_6$
104	ša$_{10}$
554	ša$_{12}$
318	ša$_{17}$(L)
455	ša$_{17}$(B)
457	ša$_{18}$
455	ša$_{19}$(L)
214	ša$_{21}$

82	ša$_{22}$
34	ša$_{23}$
115	ša$_{24}$
295k	šab
295k	ŠAB
295m	šab$_{5}$
295k	ŠABA
295f	ŠABRA
366	šad
61	šád
366	šada
366	šadi
115	šag
295	šàg
428	ŠAGAN
444	ŠAGAN$_{2}$#
50	ŠAGAN$_{2}$#
208	ŠAGAN$_{3}$#
50	ŠAGAN$_{3}$#
53	šaḫ
53	ŠAḪ
467	šáḫ
467	ŠAḪ$_{2}$
115	šak
295	šàk
592	šak$_{6}$
428	ŠAKAN
152	ŠAKAR (LM)
331e	ŠAKAR
46	ŠAKIR
42	ŠAKIR$_{3}$
34	ŠAKIR$_{3}$ (LM)
34	ŠAKIR$_{4}$ (?)
554	šal
554	ŠAL
62	šál
231	šàl
87b	ŠALLAM (?;B)
87m	ŠALLAM (?;L)
318	šam
187	šám
187	ŠAM$_{2}$
178aa	šàm
178aa	ŠAM$_{3}$
79	šam$_{4}$
428	ŠAMAN$_{2}$
178aa	šan
180	šan (LI)
572	ŠANABI
473	ŠANABI$_{2}$
356	ŠANGA
295k	šap
295m	šáp (L)
295m	šap$_{5}$ (B)
115	šaq
295	šàq
219	ŠAQA$_{2}$
331e	šar
396	šár
396	ŠAR$_{2}$
151	šàr
471	šar$_{4}$
399	šar$_{5}$
399	ŠAR$_{5}$
12	šar$_{7}$
292	ŠARAN
290	ŠARIN
151	šarri
151	šarru
471	šárru
331	šas
366	šas (LI)
331	šaṣ
331	šaš
366	šaš (LI)
366	šat
366	šaṯ (L)
61	šát
355	ŠATAM
366	šaṭ
367	še
367	ŠE
112	šé
536	ŠE$_{3}$
103b	ŠE$_{4}$
172	ŠE$_{6}$
103a	ŠE$_{12}$
82	še$_{18}$ (L)
592	še$_{19}$ (L)
164	še$_{19}$ (B)
449	še$_{20}$
164	še$_{21}$ (L)
82	še$_{21}$ (B)
103b	ŠED$_{7}$
582	ŠEDU$_{3}$
508	ŠEDUR
579b	ŠEG$_{3}$
579f	ŠEG$_{4}$
172	ŠEG$_{6}$
551	ŠEG$_{9}$
554	šel$_{4}$
215	ŠEM
424	ŠEM$_{3}$
426	ŠEM$_{4}$
423	ŠEM$_{5}$
219*	ŠEMBI
216	ŠEMBULUG$_{2}$
222	ŠEMEŠAL
219*	ŠEMKAŠ
218	ŠEMMUG
8	ŠEN
228	ŠENNUR
532	šep
71	šer
152	ŠER$_{3}$
331e	šer$_{9}$
492	ŠERIMSUR
492	ŠERINŠUR$_{2}$
331	šes
331	ŠEŠ
544	ŠEŠ$_{2}$
541	ŠEŠ$_{4}$
579c	ŠEŠ$_{5}$
65	ŠEŠLAM
449	ši
449	ŠI
112	ší
592	šì
536	ši$_{4}$

113	ši$_5$
215	ši$_6$
351	ši$_7$
24	ŠI$_7$(LM)
351	ŠI$_7$
532	šib
413	ŠIBIR
54	ŠIBIR$_2$
314	šid
314	ŠID
63a	šíd
63d	šìd
440	ŠIDIM
53	šiḫ
313	šíḫ
592	šik
539	šík
55	ŠIKA
12	šil
87b	ŠILAM
44	ŠILIG
215	šim
215	ŠIM
79	ším
318	ŠIMBIRIDA#
366	ŠIMBIRIDA#
328	ŠIMBIRIDA#
216	ŠIMBULUG$_2$
219*	ŠIMKAŠ
218	ŠIMMUG
8	šin
570	šina
93	ŠINIG
295k	šip(B)
532	šip(L)
395	šìp
295k	šip$_4$(L)
592	šiq
539	šíq
24	šiq$_4$
71	šir
71	ŠIR
371	šír
152	šìr
152	ŠIR$_3$
171	šir$_4$
373	šir$_8$
331e	šir$_9$
374	šir$_{10}$
171	šira
171	širi
331	šis
331	šiṣ
331	šiš
314	šit
63d	šít(LI)
63d	šìt
233	ŠITA
233a	ŠITA$_2$
83	ŠITA$_3$
442	ŠITA$_4$
314	ŠITA$_5$
62	ŠITA$_6$
314	šiṭ
63d	šíṭ(LI)
63d	šìṭ
331	šiz
354	šu
354	ŠU
545	šú
545	ŠU$_2$
411	šu$_4$
411	ŠU$_4$
520	ŠU$_5$
521	ŠU$_6$
113	šu$_7$
61	šu$_{10}$
7	šu$_{11}$
26	ŠU$_{12}$
214	šu$_{13}$
126	šu$_{14}$
68	šub
68	ŠUB
295k	šùb(B)
457	šùb(L)
586	ŠUBA#
102	ŠUBA#
13	šubul
53	ŠUBUR
53	ŠUBURA
373	šud
371	šúd
26	ŠUD$_3$
549	ŠUDUN
469	šug
469	ŠUG
102	šuḫ
53	šúḫ
547	ŠUḪUB
469	šuk
3	šúk
467	šul
467	ŠUL
126	šum
126	ŠUM
164	šúm
61	šùm
69	šum$_4$
61	šúmu
459b	ŠUMUNDA
8	šun
429	šùn
68	šup
1	šùp(L)
295k	šùp(B)
469	šuq
101	šur
101	ŠUR
329	šúr
329	ŠUR$_2$
71	ŠUR$_3$
482	šur$_4$#
331e	šur$_4$#
482	šur$_4$#(LM)
152	šur$_4$#(LM)
481	šur$_5$#
483	šur$_5$#
290	ŠURIN$_5$
494	ŠURUN

286	ŠURUN$_4$
7	ŠURUPPAK#
366	ŠURUPPAK#
68	ŠURUPPAK#
411	ŠUŠ
545	ŠUŠ$_2$
571	ŠUŠANA
471	ŠUŠANA$_2$
60	ŠUŠŠUB#+#
69*	ŠUŠŠUB#
364	ŠUŠUR
365	ŠUŠUR$_2$
373	šut
373	šuṭ
373	šuz
139	ta
139	TA
335	tá
126	tà
557	ta$_4$
381	ta$_5$
396	ta$_8$
124	tab
124	TAB
10	TAB$_2$
124	taba
132	TABIRA#
560	TABIRA#
63d	tad
126	tag
126	TAG
280	tág
229	tàg
63d	TAG$_4$
169	taḫ
169	TAḪ
167	táḫ
169	taḫa
126	tak
280	ták
229	tàk
63d	TAK$_4$
63d	tak$_5$
126	taka
86	tal
86	TAL
383	tál
383	TAL$_2$
1	tàl
480	TAL$_4$
86	tala
383	tála
381	tam
381	TAM
557	tám
94	tàm
207	tam$_4$
393	tam$_5$
440	tam$_6$
322	tan
575	tàn
322	tana
124	tap
396a	tàp
124	tapa
126	taq
280	táq
229	tàq
12	tar
12	TAR
12	ṯar(LM)
114	tár
114	TAR$_2$
100	tàr
12	tara
100	tàra
111	tari
111	taru
575	tas
536	TASKARIN
575	taṣ
575	taš
480	táš
339	tàš
575	taša
536	TAŠKARIN
63d	tat
63d	taṭ
575	taz
376	te
376	TE
396	té
165	TE$_3$
172	te$_4$
334a	TE$_8$
73	te$_9$
376	TEMEN
465	tén
375	ter
123	ter$_4$
575	téš
575	TEŠ$_2$
73	ti
73	TI
396	tí
94	tì
457	ti$_4$
69	ti$_5$
376	ti$_7$
334a	ti$_8$
537	tib
126	TIBIR
132	TIBIRA#
560	TIBIRA#
23	TIBIRA$_2$
352	TIGI#
355	TIGI#
106	tik
410	TIKKIN
69	til
69	TIL
459a	tíl
1	til$_4$
359	TILLA
459a	TILLU
94	tim
12	tím(L)
207	tím(B)
207	tìm

465	tin
465	TIN
537	tip
106	tiq
231	tiq(LM)
231	tíq
375	tir
375	TIR
12	tír
114	tìr
343	TIRU#
376	TIRU#
343	TIRUM#
376	TIRUM#
480	tis
575	tís
480	tiš
575	tíš
102	TIŠPAK
344	TITAB
480	tiz
575	tíz
58	tu
58	TU
381	tú
381	TU$_2$
206	tù
207	tu$_4$
354	TU$_5$#
165	TU$_5$#
16	TU$_6$
406	TU$_7$
433	tu$_8$
536	TU$_9$
89	TU$_{10}$
399	TU$_{15}$
144	tu$_{19}$(B)
230	tu$_{19}$(L)
459a	tu$_{21}$
138	tub
352	túb
58	TUD
574	tug
574	TUG
536	TUG$_2$
309	tùg
561	TUGUL
167	tuḫ
169	túḫ
167	tuḫu
561	TUḪUL
574	tuk
574	TUK
536	túk
536	TUK$_2$
309	tùk
126	tuk$_5$
574	TUKU
515	TUKU$_4$
536	tukul
536	TUKUL
296	túkul#
536	túkul#
354	TUKUMBI#
597	TUKUMBI#
144	TUKUMBI#
481	TUKUMBI#
214	TUKUMBI#
27	TUḲUR$_2$
459	tul
511	túl
511	TUL$_2$
459a	tul$_5$
207	tum
207	TUM
206	TUM$_2$
434	tùm
434	TUM$_3$
433	tum$_4$
94	tum$_8$
399	tum$_9$(B)
557	tum$_9$(L)
557	tum$_{10}$(B)
399	tum$_{10}$(L)
434a	tum$_{11}$
399	tumu
89	TUN
595	TUN$_3$
467	tun$_4$
138	tup
138	TUP
352	túp
574	tuq
536	túq
309	tùq
144	tur
144	TUR
108	túr
87a	tùr
87a	TUR$_3$
228	tur$_4$
536	tur$_7$
144	tura
144	turu
536	tus
536	tuš
536	TUŠ
536	túš
335	ṭa
139	ṭá
396	ṭà
557	ṭa$_4$
124	ṭab
537	ṭàb
63	ṭad
169	ṭaḫ
167	ṭáḫ
280	ṭak
86	ṭal
557	ṭam
381	ṭám
322	ṭan
124	ṭap
12	ṭar
114	ṭár
100	ṭàr
63d	ṭat
457	ṭe
396	ṭé

172	ṭè
172	TE$_3$
376	ṭe$_4$
338	ṭe$_5$
73	ṭe$_6$
440	ṭém
457	ṭi
396	ṭí
73	ṭì
376	ṭi$_4$
172	ṭi$_5$
537	ṭib
1	ṭil
69	ṭíl
94	ṭim
440	ṭím
465	ṭin
537	ṭip
123	ṭir
12	ṭír
101	ṭìr
114	ṭir$_4$
375	ṭir$_5$
480	ṭiš
595	ṭu
58	ṭú
206	ṭù
207	ṭu$_4$
138	ṭub
352	ṭúb
167	ṭuḫ
511	ṭul
459a	ṭùl
207	ṭum
94	ṭúm
595	ṭun
138	ṭup
352	ṭúp
108	ṭur
536	ṭúr
144	ṭùr
228	ṭur$_4$
579	ṭur$_5$
12	ṭur$_6$
536	ṭuš
411	u
411	U
318	ú
318	U$_2$
455	ù
455	U$_3$
381	u$_4$
381	U$_4$
78a	u$_5$
78a	U$_5$
449	U$_6$#
324	U$_6$#
464	u$_7$
494	u$_8$
494	U$_8$
152	u$_9$
540	U$_{10}$
78	u$_{11}$
398	u$_{13}$
134	u$_{16}$
383	u$_{17}$
49*	U$_{17}$(L)
383	U$_{17}$(B)
49*	U$_{18}$(B)
38	U$_{19}$
397	uᵓ
398	úᵓ(B)
398	ùᵓ(L)
494	ùᵓ(B)
392	uᵓ$_4$
306	ub
306	UB
536	úb
536	UB$_2$
424	UB$_3$
152^4	UBARA
1	UBU
185	UBUDILI
291	UBUR
381	ud
381	UD
122b	UD$_5$
537	UDU
495	UDUB
577	UDUG
420	UDUL#
536	UDUL#(or 537)
537	UDUL#(or 536)
406	UDUL$_2$
293	UDUL$_3$
287	UDUL$_6$
143	UDUL$_7$
415	UDUN
130	ug
130	UG
444	úg
444	UG$_2$
152^8	ug$_5$
152^8	UG$_5$
69	UG$_7$
17	UG$_8$
318	UGA#
165	UGA#
319	UGA#
499	UGRA
412	UGU
185	UGUDILI
295	UGULA
418	UGUN
417	U-GUR
398	uḫ
398	UḪ
392	úḫ
392	UḪ$_2$
562	ùḫ
17	UḪ$_4$
397	uḫ$_5$
398	UḪU
392	úḫu
470	UIA
130	uk
40	UKKIN
351	UKTIN#
358	UKTIN#

347 UKU
482 UKU$_2$#
206 UKU$_2$#
312 ùku
312 UKU$_3$
212 UKUM
343 UKUR$_2$#
53 UKUR$_2$#
550 UKUŠ$_2$
441 ul
441 UL
75 úl
228 ùl
228 UL$_3$
10 ul$_4$
10 UL$_4$
69 ULAL
228 ULLU$_2$
49* ULU$_3$
214 ULUŠIN#
339 ULUŠIN#
579 ULUŠIN#
13 ULUŠIN#
214 ULUŠIN$_2$#
339 ULUŠIN$_2$#
13 ULUŠIN$_2$#
70 ULUŠIN$_2$#
134 um
134 UM
381 úm
512 UMAḪ
92b UMBIN
314 UMBISAG
317 UMBISAG$_2$
315 UMMEDA(?;L)
134 UMMEDA#(B)
532 UMMEDA#(B)
315′ UMMEDA$_2$(L)
137 UMMEDA$_2$(B)
134 UMU
338 UMUM
411 UMUN
338 UMUN(LM)
338 UMUN$_2$
512 UMUN$_5$
509 UMUN$_6$
598c UMUN$_7$
536 UMUŠ
312 un
312 UN
40 UNKIN
195 UNU
376 UNU$_2$#
195 UNU$_2$#
420 UNU$_3$#
536 UNU$_3$#(or 537)
537 UNU$_3$#(or 536)
58 UNU$_7$(B)
337 UNU$_7$(L)
195 UNUG
196 UNUGI
411 UNUN
306 up
306 UP
536 úp
392 UPE
130 uq
152[8] uq$_5$
575 ur
575 UR
203 úr
203 UR$_2$
255 ùr
255 UR$_3$
594 ur$_4$
594 UR$_4$
401 ur$_5$
401 UR$_5$
535 URAŠ
359 URI
331 URI$_2$#
195 URI$_2$#
461 URI$_2$#
331 ùri
331 URI$_3$
331 URIM$_2$#
195 URIM$_2$#
461 URIM$_2$#
309 URRUB
309 URSUB
535 urta
535 URTA
38 URU
43 URU$_2$
331 URU$_3$
56 URU$_4$
58 URU$_5$
204b URU$_7$
186 URU$_{11}$
132 URUDU
194 URUGAL
372 us
211 ús
211 US$_2$
494 US$_5$
17 US$_{11}$
107 USAN
327 USAN$_2$
394c USAN$_3$
482 USAR#
331e USAR#
598d USSU
125e USSU$_2$
331c USSU$_3$
482 USUR#
331e USUR#
372 uṣ
211 úṣ
131 uṣ$_4$
211 uš
211 UŠ
69 úš
69 UŠ$_2$
271 UŠ$_3$
536 uš$_4$
372 uš$_{10}$(B)
372 UŠ$_{10}$(B)
372 uš$_{11}$(L)
372 UŠ$_{11}$(L)

17	UŠ$_{11}$(B)
17	UŠ$_{12}$(L)
24′	UŠ$_{13}$
28′	UŠ$_{14}$
482	UŠAR#
331e	UŠAR#
181a	UŠBAR(L)
181a	UŠBAR$_2$(B)
185	UŠBAR$_3$(L)
204b	UŠBAR$_3$(B)
413	UŠBAR$_5$
185	UŠBAR$_6$(B)
11	UŠU
472	UŠU$_3$
11	UŠUM
343	UŠUMGAL#
11	UŠUMGAL#
482	UŠUR#
331e	UŠUR#
244	UŠUŠ
381	ut
126f	UTTU
381	UTU
443	UTU$_2$
287	UTUA
281	UTUA$_2$(LM)
293	UTUA$_2$(B, LI)
577	UTUG
420	UTUL#
536	UTUL#(or 537)
537	UTUL#(or 536)
406	UTUL$_2$
293	UTUL$_3$
289	UTUL$_5$
287	UTUL$_6$
143	UTUL$_7$
381	uṭ
372	uz
372	UZ
211	úz
122b	UZ$_3$
131	uz$_4$
171	UZU
181	UZU$_2$
383	wa
231	wá(?)
342	wa$_6$
471	wan
74	war
307	wár
50	wàr
74	waš
383	we
383	wi
295	wí(?)
427	wi$_4$
210	wi$_5$
444	wir
533	wiš
383	wu
61	wu$_4$
3	wuk
374	wuš
586	za
586	ZA
229	ZA$_2$
332	zà
332	ZA$_3$
231	za$_7$(?)
393	zab
29	ZABAR(L)
29	ZABAR$_2$(B)
4	ZADIM
332	zag
332	ZAG
295	zág
172	ZAḪ
589	ZAḪ$_2$#
579	ZAḪ$_2$#
584	ZAḪ$_3$
332	zak
295	zák
231	zal
231	ZAL
393	ZALAG$_2$
231	ZANGA
393	zap
536	záp
332	zaq
295	záq
190	zaq$_4$
491	zar
491	ZAR
231	zár
72	zar$_4$
69	zaz
84	ze
147	zé
147	ZE$_2$
556	ZEḪ#
333	ZEḪ#
554	ZEḪ$_x$#
333	ZEḪ$_x$#
190	zek
72	zer
84	zi
84	ZI
147	zí
536	ZI$_3$
200c	ZI$_4$
449	zi$_5$
395	zib
395	ZIB
190	zíb
190	ZIB$_2$
15	zib$_4$
283	ZIBIN
290	ZIBIN$_2$
84	ZID
536	ZID$_2$
190	zik
592	zík
484	ZIKUM
87	zil
295bb	ZILULU
381	ZIMBIR#
228	ZIMBIR#
87	ZIMBIR#
461	ZIMBIR#

5.4 Determinatives

Determinatives by Designation

ḫi.**a**	396	after plurals and collectives (=ḫá)
	+**579**	
am	330	before vocations, clans, nationalities (=lú)
àm	579b	after ordinal numbers
ta.**àm**	139	after distributive numbers
	+**579b**	
anše/u	208	before equids
c	38	before cities (=uru)
d	13	before divinity
didli	2	after plurals
diš	480	before (mainly masc.) proper names (=I/m/p)
diš	480	indicates beginning of sentences and paragraphs
dug	309	before pots
é	324	before buildings and parts of buildings
elep	122	before ship designations (=má)
f	554	before fem. people/animals/etc (mí/munus/s/sal)
gada	90	before linen garments
gi	85	before (objects made with) grass, reeds
giš	296	before trees and wooden objects (=iṣu/w)
gud	297	before oxen and cows
ḫá	404	after plurals and collectives (=ḫi.a)
ḫi.a	**396**	after plurals and collectives (=ḫá)
	+579	
I,i	480	before (mainly masc.) proper names (=diš/m/p)
II,2	570	after duals (=min)
íd	579d	before rivers and canals
im	399	before the 4 directions, winds, clay bldgs (=tu$_{15}$)
iṣu	296	before trees and wooden objects (=giš/w)
iti/u	52	before months
kam	406	after numbers w/digits, especially ordinals
kám	143	after ordinal numbers
ki	461	after geographical and place names
kimin	464	sign of repetition
ku$_6$	589	after fish (=kua)
kua	589	after fish (=ku$_6$)
kur	366	before lands and mountains (=l)
kuš	7	before leather items, animal hide (=su)
l	366	before lands and mountains (=kur)
lú	330	before vocations, clans, nationalities (=am)

m	480	before (mainly masc.) proper names (=I/diš/p)
má	122	before ship designations (=elep)
me	532	after plur, logogr. w/D and tn verbs (=méš)
meš	533	after plurals
méš	532	after plur, logogr. w/D and tn verbs (=me)
mí	554	before fem. people/animals/etc (=f/munus/s/sal)
min	570	after duals (=II)
min	570	sign of repetition
mul	129a	before stars; NB/LB instead of ul or te
múl	376	before stars (=te)
munus	554	before fem. people/animals/etc (=f/mí/s/sal)
mušen	78	after birds
na_4	229	before stones (=zá)
nar	355	before musicians (very seldom)
p	480	before (mainly masc.) proper names (=I/diš/m)
s	554	before fem. people/animals/etc (=f/mí/munus/sal)
sa	104	before woven items and such
sal	554	before fem. people/animals/etc (=f/mí/munus/s)
sar	152	after garden plants
síg	539	before types of wool and woolen items
su	7	before leather items, animal hide (=kuš)
še	367	before grains
ši/em	215	before aromatic and resinous plants and such
ta.àm	**139** +579b	after distributive numbers
te	376	before stars (=múl)
tu_{15}	399	before the 4 directions, winds, clay bldgs (=im)
túg	536	before clothing and cloth
ú	318	before plants and (sometimes) drugs
udu	537	before sheep and goats
ul	441	before stars
uru	38	before cities (=c)
urudu	132	before copper and bronze objects
uzu	171	before parts of the body and pieces of flesh
w	296	before trees and wooden objects (=giš/iṣu)
zá	229	before stones (=na_4)
zabar	29	before copper objects (seldom)
zì	536	before types of meal
(—)	363	sign of repetition, hyphen, line break
(—)	593b	sign of repetition

Determinatives by Sign Number

didli	2	after plurals
kuš	7	before leather items, animal hide (=su)
su	7	before leather items, animal hide (=kuš)
d	13	before divinity
zabar	29	before copper objects (seldom)
c	38	before cities (=uru)
uru	38	before cities (=c)
iti/u	52	before months
mušen	78	after birds
gi	85	before (objects made with) grass, reeds
gada	90	before linen garments
sa	104	before woven items and such
elep	122	before ship designations (=má)
má	122	before ship designations (=elep)
mul	129a	before stars; NB/LB instead of ul or te
urudu	132	before copper and bronze objects
ta.àm	**139** +579b	after distributive numbers
kám	143	after ordinal numbers
sar	152	after garden plants
uzu	171	before parts of the body and pieces of flesh
anše/u	208	before equids
ši/em	215	before aromatic and resinous plants and such
na$_4$	229	before stones (=zá)
zá	229	before stones (=na$_4$)
iṣu	296	before trees and wooden objects (=giš/w)
giš	296	before trees and wooden objects (=iṣu/w)
w	296	before trees and wooden objects (=giš/iṣu)
gud	297	before oxen and cows
dug	309	before pots
ú	318	before plants and (sometimes) drugs
é	324	before buildings and parts of buildings
am	330	before vocations, clans, nationalities (=lú)
lú	330	before vocations, clans, nationalities (=am)
nar	355	before musicians (very seldom)
(—)	363	sign of repetition, hyphen, line break
l	366	before lands and mountains (=kur)
kur	366	before lands and mountains (=l)
še	367	before grains
múl	376	before stars (=te)
te	376	before stars (=múl)

ḫi.a	**396**	after plurals and collectives (=ḫá)
	+579	
im	399	before the 4 directions, winds, clay bldgs (=tu$_{15}$)
tu$_{15}$	399	before the 4 directions, winds, clay bldgs (=im)
ḫá	404	after plurals and collectives (=ḫi.a)
kam	406	after numbers w/digits, especially ordinals
ul	441	before stars
ki	461	after geographical and place names
kimin	464	sign of repetition
I,i	480	before (mainly masc.) proper names (=diš/m/p)
diš	480	before (mainly masc.) proper names (=I/m/p)
diš	480	indicates beginning of sentences and paragraphs
m	480	before (mainly masc.) proper names (=I/diš/p)
p	480	before (mainly masc.) proper names (=I/diš/m)
me	532	after plur, logogr. w/D and tn verbs (=méš)
méš	532	after plur, logogr. w/D and tn verbs (=me)
meš	533	after plurals
túg	536	before clothing and cloth
zì	536	before types of meal
udu	537	before sheep and goats
síg	539	before types of wool and woolen items
f	554	before fem. people/animals/etc. (mí/munus/s/sal)
mí	554	before fem. people/animals/etc. (=f/munus/s/sal)
munus	554	before fem. people/animals/etc. (=f/mí/s/sal)
s	554	before fem. people/animals/etc. (=f/mí/munus/sal)
sal	554	before fem. people/animals/etc. (=f/mí/munus/s)
II,2	570	after duals (=min)
min	570	after duals (=II)
min	570	sign of repetition
ḫi.**a**	396	after plurals and collectives (=ḫá)
	+579	
ta.**àm**	139	after distributive numbers
	+579b	
àm	579b	after ordinal numbers
íd	579d	before rivers and canals
ku$_6$	589	after fish (=kua)
kua	589	after fish (=ku$_6$)
(—)	593b	sign of repetition

5.5 Correspondences

Correspondences are listed in order of Borger's designations (right column)

AAH	*Borger*
60a	60,24ff(L e60)
60d	60,33ff(L e60)
66	66C(L d66)
74*	74,238f
74a	74,335
97a	97(L e97)
104a	104,6
114	v114
118	d118
124b	124,42(LM e124)
172a	172,51ff(LM e172)
187b	187(L e187)
200*	v200(L 200)
233a	233,40
482c	319,9
330b	330^6(L e330)
$354b^2$	354b(205)(L e354b)
$354b^4$	354b(206)(L v354b)
359	v359
375a	375,45(L e375)
29	381,111ff+29(LM e381)
395*	v395(L v395)
403*	v403(L v403)
403**	v403(L v403)
464	461,280+464
481c	481,73
482b	482,20(LL 482*,LM e482)
494	494+493
533a	533(L v533)
533	v533
537c	537,65+537*
543a	e543(L e543)
546a	546,6(LM e546)
554a	554,84+556,8
561	d561
569	v569
593a	593,89(L e593)
598d*	598d(L v598d)
598d	v598d
598e*	v598e

Correspondences are listed in order of Labat's designations (right column)

AAH	*Labat*
14	1+101
17	foll 16(LM)
30*	30a(LL)
38a	e38(LM)
40	foll 38(LM)
41′	42(LL)
43a	e43(LM)
49a	49*
49*	v49*(LM; LL foll 49*)
51	50,51(LI)
60a	e60(B 60,24ff)
60b	e60
60c	e60
60d	e60(B 60,33ff)
60e	e60
63a	e63
63c	e63
63d	e63
66	d66(B 66C)
78a	78*
79a	v79*
79b	v79*

B = Borger BI = Borger Index d = difference e = entry foll = following L = Labat
LI = Labat's Index LL = Labat's Liste LM = Labat's Main entry mispr = misprint v = variant

AAH	*Labat*
89a	v89
92a	92
97a	e97 (B 97)
116	d116 (LL)
124b	e124 (LM; B 124,42)
126f	e126
128a	e128
142a	foll 142 (LM)
144a	e144 (LM)
150a	e150
331e	e152
166b	e166
167a	e167
167b	e167
172a	e172 (LM; B 172,51ff)
178aa	176′
181	d181 (LL)
181a	e181 (LM)
204b	e185
187a	e187
187b	e187 (B 187)
200*	200 (B v200)
280a	e205 (LM)
211b	211a
244a	v244
250b	e252
295bb	foll 295b (LM,LL)
295cc	foll 295c (LM)
330b	e330 (B 330^{6})
334a	e334 (LM)
363a	v350
363b	v351
354	e354b (LM)
354b^{1}	e354b
354b^{2}	e354b (B 354b[205])
354b^{4}	v354b (B 354b[206])
360	362′ (LM)
371b	e371 (LL 371a)
371c	e371b
374a	foll 374 (LM; LL 165)
375a	e375 (B 375,45)
534	377*
29	e381 (LM; B 381,111ff+29)
381a	e381
381b	e381 (LM; LL 382)
394b	e394 (LM; LL 394a)
395*	v395 (B v395)
396a	foll 396 (LM)
398a	e398
403*	v403 (B v403)
403**	v403 (B v403)
405	v405
405a	405
405b	405
406a	foll 405 (LM; LL 406)
423	e424 (see LI)
443	foll 441 (LM; LL 443*)
459a	e459
481a	e481 (LM; LL 481*)
481b	e481 (LM; LL 481*)
482a	e482 (LM; LL 482*)
482b	e482 (LM; LL 482*; B 482,20)
585b	482 (LL)
486	485 (LL)
488b	485 (LI)
515a	v515 (B 515,9)
527	526 (LM)
533a	v533 (B 533)
543a	e543 (B e543)
546a	e546 (LM; B 546,6)
566	e565 (LM)
568	e567 (LM; LI 566)
575a	e575
578a	578 (LM; LL 577′)
579a	e579
579b	e579
579c	e579
579d	e579
579e	e579
593	e593
593a	e593 (B 593,89)
593b	e593
598d*	v598d (B 598d)

(?) = L and/or B uncertain on value   = graphic image of sign itself   # = number of the current sign
+ = two signs occur in sequence   x = one sign is written within the other

Combined List

Correspondences are listed in order of *AAH*'s designations (left column)

AAH	*Labat, Borger*	*AAH*	*Labat, Borger*
14	L 1+101	150a	L e150
17	LM foll 16	166b	L e166
29	LM e381, B 381,111ff+29	167a	L e167
30*	LL 30a	167b	L e167
38a	LM e38	172a	LM e172,B 172,51ff
40	LM foll 38	178aa	L 176′
41′	LL 42	181	LL d181
43	LM e43	181a	LM e181
49a	L 49*	187a	L e187
49*	LL foll 49*,LM v49*	187b	L e187,B 187
51	LI 50,51	200*	L 200,B v200
60a	L e60,B 60,24ff	204b	L e185
60b	L e60	211b	L 211a
60c	L e60	233a	B 233,40
60d	L e60,B 60,33ff	244a	L v244
60e	L e60	250b	L e252
63a	L e63	280a	LM e205
63c	L e63	295bb	LL,LM foll 295b
63d	L e63	295cc	LM 295c
66	L d66,B 66C	330b	L e330,B 330^6
74a	B 74,335	331e	L e152
74*	B 74,238f	334a	LM e334
78a	L 78*	354	LM e354b
79a	L v79*	$354b^1$	L e354b
79b	L v79*	$354b^2$	L e354b,B 354b(205)
89a	L v89	$354b^4$	L v354b,B 354b(206)
92a	L 92	359	B v359
97a	L e97,B 97	360	LM 362′
104a	B 104,6	363a	L v350
114	B v114	363b	L v351
116	LL d116	371b	L e371,LL 371a
118	B d118	371c	L e371b
124b	LM e124,B 124,42	374a	LL 165,LM foll 374
126f	L e126	375a	L e375,B 375,45
128a	L e128	381a	L e381
142a	LM foll 142	381b	LL 382,LM e381
144a	LM e144	394b	LL 394a,LM e394

B = Borger BI = Borger Index d = difference e = entry foll = following L = Labat
LI = Labat's Index LL = Labat's Liste LM = Labat's Main entry mispr = misprint v = variant

AAH	*Labat, Borger*
395*	L v395,B v395
396a	LM foll 396
398a	L e398
403*	L v403,B v403
403**	L v403,B v403
405	L v405
405a	L 405
405b	L 405
406a	LL 406,LM foll 405
423	L e424 (see LI)
443	LL 443*,LM foll 441
459a	L e459
464	B 461,280+464
481a	LL 481*,LM e481
481b	LL 481*,LM e481
481c	B 481,73
482a	LL 482*,LM e482
482b	LL 482*,LM e482, B 482,20
482c	B 319,9
486	LL 485
488b	LI 485
494	B 494+493
515a	L v515,B 515,9
527	LM 526

AAH	*Labat, Borger*
533	B v533
533a	L v533,B 533
534	L 377*
537c	B 537,65+537*
543a	L e543,B e543
546a	LM e546,B 546,6
554a	B 554,84+556,8
561	B d561
566	LM e565
568	LM e567,LI 566
569	B v569
575a	L e575
578a	LL 577′,LM 578
579a	L e579
579b	L e579
579c	L e579
579d	L e579
579e	L e579
585b	LL 482
593	L e593
593a	L e593,B 593,89
593b	L e593
598d	B v598d
598d*	L v598d,B 598d
598e*	B v598e

(?) = L and/or B uncertain on value = graphic image of sign itself # = number of the current sign
+ = two signs occur in sequence x = one sign is written within the other

5.6 Summary of Disagreements Within and Between the Lists of Labat and Borger

398	ᵓú(B)
398	ᵓù(L)
494	ᵓù(B)
330b	ad$_5$(L)
330b	AD$_5$(L)
318	AD$_5$#(B)
10	AD$_5$#(B)
330b	ad$_6$(B)
330b	AD$_6$(B)
60	aḫ$_4$(L)
397	aḫ$_4$(B)
331	aḫi(B)
334	aḫi(?;LI)
323	ALAD(B)
323	ALAD$_3$(L)
109	ALAMMUŠ
141a	ALAMMUŠ(LI)
339	áša
579	áša(LI)
330b	at$_5$(L)
330b	at$_6$(B)
133	bába(B)
133	bàba(L)
54	BAR$_8$(B)
54	BAR$_{12}$(L)
344	BARA$_2$
69	BARA$_2$(LI)
280	BARA$_3$
488b	BARA$_3$(LI)
19	bù
19	bu$_6$(LI)
318	bu$_8$(L)
318	bu$_{11}$(B)
30	BU$_{13}$(B)
11	BU$_{13}$(?;LI)
60e	BULUG$_4$(L)
560	BULUG$_4$(B)
69*	BURU$_7$(LM)
311	BURU$_7$
449	DALA#(L)
230	DALA#(L)
449	DALA$_2$#(B)
230	DALA$_2$#(B)
255	DAN$_3$(L)
341	DAN$_3$(B)
114	dàš(L)
339	dàš(B)
12	dim$_5$(L)
352	dim$_5$(B)
63e	EGA$_2$(L)
87c	EGA$_2$(B)
207	EGIR$_3$(L)
554a	EGIR$_3$(B)
207	EGIR$_4$(B)
554	EMEŠ#
548	EMEŠ#
562	EMEŠ(LI)
38	eri(B)
38	ERI(B)
38	eri$_4$(L)
38	ERI$_4$(L)
212	eš$_{16}$(LI)
325a	EŠ$_{16}$(B)
360	eš$_{18}$
480	EŠ$_{18}$(LM)
482c	GAR$_2$
319	GAR$_2$(LM)
257	GAZI(L)
252	GAZI(B)
252	GAZI$_2$(L)
361	GE$_{22}$(B)
360	GE$_{22}$(L)
360	GE$_{23}$(B)
361	GE$_{23}$(L)
296b	GIŠḪAR(B)
296b	GIŠḪAR$_2$(L)
568	GUḪŠU(B)
566	GUḪŠU(L)

566	GUḪŠU$_2$(B)
568	GUḪŠU$_2$(L)
69*	GURUN(LM)
311	GURUN
32	im$_4$(L)
206	im$_4$(B)
32	IM$_4$(L)
206	IM$_4$(B)
51	ir$_{11}$(B,LI)
50	ir$_{11}$ (LM:50x367)
367	ir$_{11}$ (LM:50x367)
51	IR$_{11}$(B,LI)
50	IR$_{11}$ (LM:50x367)
367	IR$_{11}$ (LM:50x367)
252	IŠḪARA(LM)
252	IŠḪARA$_4$
31	KAN$_4$(L)
133	KAN$_4$(B)
192	kaṣ(L)
192	kàṣ(B)
354	kat$_6$(L)
354	kat$_7$(B)
313	ki$_4$(B)
326	ki$_4$(L)
548	KIBIR(L)
548	KIBIR$_2$(B)
345	kuk(L)
468	kuk(B)
345	kúk(B)
468	kúk(L)
295	KUNGA(L)
547	KUNGA(B)
547	KUNGA$_2$(L)
74	KUNGA$_2$#(B)
13	KUNGA$_2$#(B)
435	la$_{11}$(L)
435	la$_{12}$(B)
322	LAMA$_2$(L)
322	LAMA$_3$(B)
597	LIMMU
473	LIMMU(LM)
215	LUMGI(B)
225	LUMGI(L)
225	LUMGI$_3$(B)
224	LUNGA(L)
224	LUNGA$_2$(B)
144	maru(LM)
144	maru$_5$
337	MURU$_2$(B,LI)
204b	MURU$_2$(LM)
204b	MURU$_4$(B,LI)
192	NAGA$_2$(L)
192	NAGA$_3$(B)
433	nàm
433	nam$_4$(LI)
131a	NIB(B)
131a	NIB$_2$(L)
133	pápa(B)
133	pàpa(L)
381	para(B)
74	para(L)
74	pára(B)
344	pára(L)
280	pàra(B)
280	PARA$_3$(B)
488b	PARA$_3$(LI)
488b	PARA$_5$(B,LI)
280	para$_{10}$(L)
344	PARA$_{10}$(B)
381	para$_{11}$(L)
19	pù
26	pù(LI)
19	PU$_3$
26	PU$_3$(LI)
19	pu$_4$(LI)
318	pu$_8$(L)
318	pu$_{11}$(B)
430	qìr(?;LI)
483	qìr
191	ri$_{12}$(L)
230	ri$_{12}$(B)
230	ri$_{13}$(L)
597	sa$_{15}$(B)
381	sa$_{15}$(?;L)
597	sa$_{16}$(?;L)
381	sa$_{16}$(B)

152	SAḪAR$_2$(LM)
331e	SAḪAR$_2$(B)
309	SAḪAR$_2$#(LI)
152	SAḪAR$_2$#(LI)
138	SAMAG(B)
136	SAMAG(L)
135	SAMAG$_2$(B)
138	SAMAG$_2$(L)
135a	SAMAG$_3$(B)
314	SAMAG$_3$(?;L)
363	sìp(B)
395	sìp(L)
224	SIRIS(LM)
224	SIRIS$_2$(B)
164	su$_{12}$(B)
123	su$_{12}$(L)
26	SUD$_4$(L)
371	SUD$_4$(B)
135	SUMUG(L)
138	SUMUG(B)
138	SUMUG$_2$(L)
18*	SUN$_4$
18*	SUN$_8$(LI)
12	ṣìl(L)
13	ṣìl#(B)
329	ṣìl#(B)
318	ša$_{17}$(L)
455	ša$_{17}$(B)
455	ša$_{19}$(L)
152	ŠAKAR(LM)
331e	ŠAKAR
42	ŠAKIR$_3$
34	ŠAKIR$_3$(LM)
34	ŠAKIR$_4$(?)
87b	ŠALLAM(?;B)
87m	ŠALLAM(?;L)
178aa	šan
180	šan(LI)
295m	šáp(L)
295m	šap$_5$(B)
331	šas
366	šas(LI)
331	šaš
366	šaš(LI)
82	še$_{18}$(L)
592	še$_{19}$(L)
164	še$_{19}$(B)
164	še$_{21}$(L)
82	še$_{21}$(B)
351	ši$_7$
24	ŠI$_7$(LM)
351	ŠI$_7$
295k	šip(B)
532	šip(L)
295k	šip$_4$(L)
63d	šít(LI)
63d	šìt
63d	šíṭ(LI)
63d	šìṭ
295k	šùb(B)
457	šùb(L)
1	šùp(L)
295k	šùp(B)
482	šur$_4$#
331e	šur$_4$#
482	šur$_4$#(LM)
152	šur$_4$#(LM)
12	tím(L)
207	tím(B)
106	tiq
231	tiq(LM)
231	tíq
144	tu$_{19}$(B)
230	tu$_{19}$(L)
399	tum$_9$(B)
557	tum$_9$(L)
557	tum$_{10}$(B)
399	tum$_{10}$(L)
49*	U$_{17}$(L)
383	U$_{17}$(B)
49*	U$_{18}$(B)
398	úʾ(B)
398	ùʾ(L)
494	ùʾ(B)
315	UMMEDA(?;L)
134	UMMEDA#(B)

532	UMMEDA#(B)
315′	UMMEDA$_2$(L)
137	UMMEDA$_2$(B)
411	UMUN
338	UMUN(LM)
58	UNU$_7$(B)
337	UNU$_7$(L)
372	uš$_{10}$(B)
372	UŠ$_{10}$(B)
372	uš$_{11}$(L)
372	UŠ$_{11}$(L)
17	UŠ$_{11}$(B)
17	UŠ$_{12}$(L)
181a	UŠBAR(L)
181a	UŠBAR$_2$(B)
185	UŠBAR$_3$(L)
204b	UŠBAR$_3$(B)
185	UŠBAR$_6$(B)
281	UTUA$_2$(LM)
293	UTUA$_2$(B,LI)
29	ZABAR(L)
29	ZABAR$_2$(B)